UNIVERSITY OF NORTH CAROLINA AT CHAPEL HILL
DEPARTMENT OF ROMANCE LANGUAGES

NORTH CAROLINA STUDIES
IN THE ROMANCE LANGUAGES AND LITERATURES

Founder: URBAN TIGNER HOLMES
Editor: MARÍA A. SALGADO

Distributed by:

UNIVERSITY OF NORTH CAROLINA PRESS
CHAPEL HILL
North Carolina 27514
U.S.A.

NORTH CAROLINA STUDIES IN THE
ROMANCE LANGUAGES AND LITERATURES
Number 228

HALF-TOLD TALES

HALF-TOLD TALES:
DILEMMAS OF MEANING IN THREE FRENCH NOVELS

BY
PHILIP STEWART

CHAPEL HILL

NORTH CAROLINA STUDIES IN THE ROMANCE
LANGUAGES AND LITERATURES
U.N.C. DEPARTMENT OF ROMANCE LANGUAGES

1987

Library of Congress Cataloging in Publication Data

Stewart, Philip.
 Half-told tales.

 (North Carolina studies in the Romance languages and literatures; no. 228)
 English and French.
 Includes bibliographical references.
 1. French fiction — 18th century — History and criticism. 2. Marivaux, Pierre Carlet de Chamblain de, 1688-1763. Vie de Marianne. 3. Rousseau, Jean Jacques, 1712-1778. Nouvelle Héloïse. 4. Diderot, Denis, 1713-1784. Religieuse. I. Title. II. Series.

PQ648.S68   1987   843'.5'09   87-10833
ISBN 0-8078-9232-7

© 1987. Department of Romance Languages. The University of North Carolina at Chapel Hill.

ISBN 0-8078-9232-7

DEPÓSITO LEGAL: V. 258 - 1987   I.S.B.N. 84-599-1893-9
ARTES GRÁFICAS SOLER, S. A. - LA OLIVERETA, 28 - 46018 VALENCIA - 1987

CONTENTS

	Page
FOREWORD	11
LA VIE DE MARIANNE	15
LA RELIGIEUSE	83
JULIE, OU LA NOUVELLE HÉLOÏSE	115
CONCLUSION	211
WORKS CITED	215

Pour Justin

FOREWORD

My title is, of course, a sort of play on words. Of the three novels discussed here, only the first is, as a story, incomplete. (And in the other two the heroine dies as the story concludes.) Indeed in one sense they are all over-told: repetition and recapitulation play a significant thematic role in all three cases, and the narrative is forever working variations on itself.

What is half-told about them is that the heroine's sincerity, established through large-caliber rhetorical apparatus, does not prevent some of the most important elements of her story from being obscured. On the surface, the thesis is in each case quite clear and most of the problems clearly enunciated. Despite that, however, an ambiguity creeps into the discourse, compromising if not subtly contradicting its most obvious premises. The reading practiced here attempts to tease out of the text, as it were, these countercurrents or repressive strategies, and situate them within the broader thematics of the work. Aside from that central concern, these chapters are separate discussions of three marvelously complex eighteenth-century novels.

To schematize this undermining or problematizing process, one might conceive of the textual machinery as operating on three distinguishable levels, each having a quite different effect on what one might call the rhetorical "momentum" of reading:

1) Insofar as there is an ostensible argument, a thesis that seems to command the locomotive force for the plot (two of the novels discussed here have often been considered *romans à thèse*), the rhetoric seems streamlined, and tends to make the text run like an express train. It supplies for the reader, in directly accessible form, the *predetermination* of meaning.

2) In function of that argument, the text has a maintenance job to perform; at subtler levels of rhetoric, it urges reading of the text's episodic details as realizations, direct or indirect, of the thesis. In the case of *Julie,* the thesis is the value of the virtuous life, and the plot corresponding to it transforms the seductive enticements of love into the superior happiness of virtue; the second level is, then, a kind of *Textarbeit* of redemption, the gradual elevation of a once-fallen Julie to angelic perfection. To uncover moments in this process is admittedly to make the text appear less streamlined, more like a freight train. In forms that may or may not be predominantly perceptible in cursory reading, this level of signification amounts to the *determination* of meaning.

3) The process, largely unproblematic up to this point, sooner or later encounters a kind of turbulence resisting or obstructing its heretofore univocal thrust. This counterforce may come close to the surface of the text but is rarely acknowledged by it explicitly, since it would tend to contradict level one and thus compromise the fabled "unity" of the text. One might call this the commuter train (commute='exchange', 'substitute') or, better, the commutator train. To return to the example of Julie, this process involves the heroine's fear of defeat and flight from life, the radical doubt which creeps into and poisons her total sense of value and mission. Insistent detection of such indices brings to light a paradoxical and unnerving *indetermination* of meaning.

These are of course not to be thought of as progressive steps in the linear development of a text; they are better likened to successive readings of the same text, but even then they need not be detached mechanically in the course of analysis. While I will occasionally point to relatively specific shifts between them, the principal intention is just to keep them in mind, calling on them to inform but not wholly shape what I intend to be a flexible, essay approach to the novels.

A further clarification of intention may be useful. The reading of a text solely on its own terms does not necessarily proceed from an idealization of textual unity as a seamless fabric, in which any snags must appear as flaws. It is perfectly possible to conceive of the text as at once self-contained and self-undermining. Unity in the classical sense is not the point; that the text is a defineable entity, however, can hardly be doubted. Any number of perspectives (social, historical and so on) can be brought to bear on it; this a textual reading does not deny. What it does do, as a counterweight to the frequent tendency to read "between the lines" without always reading the text itself well enough, is to put aside temporarily these broader frameworks of interpretation. To dissect a butterfly with the help of a microscope and other appropriate tools is not to remove it from other contexts of study — as part of an ecosystem or as a link in an evolutionary chain of similar and dissimilar entities — nor for that matter from aesthetic wonderment at its beauty. But even if the literary text were approached as the product of its author's personality or of a social class, it would, when questioned closely enough, be revealed as an only partially successful attempt to resolve certain kinds of tensions. Deconstruction, which situates the impossibility of complete resolution within language itself, is by no means the only kind of analysis which recognizes that perplexing eddies are inherent in the very nature of the utterance.

The fact that these three novels all concern women protagonists is not meant to hint at an inchoate feminine theory lurking behind the ostensible discussion. If I had a theory of the feminine subject worth putting forward, I would do so purposefully and might very well use other books as examples. I am more concerned here with how the narrative behaves than how the heroine behaves, and have no reason to assert that the substitution of a masculine hero would entail any fundamental change in that behavior. Certainly it is possible to examine these novels as examples of the way the male author construes women or their fictional function, and I have no quarrel with a valorization of the "heroine's text" (as Nancy Miller has called it). That is simply not the subject here. What the common aspects of the three texts do allow is a certain degree of thematic coherence, suggesting interesting comparisons in a study which is otherwise essentially separated into discrete chapters. Coincidentally, they are all alike too in that the heroine tells, at least in large part, her own story: and that adds a dimension to the sense in which each story is but half told.

Two brief clarifications about my critical procedure. 1) Some of the analytical terminology is borrowed from Gérard Genette's "Discours du récit" in *Figures III* (Paris: Seuil, 1972). 2) Italics being relatively rare in the texts under consideration, I have used them freely to underscore important terms for the argument; therefore, italics are my own unless otherwise indicated.

LA VIE DE MARIANNE

Origins were a preoccupation of the eighteenth century, perhaps by way of filling the void left where intellectual confidence in *the* origin of all things retracted. Both historical and abstract inquiries about origins proliferated: Montesquieu devoted over a book of *L'Esprit des lois* to discussion of the origins of the monarchy and other governmental institutions, including the much debated matter of the origin of the nobility, a question inevitably linked to that of its authority and privileges; thanks to Rousseau's *Discours sur l'inégalité,* the problem of class origins, as raised for contest purposes by the Académie de Dijon, is well known, and more recently renewed attention has been paid also to his *Essai sur l'origine des langues.* Although the subject in general may now seem to be one of Rousseau's particular obsessions, it was not his alone. With this in mind, one is not surprised to note the regularity with which novels of the period addressed themselves to the question not only of origins but of their own origin: how to posit their somewhat unauthorized existence in the world of culture which by classical standards had no clear place for them. *La Vie de Marianne* is involved, in both narrative frame and plot, in all these levels of challenge and inquiry.

In the beginning was the story. Even before the fundamental enigma of Marianne's birth is described, that of the text is doubly founded through two levels of introduction by an "author" and his secondary foil, the "friend" who found the manuscript in an old cupboard. The *je* who speaks in the first of these is, by virtue of the

---

Pierre Carlet de Marivaux (1688-1763), *La Vie de Marianne, ou les aventures de Madame la comtesse de* ***, parts I-VIII, 1731-1737; parts IX-XI, 1742. Edition: Classiques Garnier (ed. Frédéric Deloffre), 1963.

title page, named "Marivaux"[1] who is known to the public as an author: but he admits to authorship only of the "Avertissement" and removes himself from consideration as the author of *La Vie de Marianne*,[2] to be replaced by the non-author ("je ne suis point auteur") of the first four paragraphs of the text proper. It is the latter who details the fictional history of the "manuscript" to follow, establishing the anteriority of a story which, written forty years earlier (thus about 1690) by a countess age fifty, had to have taken place for the most part in the vicinity of 1655. But like Marianne's own origins, the text's are obscured in the past and inaccessible: Marianne never gives her full name, and that of the marquise she addresses (p. 375) is left blank.[3] There is no birth in either case; there is only a prehistory which has mysteriously left as its trace a story. The fiction is anterior to its pretexts.

For Marianne too is a non-author ("ce n'est point un auteur" [p. 55]), uncertain with regard to a style certified by "Marivaux" as negligent in the original version.[4] The "comtesse de ***" of the subtitle is, however, not the sign of discretion but of an unknown: "nous ne savons qui elle était." On the other hand, this guarantee that Marianne has become a countess is not purely a function of the subtitle; it is also an indication that the total manuscript is not delivered in the eleven parts of *La Vie de Marianne,* for its possessor tells us — without explaining how, of course — that "elle prend ensuite le titre de comtesse." The "Avertissement" also affirms that

---

[1] I use quotation marks to indicate the equivalence to a character role: Marivaux's name appears on the first edition, but the function assumed is not necessarily identical with that of the historical personage. The "Avertissement" of part two appears once more to present "Marivaux" as speaker, after which he is silent.

[2] It is not of course a question of who, historically, authored the book, but of who is speaking in terms of the fictional framework, where "Marivaux" did not write the story, but Marianne; and the "manuscript" in question too is hers.

[3] "Dont le nom est en blanc" (p. 8) is ambiguous. It could mean that the speaker has removed the name, as he has changed two others (p. 7); but in fact there is no objective "blank" in the text designating the addressee. Or it could mean that the "blank" is on the original manuscript. But the title, he suggests, is not part of the manuscript, and must therefore be his contribution: "C'est la *Vie de Marianne*; c'est ainsi qu'elle se nomme elle-même."

[4] "Je n'y ai point d'autre part que d'en avoir retouché quelques endroits trop confus et trop négligés" (p. 5).

the countess Marianne is in retreat, which again must be information drawn from that remainder of the manuscript which, though never published, was known to "Marivaux" and his friend. Thus the end is in the beginning, even if that "end" is diegetically, in terms of the story line itself, unreachable: although in principle the memoir form should lead us to the eventual coincidence of Marianne with the Countess, a gap persists which can never be filled.[5]

The voice of the Comtesse de *** (which I will call Marianne II, to distinguish her when useful from the protagonist of fifteen, Marianne I) is everywhere present in the narrative, but disembodied: a present is always implied in her apostrophes to the Marquise, but its modalities are never made explicit. It enters tangentially, not through the dimension of Marianne II watching Marianne I, but in Marianne II's comments relative to Marianne II herself.[6] Even on this level there is ironic distance, just as there is with respect to Marianne I; she lays claim perhaps to all the *esprit* of a certain former self, but not to its charms, for a woman of fifty is entitled only to the coquettishness of wit and not that of beauty.[7] The diegetic actualization of Marianne II may be "impossible" in terms of a continuous linkage with Marianne I,[8] but they are joined by a consistency of personality. A degree of flippancy in depicting herself,

---

[5] Cf. Sylvère Lotringer: "La surimposition de la vieille Marianne sur la jeune et du point d'arrivée sur le point de départ ne cessent en effet de renvoyer le passé au présent de la narration, d'ôter à chaque moment du récit sa part d'inconnu puisque aussi bien l'issue précède le cheminement"; there is, in other words, "une intrigue de causalité ... imbriquée dans une intrigue de prédestination (on sait que l'héroïne deviendra cette comtesse qui parle" ("Le Roman impossible," *Poétique,* 3 [1970], 297-321, p. 318).

[6] Cf. Henri Coulet, *Marivaux romancier* (Paris: Armand Colin, 1975), pp. 229-30.

[7] "Je badine un peu sur notre science, et je n'en fais point de façon avec vous, car nous ne l'exerçons plus ni l'une ni l'autre" (p. 50). René Démoris compares thus the separate "seductive" projects of the two Mariannes: "Car il s'agit bien de séduction, la seule qui soit encore permise à un personnage vieillissant, qui entend se parer de sa jeunesse, aux dépens, s'il le faut, de celui qu'il fut. L'écrivant triomphe ainsi de son propre personnage: on peut douter de la vertu passée de Marianne, mais non de son esprit présent.... Les moyens seuls de la séduction ont changé: le corps a laissé place à l'écriture" (*Le Roman à la première personne,* Paris: Armand Colin, 1975, p. 413).

[8] The term "impossible" is used by Lotringer to indicate the structural incompatibility preventing a narrative joining of the two Mariannes; I shall return later to some aspects of his argument.

from the outset, differs notably from the perspective of Marianne I alone in that the element of risk has been surmounted; other than that, the tone and even the constant irony of Marianne II is not foreign to the traits manifested by her earlier version. Just as the latter is, for instance, capable of appearing tender, modest, serious, nonchalant, or sexy, so can Marianne II insist — in referring to some non-diegetic time subsequent to the chronology of the text — on her own capacity for strategic metamorphosis.[9] The two Mariannes are alike too in their instinctually quick analysis, and even more so in the priority they accord to inner feeling.[10]

But of course the different levels interfere with each other, and in the first instance because Marianne I is accessible to us only through the discourse of Marianne II; the distinction between them constitutes what Jean Rousset, in a well-known study, called the double register.[11] There are many variations on this original theme. The narrative is hardly pure, in that the narrator never maintains for long a discursive silence granting the diegesis itself full stage. Marianne's discourse is flooded with its own metadiscourse, her unending commentary not on the world, which is on an altogether different level, but on her own loquaciousness, industry, or laziness, and so forth. Unlike that of Scarron and Furetière, though, such metadiscourse no longer serves as satire of conventional narrative procedures but rather as a constituent of narrative, an aspect of the character and concerns of the intradiegetic narrator (whose existence is posited within the framework of the story). Yet it is echoed on an extradiegetic register; compare the editor's remarks with Marianne's:

> Voilà tout ce que j'avais à dire: ce petit préambule m'a paru nécessaire, et je l'ai fait du mieux que j'ai pu, car je ne suis point auteur, et jamais on n'imprimera de moi que cette vingtaine de lignes-ci. [p. 7].

> Il y a si longtemps, madame, que vous attendez cette suite de ma vie, que j'entrerai d'abord en matière; point de

---

[9] "Je savais être plusieurs femmes en une.... Tous les jours je lui renouvelais sa maîtresse, et c'était comme s'il en avait changé" (p. 51).

[10] Marianne I: "j'avais le cœur plus fin et plus avancé que l'esprit" (p. 18); Marianne II: "Je pense, pour moi, qu'il n'y a que le sentiment qui puisse nous donner des nouvelles un peu sûres de nous" (p. 22).

[11] "Marivaux ou la structure du double registre," ch. 3 in *Forme et signification* (Paris: José Corti, 1962).

préambule, je vous l'épargne. Pas tout à fait, me direz-vous, puisque vous en faites un, même en disant que vous n'en ferez point. En bien! je ne dis plus mot. [p. 429]

Just as notable is the degree to which the diegesis is dramatized through the metadiegetic voice of Marianne II in the present: "Oh! voyez combien il [= Valville] sera surpris; et si moi [= Marianne I], qui prévois sa surprise, je ne dois pas frémir plus que jamais de la lui donner!" (p. 82). This is a substitutive, projective function of narration: there is a dramatization before there are dramatic (diegetic) facts.

There are even whole scenes built around the conjecture concerning what might have been (or, anticipatorily for Marianne I, of what might take place), like the two pages describing her apprehensions of the upcoming encounter with Climal (pp. 241-42); there ensues a scenario, different contingent strategies, and the resultant tension: "je sortis du carrosse avec un tremblement digne de l'effroyable scène à laquelle je me préparais." It is a sort of prolepsis — narration by anticipation — but rather special in that the events are diegetically nil, never occurring actually in the story. A not insubstantial part of Marianne's narration is built around these imaginative projections or offshoots of the kernel story.[12] They frequently cannot be neatly situated on the level of either Marianne alone, inasmuch as they could be attributed to the thought processes of the one or the other.[13] Analysis of thought in *La Vie de Marianne* tends toward the diegetic stasis; the device is not new here except in the extent of its use, which makes time seem to flow in slow motion. Marianne II is quite aware of this disparity (*anisochronie*, in Genette's terms) between narrative time and diegetic time: "tout ce qui me vint alors dans l'esprit là-dessus, quoique long à dire, n'est qu'un instant à être pensé" (p. 72); this remark comes in the middle of a long passage devoted to the problem of what address Marianne I can

---

[12] Cf. p. 303: "Voyez, je vous prie, à quoi l'on va penser dans de certaines situations. Il n'y a point d'accident pour ou contre que l'on n'imagine, point de chimère agréable ou fâcheuse qu'on ne se forge."

[13] "Il ne lui était plus possible, *à mon avis*, d'aimer Mlle Varthon d'aussi bon cœur qu'il aurait fait" (p. 407): the italicized expression has no local tense, and therefore cannot be assigned clearly to either Marianne I or Marianne II.

give Valville before she finally pronounces the name of Mme Dutour — thirteen pages to describe a few minutes' embarrassed conversation, containing a major drama complete with its reflections, its "mortifications," its distresses.

Finally, to finish with this overview of narrative interplay, there are moments of explicit overlap between the narrative and diegetic levels (between *énonciation* and *énoncé*) which, although they pass as a function of Marianne's playfulness, reflect their complicated thematic relation. "Finissez donc, me diriez-vous volontiers; et c'est ce que je disais à Valville" (p. 75): here a word is uttered by the addressee or *narrataire* and passes, via the slippage of the conditional and imperfect tenses, through the narrative wall to Marianne I and becomes hers. The summary recited at the beginning of part seven of the rhythm of installments delivered to the Marquise is suspiciously parallel to that of the actual publication year by year of the different volumes up to that point, just as Tervire's "j'ai quelque confusion de vous parler si longtemps de moi" (p. 539) suggests a transfer from the diegetic plane to the instance of primary enunciation, and thus an allusion to the fact that the primary narrative (Marianne's) has been usurped by the second (Tervire's).

A sense of infinite gradations is the most fundamental form of identity between the two Mariannes, and is tied to the theme of inborn values. An intrinsic delicacy (p. 32) or "goût naturel" (pp. 212, 262) are aspects of Marianne I's revulsion for all signs of crudeness (Mme Dutour manifests "quelque chose de grossier qui me rebutait" [p. 32; cf. p. 309]). Especially is she sensitive to whatever wounds pride, the "discours mortifiants" [14] which turn charity into a brutal and hateful act and overlay the word itself with odious connotations (p. 29); she reacts to such insistence on her indigence as if she were being stripped in public; "on avait épluché ma misère pendant une heure" (p. 29). But the more benevolent curiosity manifested in the convent repels her too (p. 233) by its utter lack of tact.

---

[14] Cf.: "Ah! *l'humiliant discours!*" (p. 70); "j'aime encore mieux y renoncer, n'avoir rien et sortir de chez vous, que d'y demeurer exposée à des *discours aussi désobligeants*" (p. 98); "Vous savez que je sors d'entre les mains d'une fille vertueuse qui ne m'a pas élevée pour entendre *de pareils discours*" (p. 116).

The banter about her vanity shades into a serious and essential expression of self-worth: "j'avais l'âme un peu fière" (p. 29). All this ties in too with her instinctive rejection of domestic contamination, which in turn is part of the latent noble pretention: "j'aimerais mieux mourir que d'être chez quelqu'un en qualité de domestique; et si j'avais mon père et ma mère, il y a toute apparence que j'en aurais moi-même, au lieu d'en servir à personne" (p. 28). Even a shop is, of course, distasteful to her, and along with this automatic reaction, the further fact that she is awkward with her fingers seems to corroborate her unhesitating resentment at being "déplacée" in her life's station.[15] For even before these humiliations, her soul had risen spontaneously to the call of Parisian luxury:

> Dans ces rues il y avait des personnes de toutes espèces, il y avait des carrosses, et dans ces carrosses un monde qui m'était très nouveau, mais point étranger. Et sans doute, il y avait en moi *un goût naturel* qui n'attendait que ces objets-là pour s'y prendre, de sorte que, quand je les voyais, c'était comme si j'avais rencontré ce que je cherchais. [p. 33]

The sense of destiny in the novel is already strongly fixed in a passage such as this: Marianne has found her proper medium.

Even though begun on a note of amused detachment, the relationship of these fine qualities to high station is soon indirectly induced: "J'étais jolie, j'avais l'air fin; vous ne sauriez croire combien tout cela rendait *noble* et *délicat* l'attendrissement qu'on sentait pour moi. On n'aurait pas caressé une petite *princesse* infortunée d'une façon plus digne; c'était presque du *respect* que la compassion que j'inspirais" (p. 13). Such terms can hardly be innocent in a story where they correspond to the main concern of the plot: *noble* as epithet is a way of hedging towards its other semantic implications.[16]

---

[15] One of the signs of Climal's antipathetic role is precisely that he means the contrary of what Marianne means when he says, "vous n'êtes point née pour être lingère"; and from her lack of dexterity too he draws the opposite conclusion: "vous n'y feriez aucun progrès ... vous seriez donc toujours fille de boutique" (p. 116).

[16] There are other indirect ways of suggesting the connection, especially ambiguous terms such as the following: "il valait mieux qu'une fille *comme moi* mourût d'indigence que de vivre aussi *déplacée* que je l'étais" (p. 45).

In the company of like people, something telepathic takes place: "Les gens qui ont eux-mêmes un peu de *noblesse* de cœur se connaissent en égards de cette espèce, et remarquent bien ce qu'on fait pour eux" (pp. 154-55). "Nobility" plays on both sides of the register here, since only nobles possess (but do not *display*) such qualities and can decode their muted expression. It is paramount that Marianne's behavior have this particular "noble" quality,[17] and that it be recognized in turn by others: "en vérité je ne sache point de figure plus aimable, ni d'un air plus noble" (Mme Dorsin, p. 172); "vous ne sauriez croire combien je l'ai trouvée noble, généreuse et désintéressée" (Mme de Miran, p. 324). Such words are tendencious: they forcefully imply, in the surface movement of the text, nobility of blood. This is indeed the conclusion that Mme de Miran, with admirable rhetorical flourish, draws from these very facts in the family council:

> Je puis vous assurer que, par son bon esprit, par les qualités de l'âme, et par la *noblesse* des procédés, elle est *demoiselle* autant qu'aucune fille, de quelque rang qu'elle soit, puisse l'être. Oh! vous m'avouerez que cela impose, du moins c'est ainsi que j'en juge; et que ce [que] je vous dis là, elle ne le doit ni à l'usage du monde, ni à l'éducation qu'elle a eue, et qui a été fort simple: *il faut que cela soit dans le sang*; et voilà à mon gré l'essentiel. [p. 329]

Although this too is based on a hedge, it is meant to imply, in the absence of objective proof, that *sang* thus qualified can only be of one kind.[18]

Similarly, Marianne, who does not dare assert that a marriage with the likes of Villot is socially beneath her, tactfully advances her rejection under the cover of sensitivity, which comes to the same thing: "je suis née avec *un cœur* qu'il ne faudrait pas que j'eusse, et qu'il m'est pourtant impossible de vaincre. Jamais, *avec ce cœur-là*, je ne pourrai aimer le jeune homme qu'on me présente, jamais. Je sens que je ne m'accoutumerais pas à lui, que je le regarderais comme un homme qui ne serait *pas fait pour moi*" (p. 333).

[17] "Cette dernière réflexion ... avait quelque chose de noble qui m'y attacha" (p. 386); "la noblesse de mon procédé" (p. 407). There is perhaps some irony in the pun, "cette idée d'être véritablement aimée de Valville ... me fit penser si *noblement* ..." (p. 178).

[18] My conclusions here are in essential agreement with those of Lotringer: "La *Marianne* ménage un silence originel et qui l'est ici doublement puisque silence sur des origines que tout le récit a pour fonction d'interroger, que

Likewise, relatively banal phrases like "*née* si reconnaissante" (p. 122) and "*née* pour avoir du *goût*" (p. 211) are charged with noble connotations in a society where birth is the fundamental claim for consideration. There can only be an underlying irony in the repeated allusions to her luck — but always coming from people of low station — expressed "il faut que vous soyez *née coiffée*" (Mme Dutour, p. 43; Cathos, p. 306). From such an ambiguous phrase her religious friend (Tervire) draws the inference that expresses this essential tautology: "une fille aussi *bien née* que vous l'êtes ... ne peut assurément venir que de très bon lieu" (p. 236).[19]

Marianne's is a kind of limit case, since an unsolvable enigma envelops her origins while the truth, known to Marianne II, is posited from the start without being ever divulged to the reader. Thus her whole story of aspiration to noble acceptance can only be an adventure. For an orphan, by definition, cannot be noble: nobility is determined by one's relatives, and no one without them can possibly be anything but nothing. And she is more extremely divorced from social definition than even that alone suggests, since she is also cut off from her *pays*. She is thus doubly originless, someone with neither blood nor country, come literally from *nowhere*; she has no one to go to, and nowhere to go: "et moi, je ne sais *où aller, on ne m'attend nulle part*" (p. 135). She is afflicted with a rare social disease of which one can scarcely even speak without euphemism: "est-ce qu'on ne sait pas la conséquence de ces choses-là?" (p. 232). In the society of her time, Marianne is a freak.

Is anything about Marianne's birth knowable? Does it matter?

The specific irresolution with which the text leaves us is, I think, undeniable: Marianne's story is not a puzzle where one can hope to find the missing pieces. This does not mean, however, that

---

rien, on le sait, ne pourra jamais mettre à jour.... Toute recherche deviendrait impossible si la différence sociale n'était déjà signifiée à chaque instant par la noblesse naturelle de Marianne. Ce que Marivaux désigne par l'*âme,* ou le cœur. L'itinéraire de l'héroïne consiste par suite à faire coïncider noblesse naturelle et noblesse de naissance, le cœur qu'elle a avec la condition qu'elle n'a pas" (p. 306).

[19] *Né coiffé*: "toutes choses lui succèdent heureusement"; *bien né*: "bonnes inclinations"; *bon lieu*: "on dit qu'un homme vient de *bon lieu,* ou de *bas lieu,* selon qu'il est de bonne, ou de basse naissance" (Furetière, *Dictionnaire universel*). Cf., in Tervire's own story: "une fille née ce que tu es" (p. 488), "j'étais née douce" (p. 494); Tervire of course is authentically noble.

there is no determination of the question within its dynamics. Marianne, in aspiring to noble recognition, enters a world of very strict rules which explicitly exclude her, where there can be no such thing as a presumption of nobility. True nobility is always demonstrable. And the point is not that her birth is irrevocably undecidable, once a total reading is taken into account, but that, for purposes of the plot, the proof is irremediably lost.[20]

All of the "noble" qualities to which I have alluded tend in one clear direction, which is to signify, indirectly to be sure, the latent "quality" of birth which can only in time be authenticated — although at some point beyond the diegetic limits of the text, when Marianne is about thirty-five.[21] But there are telling clues in the terminology of Marianne II's text, if one looks at it closely. Take, for example, a symptomatic remark of Mme Dorsin's: "Y a-t-il rien dans la physionomie de mademoiselle qui pronostique les infortunes qu'elle a essuyées? ... Mais il faut tôt ou tard que chacun ait ses malheurs dans ce monde; et voilà les siens passés, j'en suis sûre" (p. 172). Here we have the curious combination of a "prognostic" about the *past* and a reassurance about the future, which may be subtly revealing. What does it mean to "prognosticate" the past? Unless, of course, it lies in the future? Diegetically, Marianne's nobility is not in the past, where it is effaced, but in the future where it will be discovered: her noble *origins* are, paradoxically, *predictable*. One really cannot know whether merit or birth is principally at issue:

---

[20] Cf. Lotringer: "Marianne doit, c'est là le paradoxe fondateur du roman, partir à la recherche non de ce qu'elle n'est pas, mais de ce qu'elle est sans le savoir, non d'une différence absente du champ dénoté, mais présente au contraire pour elle tout au long *sur le mode de l'absence*" (p. 306).

[21] "The aristocratic principle is inherent to Marianne," writes Peter Brooks; "never do we as readers question the nobility of Marianne's birth.... Marianne discovers in herself aristocratic origins" (*The Novel of Worldliness*, Princeton, 1969, p. 97). The merit of Lotringer's position is to be based not just on such an intuitive judgment but on an argument concerning structures: "dans un roman fondé sur la différence des 'conditions', la vertu est l'apanage exclusif du secteur marqué [la noblesse].... Tout personnage vertueux est nécessairement noble, mais tout noble n'est pas nécessairement vertueux. Les droits de Marianne à la naissance sont, bien que laissés en suspens, incontestables puisque d'ordre structural" ("Manon l'écho," *Romanic Review*, 63, No. 2 [1972], p. 102). Cf. too the remark by Démoris: "Il est sans doute tout à fait arbitraire de la part de Marianne de se croire un destin: mais cette illusion n'est peut-être aussi que le fait d'une personne de qualité" (p. 412).

the first seems to gain ground on the second as the story progresses, but ultimately the second comes to corroborate the first.

Moreover, bearing in mind that Marianne II knows the answer, what but nobility can be implied by the symbolism of the affirmation that her (putative) mother "m'avait baignée de son sang" (p. 11)? Could Marianne II say, of Mme Dutour's shop, "j'étais déplacée, et je n'étais pas faite pour être là" (p. 32) if her ulterior knowledge branded her as a bastard or commoner? Even the carefully balanced terms in which the "factual" enigma is placed yield to scrutiny. "Il y a quinze ans que je ne savais pas encore si le sang d'où je sortais était noble ou non, si j'étais bâtarde ou légitime" (pp. 9-10): to this, Henri Coulet says: "le lecteur est mis devant quatre hypothèses sans qu'on lui laisse entendre quelle est la bonne."[22] This is to refuse to *read the terms,* merely because the syntax is symmetrical. Indeed it is, yet these are not merely four alternatives; the very way they are put betrays a privileged perspective from which the (non-) mystery is posed. "Noble ou non" are not the terms in which a disappointed aspirant would chose to frame the question, for they make *noble* the pivot; and "bâtarde ou légitime" would hardly suit, if the first adjective were really applicable, the Marianne who cringes when a Mme Dutour says to her, "J'aimerais autant qu'on me dît que je suis bâtarde" (p. 43). One must not suppose that stylistic equilibrium makes the terminology neutral: the implicit connotations of the chiasma make Marianne *noble et légitime*. Another instance:

> Je me disais déjà que dans le monde, il fallait qu'il y eût quelque chose qui valait mieux que cela [=Mme Dutour]; je soupirais après, j'étais triste d'être privée de ce mieux que je ne connaissais pas. Dites-moi d'où cela venait? Où est-ce que j'avais pris mes délicatesses? *Étaient-elles dans mon sang?* cela se pourrait bien; venaient-elles du séjour que j'avais fait à Paris? cela se pourrait encore. [pp. 32-33]

---

[22] Coulet, p. 409. Coulet maintains steadfastly that, since the novel was not completed, the answer cannot be known, or more exactly does not exist. He therefore insists more firmly on Marianne's radical lack of essence: "Son néant est ce qu'elle a de plus sûr"; "le sujet de *Marianne* n'est pas: comment une orpheline découvre qui elle est, mais: comment être soi quand on n'est personne" (pp. 222, 224).

Once again, we have here a theoretical hesitation, blood being only one possible explanation of two. But what makes it a *possible* explanation? For though one can contest whether, in this overall rhetorical framework, "noble" qualities necessarily imply blood nobility, there is no way to maintain that they could derive directly from a blood which is base. Marianne cannot even pose a variant of the fundamental question without privileging in some way the marked response.

At this point, we can viably distinguish what I referred to in my Foreword as the first two levels of the textual process. There is no ambiguity, from the very outset, about the plot: Marianne relates "how I got to be what I am" — that is, Countess Marianne. The thesis too behind that plot could not be much clearer: Marianne II is obviously, one way or another, noble; and that is as it should be because Marianne I is "noble" in character and thus worthy of being ennobled. Level two, which will be further elaborated as this discussion continues, synthesizes traces of exterior evidence, Marianne's qualities of character, and eventual "factual" confirmation of her origins, in a slightly oblique rhetorical process tending to one ultimate, complete realization of essence: Marianne simply *is* noble, at all times and in every sense of the term.

This does not affect the scrupulous neutrality of the diegetic facts concerning her parentage, and which in truth are not facts but only tokens modulated in function of the multiple metamorphoses of narration. The data are too far removed, too obstructed by hearsay, absolutely lacking in evidence.[23] The story never can change, and yet it evolves constantly in its incessant retellings: thirteen versions, by Annick Jugan's count, "sans qu'il lui soit rien ajouté, sans qu'il soit touché à ce jeu d'éléments donnés une fois pour toutes et qui se veut jusqu'à la fin sans surprise, ayant pour seul maître le récit et non l'histoire."[24] "Il peut y entrer," as Valville

---

[23] Even collateral information yields like quicksand; Marianne's protectors in her youth, besides the fact that they drop simultaneously into oblivion without a trace, were themselves all but traceless, known, like Marianne, only by bits of hearsay allowing a presumption of their "très bonne famille."

[24] "*La Vie de Marianne* de Marivaux: l'équivalent littéraire d'un art de la fugue," *Degré Second*, No. 1 (1977), 59-95, and No. 2 (1978), 67-99; No. 1, p. 88. She remarks further on the impossibility of a "neutral" version of this theme: "on ne peut prétendre le saisir à nu quand il existe non en lui-même

puts it, "une infinité de circonstances qui changent considérablement les choses" (p. 277). But in reality the crux is not the "circonstances," but rather the perspective. Valville himself illustrates this beautifully by his narration of Marianne's "story" to Mlle de Fare in reply to the immediately previous version of Mme Dutour (pp. 262-67): besides the fact that all the inferences are reversed in his telling, the role of Mme Dutour herself is totally eclipsed — although there could be no question, objectively speaking, of denying it.

Marianne's own narrations of the "story" evolve tendenciously: at first she allows an uncertainty about which woman in the carriage (indeed, if either) was her mother, but to the abbess she solves this question without further ado and adds that her parents' domestics as well as her parents themselves too lost their lives (p. 151). There is a practical shrewdness involved here: Marianne has sensed that to seek to restore the neutral facts in all their ambiguity can only be an error, and henceforth she never retreats on this movement toward emphasizing their favorable implications — except, of course, ironically, as when she wants to shame someone for ill-treatment of her by rehearsing her "moi qui ne suis rien" routine. Indeed, Marianne has no use for witnesses, who can only shed doubt on her preferred inferences;[25] nothing in her path depends for favorable resolution upon the availability of witnesses,[26] but only on favorable reception of a certain rhetorically disposed apparatus which is Marianne's only real birthright. If one looks at Mme de Miran's narration to the assembled family in part seven, one finds all the uncertainties turned into "des indices presque certains," and, for

---

mais seulement sous ses formes diverses où il se dérobe sans cesse.... Le formuler de façon neutre ou abstraite n'est qu'une nouvelle variante" (No. 2, p. 95). I will not pursue here the matter of the story's permutations, which Jugan has analyzed shrewdly and perceptively.

[25] She refers to Valville's lackey, who has followed her, as "un témoin de plus de la petitesse de mon état" (p. 91); the deadly effects of Mme Dutour's testimony need no elaboration: "passer ainsi à travers la vie d'une Mme Dutour, signifie pour l'histoire être pulvérisée puis amalgamée à tout un au jour le jour d'insignifiance, de prosaïsme et de trivialité" (Annick Jugan, ibid., No. 1, p. 84).

[26] If there is an exception it appears to be the availability of Mme Dutour as character witness, based upon her few days' acquaintance with Marianne, the night she is taken into the convent under Mme de Miran's protection (pp. 155-56).

good measure, the parents' one lackey is now two (p. 328). Although specious, this argument is capital in the plot: if Marianne emerges a recognized aristocrat, it is not alone because of her noble behavior, nor certainly because of any hard (and much less, new) evidence, but because someone appeared at the right time and place to thus "prove" her nobility. Although she has for her objectively only "tous les préjugés," this crucial intervention reverses her position and transforms her from an ambitious nothing into an unfortunate, deprived aristocrat: and only by virtue of her *malheur* thus framed is she entitled to touch and provoke tears of sympathy.

Mme de Miran herself, however, initially took an interest in Marianne only because she too received the story as it was intended by Marianne. For even she and Mme Dorsin, when discussing Marianne from a purely exterior, hearsay standpoint because unaware of the character's identity (pp. 175-76), call her a "grisette," "une fille de cette sorte-là," "la petite aventurière": [27] indication enough of the normal construction one of their society would make of Valville's encounter with her. It is far from their minds that Marianne, by class, could possibly be a *grisette;* and though their perceptions are subsequently corrected in *her* regard, they think none the better of *grisettes* for it. The terms of Mme de Miran's offer of protection sufficiently reveal that only the positive presumption of birth determines her compassionate intervention: "je ne souffrirai point qu'une fille *aussi bien née* y soit jamais réduite [à demander l'aumône]" (p. 154); and at the same time, it is precisely this sympathy predicated on like birth which marks her as a good soul in the overall rhetorical structure of the novel.

For this purely attitudinal question is the key to every character's position. Either a given hearer to whom it is exposed takes her story to mean (negative mark) that she is simply without birth — that is, nothing, and with claim to nothing; or that contrariwise (positive mark) she is a tragically stricken noble, in which case to treat her as a commoner would be unworthy and even unjust. Her *malheurs* take on irreducibly opposing meanings at this point, which splits the novel's society into two camps. Mlle de Fare, for example,

---

[27] The term is ominous enough to make Marianne fear her enterprise is sunk: "Petite aventurière! le terme était encore de mauvais augure. Je ne m'en tirerai jamais, me disais-je" (p. 176).

is as spontaneously recognized as a friend and ally as her mother is as an adversary, and one evidence of her fine character is that she comes up on her own with the idea which by romantic definition is a good one, of Marianne's marrying Valville (p. 259). Climal, on the contrary, keeps referring to Marianne's sorry *état* (pp. 28, 111) with no reference to her birth, which is where Marianne wants to play the stakes. Cathos as well: "entre nous, qu'est-ce qu'on devient avec cela? On reste sur le pavé; on vous en montrera mille comme vous qui y sont"; she is fortunate enough to be offered a husband "dont une belle et bonne fille de bourgeois s'accommoderait à merveille" (p. 306) — *fille de bourgeois* signifying in this context what Marianne is *not even*.

Like Mme Dutour and Saint-Vincent, whose place between the two groups is mixed,[28] these characters lack the privileged, decisive vision to discern the truth — essential, not factual — of (not *about*) Marianne. Their affective role is indissociable from this petty perspective of theirs. Villot, the symbol of what in bourgeois terms would be the lucky marriage, provokes a visceral repulsion when he starts to kiss Marianne's hand: "le cœur m'en souleva" (p. 310); and it is he who, spurned, reveals the proprietary bias with respect to relatives which assumes the right to stigmatize and insult her through what she lacks.[29] Other ironies, situational, similarly draw attention to this radical absence: the abbess's saying, "je gagerais qu'elle est fille unique, et qu'on la veut marier malgré elle"[30] (p. 150).

---

[28] They are at least not hostile, although neither manages to help very much, and their vision is similarly limited on this score: at times Mme Dutour returns with almost every sentence to her obsessive reminders: "vous n'avez ni père ni mère," "vous ne connaissez point vos parents," "vous ne l'êtes [= parente] ni de près ni de loin, ni à nous ni à personne" (pp. 98, 99, 127); as for Saint-Vincent, the absence of relatives raises for him only the question of charity, and he can never imagine her parents as even potentially noble, which would give her a positive claim to something.

[29] "Ce n'est pas que je sois en peine de trouver une femme; il n'y a pas encore plus de huit jours qu'on parla d'une, qui aura beaucoup de bien d'une tante, et qui d'ailleurs a père et mère" (p. 311).

[30] A further irony here, anticipatory: although the total opposite of a *fille unique,* Marianne will be none the less subjected to the duress of a marriage intended *malgré elle.* Cf. Mme de Fare: "Est-ce qu'elle a envie d'être religieuse?... C'est peut-être qu'elle y a quelque parente?" (p. 255). By situational irony I refer not to any extralinguistic phenomenon, but to what is neither enunciated by Marianne (although reported and perhaps appreciated

Although such words are not necessarily purposefully harmful, they come only from members of the unsympathetic cast of characters; the true friends seem inherently incapable, even in ignorance, of such awkward and wounding remarks.[31] In any event, the injury consists, as Mme de Miran's rhetorical tour de force establishes, in a failure to recognize Marianne's nobility: "Il n'est donc point ici question de galanterie, mais d'une *justice* que tout veut que je lui rende" (p. 328). And justice is the name of a reintegration of Marianne into her home class: "Je vous rends justice" (p. 338), says the minister, who functions here as a tribunal and decides the matter, authoritatively, in her favor, both on the grounds of the supposed evidence — "ce ne sera pas moi qui lui refuserai le titre de mademoiselle, et je crois avec vous qu'on le doit même à la condition dont elle est" (p. 331) — and on those of inherent qualities — "La noblesse de vos parents est incertaine, mais celle de votre cœur est incontestable" (p. 337). Thus, although in the absence of official documentation, Marianne is afforded immanent right of entry to the promised land.

No one in Marianne's day could have formulated the incongruous modern proposition that existence precedes essence. Birth, in the world view of this novel, is the ontological origin of being; without it, it is impossible to know oneself — what one *is*. It is to be originless, "inconnue sur la terre" (p. 135); there is indeed something almost existential in Marianne's "*effroi* d'être *étrangère* à tous les hommes, de ne voir la source de mon sang *nulle part*" (p. 46). Literally nothing can be known by others either about a person in these conditions: "on ne sait d'où elle sort, on n'est sûr de rien avec elle, à moins qu'on ne devine" (p. 327).[32] *La Vie de Marianne* can equally well be called a novel about origins or a novel about

---

by her) nor intended ironically by the enunciator, to whom the ironic relation to the facts of Marianne's case are at the time unknown.

[31] There is of course situational irony too in Valville's "vous et vos parents me serez éternellement inconnus, à moins que vous ne me disiez votre nom" (p. 78), but it is not he who introduces it: when he says this, Marianne is already in the midst of a long meditation on the quandary of the name.

[32] Saint-Vincent likewise reflects the sense that something about Marianne upsets the stability of normal perceptions and established identities: "Que faut-il que je pense? et qu'est-ce que nous, bonté divine?... Si vous dites vrai, à qui se fiera-t-on?" (p. 143). An epistemological dilemma is posed by her discourse, with its strange undertones of challenge to the known world.

essences, because origins and essences are so inextricably interrelated: essence is not invented, but given or potentially even rediscovered in an origin. What Marianne is and where she comes from are but two facets of the same question: *qui je suis.*

Thus the emphasis on the missing threads, which leave Marianne adrift: "Je ne sais point de qui je suis née" (p. 193); "je ne suis la fille ni la parente de qui que ce soit" (p. 24); "[elle] ne connaît ni ses parents ni sa famille" (p. 289); and so forth (note the delicacy of the way Tervire phrases it: "vos parents vous ont perdue" [p. 236]). Such a gap inevitably entails a doubt as to the ground of being, expressed by significant and insistent clusters of related expressions:

> ... une pauvre fille *qui n'est rien* ... [p. 185]
> Il n'y a ni père ni mère, on ne sait *qui elle est.* [p. 156]
> Elle ne sait *qui elle est.* [pp. 264-65]
> On ne sait ni d'où vous venez, ni *qui vous êtes.* [p. 306]
> Vous n'avez ni père ni mère, et ne savez *qui vous êtes.* [p. 317]
> Une fille qui ne sait *qui elle est!* [p. 391]
> ... étant née *ce qu'elle était* ... [p. 227]
> Examinez *ce que vous êtes.* [p. 298]
> Je ne sais que trop *ce que je suis.* [p. 298]
> Dieu nous a caché *ce qu'elle est.* [p. 328][33]

Qui je suis, evidently enough, is in her case a signifier with no signified: "quand je vous dirais qui je suis, je n'en serais pas plus connue de vous, madame" (p. 149). On the contrary, *être* is full of content for the person who knows "who he is," as illustrate Mme Dorsin's remarks about Valville's lovesick behavior: "qu'en concluez-vous? ... qu'il va oublier ce qu'il est, ce qu'il vous doit, ce qu'il se doit à lui-même ... ?" (p. 176). Not just *être* but *devoir* and *se devoir quelque chose* are noble categories of thought, indices of an existence infused with essence. And Marianne shares them, implicitly: her problem is to demonstrate that they are meaningful to her as well.

---

[33] Climal, to whom Marianne is a desired object, interestingly construes her *être* in terms reflecting that fact: "[Valville] vous a trouvée ce que vous êtes, c'est-à-dire belle, aimable, charmante" (p. 110); they also betray an underlying concern, not only to hide his unworthy deeds, but to hide his prize from the sight of other aspirants.

All this connects, of course, to the question of a name. Marianne's putative parents bore a "nom assez étranger" possibly not their true one, which symbolizes in itself her equivocal status as a (perhaps) outsider, the authenticity of even that being uncertain. Marianne of course has no name but Marianne, which is the same thing as being no one:[34] whenever she writes a letter, she must sign simply *Marianne* (pp. 155, 189, 360), having nothing else to sign—practically the only word so italicized in the text. Indeed, *La Vie de Marianne* too has no other, and yet, as Mme Dutour points out (p. 265), even it is not her true (original) given name. Noble girls, in the social universe of the novel, are never called by a first name: nothing more than this fact is needed to understand "j'ai si peu l'air d'une Marianne" (p. 82), or "prendre ce nom-là, c'était presque déclarer Mme Dutour et sa boutique" (p. 79). Mlle de Fare's riposte to Mme Dutour, "Mademoiselle n'est pas cette Marianne pour qui vous la prenez" (p. 264) reflects the assumption that her new friend, obviously (to her) noble, *cannot* be "Marianne" to a Mme Dutour; but Mme Dutour, for her part, is equally uncomprehending, for Marianne (to her) *cannot* be "Mademoiselle," whence her insistent reply: "En un mot comme en cent ... c'est Marianne; et quoi encore? Marianne. C'est le nom qu'elle avait quand je l'ai prise; si elle ne l'a plus, c'est qu'elle en a changé, mais je ne lui en savais point d'autre, ni elle non plus" (p. 264).[35]

The abbess has no difficulty reading an identity into her *prédestinée*'s features ("il est certain que votre vocation est écrite sur votre visage") but it evaporates as soon as she discovers that Marianne has no patronym; only nobles can be *prédestinés*, it appears, and such lack of identity is properly incomprehensible: "Jésus, mademoiselle! ... voilà qui est bien fâcheux, point de parents!" (pp. 150-51). For the Church is a purely social institution in *La Vie de Marianne,* endowed with no special powers of spiritual vision. And

---

[34] Cf. Tervire's remarks about the old and faithful chambermaid: "C'est une amie d'une espèce unique ... qui n'est, pour ainsi dire, *personne* pour vous ... une amie qui *n'en a pas même le nom*" (p. 499).

[35] One of the reasons for her ungracious insistence is of course that titles and names are an aspect of her own fierce class pride, which Marianne hears her exclaim vociferously to the *fiacre*: "[je] ne suis pas une chiffonnière, mais bel et bien Mme Dutour, madame pour toi, madame pour les autres, et madame tant que je serai au monde" (p. 97).

Marianne, always attentive to slight nuances of name and title, comments on the linguistic effect of this unanticipated disorientation on the abbess: "Ainsi de tous côtés vous voyez notre impuissance, dont je suis vraiment mortifiée; car vous m'affligez, ma pauvre enfant (ma pauvre! quelle différence de style! Auparavant elle m'avait dit: ma belle),[36] vous m'affligez, mais que ne vous êtes-vous adressée au curé de votre paroisse?" (p. 153). And there the vicious circle begins anew, for the parish supposes an identity and a home, and the nun cannot conceive of someone who has no name and in addition comes from nowhere.

Adoption by Mme de Miran confers a sort of name: that of a daughter. "Ma mère, vous voyez ce que c'est que Marianne" (p. 197) weighs the terms on the two syntactic ends of a scale which in this instance is tipping to the left. But for the society at large a mere adoption will not stand in lieu of patronym, and the introduction of Marianne therefore depends upon inventing for her an *origin,* both name and place: "je t'y mènerais comme la fille d'une de mes meilleures amies qui est morte, qui était en province, et qui en mourant t'a confiée à mes soins" (p. 210). The subterfuge is double, taking in both the social circle, and on the other hand the reader: for this makes someone of Marianne, but Mademoiselle *who?* We do not know whether a (another) name was actually invented for her, or whether — equally significantly — "mademoiselle" as title simply suffices as its own self-sufficient guarantee of the authenticity of the "name" unspoken: paradoxically, if one has a name it need not be used. The real symbolic conferral of letters of nobility on Marianne comes from the simple and repeated term "ma fille," which in effect makes her marriageable to a noble (Valville). It changes the signified of *être:* "elle m'a même défendu de songer que je suis orpheline, et elle a bien raison; je ne dois plus me ressouvenir que je le suis; cela n'est plus vrai" (p. 195). And this too is sanctioned by the minister, when he dismisses the family saying to Mme de Miran, "je vous rends votre fille" (p. 337). Yet despite the efficacious grace of this quasi-official adoption, *fille* is not a *proper* name (in every weighty sense of the word *proper*), and a certain fearful void still yawns beneath Marianne the tightrope-walker, again expressed in terms of

---

[36] Mme de Fare, after the fall, calls her "ma belle enfant," but this is a pointed demotion from "mademoiselle" (pp. 274-75).

the name, when the marriage founders: "Cette mère si tendre croit venir voir sa fille, me dis-je, et elle ne sait pas qu'elle ne vient voir que Marianne, et que ce sera toujours Marianne pour elle" (p. 395). [37]

In this position, Marianne is not devoid of a degree of aggressiveness, which she more often than not discounts as an effect of her petty vanity; and her most violent weapon is her beauty. When she says, "j'effaçais si fort la pauvre Toinon que j'en avais honte" (p. 51), the humane *honte* serves to attenuate the ferocity of the *j'effaçais* crushing this inferior. With more worthy competition, at church, the terms are more gallant but the result more significant; all the elegant ladies are suddenly ignored when Marianne appears: "Elles s'aperçurent... que la désertion était générale" (p. 60). This scene is represented as an intricate drama, a battle really, but disguised by the subtlety and femininity of the arms and the tacit nature of the victory. Although its erotic implications are hardly negligible, beauty is essentially the displaced terrain of an assault on the bastion of rank which Marianne is in no position to launch frontally. Thus the sister-inmate who pulls rank on her with a "ton de princesse" is furious in fact, as Tervire says, to find herself jealous on the grounds which are Marianne's strength, and where she becomes the (losing) challenger: [38] Marianne does not fail to signal again her triumph, sealed by sentiment. [39] Similarly, her cold war with Varthon is waged on grounds of beauty, this time with a handicap: "je me sentis

---

[37] Symbolically, since Mme de Miran and her son bear different names (not an uncommon phenomenon among the nobility), the "name" has a different value according to which attachment predominates: to be the daughter of Mme de Miran is rather different from being Mme de Valville.

[38] "[Elle] ne pouvait pas me pardonner d'être, peut-être, aussi belle qu'elle. Quand je dis peut-être, c'est pour parler comme elle.... Il est vrai que j'étais brillante" (p. 234).

[39] Marianne's control and understatement dissimulate a deadly counter-aggression: "Non, ma mère, répondis-je [à Tervire] d'un air doux, mais contristé; je n'ai rien, Dieu m'a tout ôté, et je dois croire que je suis au-dessous de tout le monde; mais j'aime encore mieux être comme je suis, que d'avoir tout ce que mademoiselle a de plus que moi, et d'être capable d'insulter les personnes affligées. Ce discours et mes larmes qui s'y mêlaient émurent le cœur de mes compagnes, et les mirent de mon parti" (pp. 236-37). Marianne is of course also good with words, and demonstrates her sarcasm with particular skill in quoting to Valville the injurious things said by his friends, and relayed through Varthon by himself (pp. 392, 404-5).

mortifiée, je vous l'avoue, de paraître avec tant de désavantage auprès d'elle.... Elle était plus brillante que moi" (p. 400). But the intricate game of subtleties, always rationalized via the code of femininity as an effect of fine, virtually inherent sensitivity, all but swings this disadvantage to the other side.[40]

Garments are a critical intermediary, because they are one of the means by which one visibly bears one's pedigree. Therefore the dress from Climal, an essential vehicle for one all-important day, is on the one hand a fraud, but on the other a sort of restitution of the value represented by her original dress: "j'étais vêtue d'une manière trop distinguée pour n'être que la fille d'une femme de chambre" (p. 11). Whence, despite the conditional tense which attenuates any direct equivalence, the socially symbolic description, "L'habit ... était *noble* et modeste, et tel qu'il aurait pu convenir à *une fille de condition* qui n'aurait pas eu de bien" (p. 38). Marianne feels fully valorized only when appropriately (by her standards) dressed, which is why Climal's gift is a transfusion to her spirits. The church performance, which creates the bridge from Climal to Valville and a noble future, rides on it: it is considered as borrowed, in effect, with some shame for the economic implications, and returned at day's end because another source of new clothes has been found.[41] It is thus the pivotal element in the transition which brings her back to Mme Dutour's, like Cinderella, altered and unrecognizable: "Je l'aperçus de loin qui me regardait dans le carrosse où j'étais, et qui m'y voyait, non comme Marianne, mais comme une personne qui lui ressemblait tant, qu'elle en était surprise; et mon carrosse était déjà arrêté à la porte, qu'elle ne s'avisait pas encore de croire que ce fût moi" (pp. 90-91). Marianne speaks as one promoted to a completely dif-

---

[40] "J'étais dispensée d'avoir mes grâces, et elle était obligée d'avoir les siennes; aussi les avait-elle, et voilà jusqu'où elles allaient, pas davantage; au lieu qu'on ne savait pas jusqu'où iraient les miennes, quand elles seraient revenues" (pp. 400-401).

[41] "Ma bienfaitrice m'y fit habiller comme si j'avais été sa fille" (p. 160). Lotringer has underscored this function, to which I shall return below: "l'argent, du fait qu'il subvient aux besoins, participe du peuple tandis que la robe par son luxe, sa superfluité, désigne déjà le rang auquel elle aspire.... M. de Climal n'a donc pu exposer l'orpheline à l'Échange qu'en invoquant la différence sociale (vanité) contre la différence morale (vertu). Marianne a dû anticiper par sa toilette le rang qui lui est encore refusé" ("Le Roman impossible," p. 307).

ferent plane, now a stranger on the previous one.[42] Whenever this kind of transfiguration occurs in literature, a certain mortgage has been entailed and a possibly evil bargain threatens to exact its toll: in Marianne's case, Climal's role compromises the purity of an accession which he has unwittingly made possible by wanting to prettify her exclusively for his own private consumption. From his standpoint too, then, something has at this juncture gone badly awry; three "scenes" — the two chance meetings with Valville, and Mme Dutour's quarrel with the coachman — have threatened to publicize a transaction which depended on secret.[43] That secret, though, now appears to Marianne as an implicating liability, and no risk equals that of maintaining it henceforth.[44]

In this, of course, despite some complicity between them (for example, in their tacit agreement not to recognize each other at Valville's), their wavelength is absolutely different. Marianne is preoccupied with the effects on herself — "voulez-vous que je sois la victime de ceci? Que va-t-il [= Valville] penser de moi? pour qui me prendra-t-il?" (p. 121) — which are of no interest to Climal. Still, greed (sexual in this case) is strong, and he will accept some risk provided his semantic transition from *charité* to *amitié* to *amour* is properly requited. Marianne now will not allow the slippage, and rivets him to the primary signifieds: "je compte sur votre amitié, monsieur, et sur la vertu dont vous faites profession, ajoutai-je pour

---

[42] Marianne's path is of course wholly incomprehensible to Mme Dutour. How, after all, could she imagine that Marianne would return in a coach? She not unnaturally supposes that Marianne's falling-out with Climal means she is going into a *decline,* and offers to buy the dress which "serait trop belle pour vous" (p. 127); and after that, she knows only that Marianne has entered a convent: hence, on both scores, her unbelieving exclamations at the De Fare encounter in part six.

[43] "Il vaut mieux, et pour vous et pour moi, qu'on ignore les liaisons que nous avons ensemble" (p. 109); "c'est dans le secret que je prétends réparer vos malheurs, et vous assurer sourdement une petite fortune" (p. 115). His remark to Mme Dutour, "ce sont là de ces scènes qu'il faut éviter le plus qu'on peut" (p. 106), reflects also this concern, but in addition the more general noble attitude that such scandal is distasteful: better to pay than quarrel, money not being the essential. Preoccupation with money is bourgeois and Marianne does not share it either: "Vous voyez bien ces vingt sols-là, Marianne, je ne vous les pardonnerai jamais ... car l'intérêt de Mme Dutour ne s'étourdissait de rien" (p. 97).

[44] "J'irai où vous voudrez, je vous obéirai en tout ... pourvu qu'à présent vous ne fassiez plus mystère de cette charité à laquelle je me soumets" (p. 122).

lui ôter la hardiesse de s'expliquer plus clairement" (p. 113). Climal knows that there is an element of feint in Marianne's role: "vous savez fort bien ce que je veux dire par le mot d'amitié; mais vous êtes une petite malicieuse, qui vous divertissez, et qui feignez de ne pas m'entendre." Indeed she knows quite well by this point what he means, but he is caught in a web of his own making which she exploits by returning to his weak point, piety ("Laissons là ma piété"), and borrowing its language to shame him with.[45] Climal, who has never viewed Marianne as anything but a wholly dependent underling, reacts with only slightly veiled threats, like the offended noble he is who can scarcely believe he could be so defied by someone of no station.[46] In the long run, of course, the ambiguous charity with which Climal's attempt on her virtue all began comes to an ironic reversal, as Marianne is ultimately asked to grant both charity and silence for his sake.[47]

Marianne gambles, in one sense: she forces the issues when she judges they are ripe. The break with Climal furnishes the occasion for a letter to Valmont designed to "faire regretter ma perte" (p. 130), and at the same time boldly assert an only slightly oblique form of noble claim in its conclusion: "... une fille affligée, vertueuse, et peut-être votre égale" (p. 158) — note that this letter is *not* signed *Marianne*. *Peut-être votre égale* is, at the least, brave, and in the family view brazen: in terms of the social structure, it is an assertion without substance, absolutely gratuitous — though not so, to be sure, in terms of the novel's thematics and Marianne's consciousness. Its full import, however, is not immediately evident; *peut-être votre égale* does not even mean, as it first appears, "peut-être, comme vous, noble," which indeed would make little sense in the context where Valville already supposes it: she could only call her nobility into question by expressing it thus. Rather, it can only mean, "(within the nobility) of a rank equal or superior to

---

[45] "Il faut donc absolument que vous lui parliez [= à Valville], quand ce ne serait qu'à cause de moi; vous y êtes obligé par ma réputation, et même pour ôter le scandale, autrement ce serait offenser Dieu" (p. 122).

[46] "Allez, petite fille, ... je ne vous crains point, vous n'êtes pas capable de me nuire: et vous qui me menacez, craignez à votre tour que je ne me fâche, entendez-vous?" (p. 123).

[47] "Soyez discrète, la charité vous l'ordonne, entendez-vous? Ne révélez jamais cette étrange aventure à personne" (p. 144).

yours." The very use of the expression presupposes — or presumes, depending on the point of view — nobility.[48] Beginning with an objective ambiguity, Marianne decides in effect to play to the limit the as-if-noble hypothesis, to attempt at the risk of almost criminal fraudulence — double or nothing — to stake a claim to which she is not formally entitled. If the wager fails, she can always settle for less later.

Which is not to say that she does not, initially at least, obey the rule of precarious balance: never let go of anything until you have something else to hold onto. Twice she attaches herself to Saint-Vincent,[49] relinquishing her grip the second time only because Mme de Miran has intervened. Her trip to church is from all appearances a sort of fishing expedition to see what she can find, to what extent she can hope to exploit her good looks and outfit; even she does not expect the immediate concrete dividends she gets with ample help from chance. But though she needs its collaboration, her instinct is always to seek the maximum yield.[50] If the *tourière,* for example, invites her to speak with one of the religious, she instinctively goes right to the top: "Oui, madame, lui répondis-je, je souhaiterais bien parler à Madame la prieure" (p. 148). There is no sense of destiny developed in her ascension, except in a flippant sort of way; Marianne never suggests that she is really impelled by any outside force which will have its way; the gambles she takes could fail, except that they are so shrewdly calculated. She takes an existential sort of leap — entering the convent, for instance, while knowing neither its name nor that of Mme de Miran — but where little, concretely, stands to be lost. And her passivity, which she on more than one occasion emphasizes,[51] is part dissimulation. The scene in the chapel which so strikes Mme de Miran

---

[48] Tervire refers more explicitly to "égalité de condition" (p. 431), *condition* itself already signifying nobility; cf. other uses of *égal* on pp. 236, 240, 452, 571.

[49] "Ce religieux ... était dans un embarras cruel, et ... ne pouvait se débarrasser de moi" (p. 25).

[50] "Il faut lire dans l'âme des hommes, et savoir préférer ce qui la *gagne le plus* à ce qui ne fait que la gagner beaucoup" (p. 50).

[51] "J'étais si étourdie, si déconcertée, que je me laissai mener comme on voulait.... On me menait, et j'allais" (p. 90); cf. also p. 158.

is described as though Marianne had been watching her out of the corner of her eye and gauging her effect (p. 146).[52]

Inspiring compassion depends upon establishing a certain tone, that is, somewhat artfully creating a sensation of artlessness. Many a reply begins with Marianne's faithful "Hélas!" and even Marianne's declarations of candor are tinged with irony, as in the diminutives of: "Là finit mon *petit* discours ou ma *petite* harangue, dans laquelle je ne mis point d'autre art que ma douleur, et qui fit son effet sur la dame en question" (p. 153). The "dame in question," Mme de Miran, has replaced the abbess as target because Marianne has already written off the latter after sensing her withdrawal of sympathy. And, as she had with Climal, Marianne bends her vocabulary to suit the climate. "Dieu m'a inspiré la pensée de me jeter à vos pieds, ma mère, et d'implorer votre aide" (p. 152): God is only a rhetorical device, an instrument of suasion. She is capable of minor slips, but also of compensating for them. For one thing, playing one role full tilt may necessarily involve compromising another: "j'étais indiscrète, à force de candeur" (p. 182). And when her involvement with Valville surfaces, her confidence in Mme de Miran's protection is shaken, calling for repeated protestations of her submission (pp. 187-88) and emphatic renunciation of Valville who, as the lesser resource, must be sacrificed. In this instance, as well as in others, she takes to stylized self-deprecation in the interests of provoking sentiment: "Y aurait-il rien de si abominable que moi sur la terre...?" (p. 197).

There is another leap when she accepts in advance the minister's proposal on terms suggested by the second mother superior, throwing herself at first to the mercy of chance: "peut-être quelque événement favorable me délivrera-t-il," she thinks (p. 302). But Marianne has never been a loser in this kind of contest, and she soon recovers

---

[52] She later states quite explicitly, in admitting "candidly" to Climal that she has revealed his part in her story, that "je n'avais point d'autre ressource que de faire compassion" (p. 252). René Démoris too underscores Marianne's aggressiveness: "Marianne, qui éprouve une sympathie aristocratique pour les carrosses se jette sous les roues de celui de Valville et fait ainsi le premier pas qui lui permet d'en devenir l'occupante.... Il peut sembler surprenant que Marianne prenne des risques assez graves pour le seul plaisir de garder sa belle robe, mais il se trouve que cette robe lui permettra de jouer les princesses infortunées et de conquérir ainsi le cœur de Mme de Miran" (op. cit., p. 408).

her nerve by imagining and planning her role: "il me semblait impossible qu'on ne s'y rendît pas" (p. 303). The fact is that she has by this time more than once tested her verbal skills and knows how to manage her effects; [53] her enemies hardly get a word in edgewise when the confrontation occurs. Again one of her most effective weapons is to shame them in the guise of deprecating herself; addressing herself to Mme de Miran, she says: "je ne tiens sur la terre qu'à vous qui m'avez recueillie si charitablement, et qui avez la générosité de m'aimer tant, quoiqu'on tâche de vous en faire rougir, et quoique tout le monde me méprise" (p. 335). Here the telling phrases are neatly tossed off in the closing subordinate clauses. She tops off her forensic victory with a grand-effect obeisance to the minister, of which she once more underscores the success: "Il me releva sur-le-champ, d'un air qui témoignait que mon action le surprenait agréablement et l'attendrissait; je m'aperçus aussi qu'elle plaisait à toute la compagnie" (p. 337). The fact that the result is noted afterward, but still rather self-consciously, tends to render her intentions more ambiguous to the reader.

There is of course a relationship between Marianne I's diegetic situation and the discursive one of Marianne II. The complaisance of the first, looking at herself in the mirror to retouch and admire (p. 209), is not unlike the narcissicism of the second who is also, in a sense, describing — and preening — her mirror image; and she is as much conscious of being read ("les jeunes personnes à qui vous pourriez donner ceci à lire" [p. 237]) as is Marianne I of being talked about ("[l'officier] avait fort entendu parler de moi" [p. 418]): both have been "published." [54] And as Marianne I knows, the past is inaccessible in its autonomous truth; it must be reinvented. Just so, Marianne II must create her own past, and it is moot on which of these levels the calculation is most manifest. "Je n'étais rien, je n'avais rien qui pût me faire considérer; mais à ceux qui n'ont ni rang, ni richesses qui en imposent, il leur reste une âme, et c'est beaucoup; c'est quelquefois plus que le rang et la richesse, elle peut

---

[53] Cf. Varthon's reproach for her tendency to equivocate and bias: "Il y a bien de petits articles que vous ne m'avez dits qu'en passant, et qui sont extrêmement importants, qui ont pu vous nuire" (p. 391).

[54] "Madame," says the officer to Mme de Miran, "ce qu'on a *publié* de M. de Valville est-il vrai? *On dit* qu'il n'aime plus cette fille si estimable" (p. 419).

faire face à tout. Voyons comment la mienne me tira d'affaire" (p. 178). The occasion described in this passage does not exactly concern a spontaneous function of soul: it is rather like a decision to behave *as if* one had soul, that is, in function of a willed effect or "reading." *Ame* is a creation of discourse, and Marianne's action indeed generates the word as Mme Dorsin exclaims, "ce qu'elle vient de vous dire est admirable: voilà *une belle âme,* un beau caractère!" (pp. 179-80). Here, because the announcement of the target term preceded the action at least in Marianne II's discourse, Mme Dorsin can hardly be read as coming upon it unaided. To possess "soul" is to manifest certain types of coded behavior which refer back to the signified which produced them as intention. Correspondingly, when Marianne says, "En un mot, je me proposai une conduite qui était fière, modeste, décente, digne de cette Marianne dont on faisait tant de cas" (p. 386), the public echo of "faisait tant de cas" lends to what precedes a connotation to the effect: "... une conduite *qui signifie*: 'fierté,' 'modestie,' etc." The subtleties of thought and conduct in Marianne I are automatically subtleties of thought and writing in Marianne II. To what extent is the finesse of the following, as diegetic action, a discursive function in the present?

> A ce discours, je levai les yeux sur elle [= Mme Dorsin] d'un air humble et reconnaissant, à quoi je joignis une très humble et très légère inclination de tête; *je dis légère,* parce que je compris dans mon cœur que je devais la remercier avec discrétion, et qu'il fallait bien paraître sensible à ses bontés, mais non pas faire penser qu'elles me consolassent, *comme en effet* elles ne me consolaient pas. [p. 180]

This sort of parenthetical afterthought clause — here "comme en effet...," but elsewhere the familiar "je dis *x* (et cela était vrai)" — reveals that the rhetorical effect comes first, referential truth value only second.

Marianne's hopes insofar as they are tied to her marriage with Valville imply a particular kind of challenge to social order[55] which

---

[55] Lotringer argues that "la Passion, dans un roman explicitement fondé sur la division des classes, a toujours pour fonction de remettre celle-ci en question. C'est pourquoi, de *la Vie de Marianne* à *Manon Lescaut,* ou même à *Paul et Virginie,* les amants se situent nécessairement de part et d'autre de la fracture sociale" ("Le Roman impossible," p. 314).

is taken very seriously; Mme de Miran, in her infatuation with Marianne, may toss it aside somewhat cavalierly as "la folie des usages" (p. 184), but the more somber tones of the second mother superior would seem to lie closer to the social norm: "la différence des conditions est une chose nécessaire dans la vie, et elle ne subsisterait plus, *il n'y aurait plus d'ordre,* si on permettait des unions aussi inégales que le serait la vôtre, on peut dire même aussi *monstrueuses*" (pp. 297-98). If the consequences are viewed as that fundamental, it is more than just superficially that Marianne can be called "dangerous." [56] And it makes all the more bold Marianne's suggestion that the proposed marriage with Villot is itself a misalliance (p. 333). It is only on this ominous subject that the minister remains reticent. He leaves Mme de Miran free to act with a simple: "Faites comme vous pourrez, ce sont vos affaires" (p. 388); but this stops well short of approbation. He has formally sanctioned Marianne's adoptive status and right to respect as a noble, but not to family alliance with its great ramifications.

Marianne does not have much to say about eroticism, except from the point of view of coquetry; but it enters the text in other ways. At the outset, Marianne's situation is viewed by others largely in terms of her sexual vulnerability, but it is not long before two different women have occasion to remark on how "dangerous" she is. [57] The significance of Marianne's age lies primarily in its pubescent efflorescence — "cet âge où les grâces sont si charmantes, parce qu'elles sont ingénues et *toutes fraîches écloses* (p. 24) — the burgeoning of which is again evoked when Marianne is on her way to church: "je ressemblais assez à une aimable petite fille, *toute fraîche*

---

[56] One has only to look at the extremely severe terms which Mme Dursan, the reverse in this from Mme de Miran, reserves for her son's misalliance, which to forgive would be an offense "à l'ordre et à la justice humaine et divine" (p. 496); this episode in Tervire's story also makes explicit the right of authority to annul a marriage in the presence of factors including "l'extrême inégalité des conditions" (p. 485). Tervire's mother too is viewed as the beneficiary of a misalliance (p. 551).

[57] The lady (forever unidentified) who finds Valville at Marianne's feet: "Je ne vous plains point, monsieur, vous êtes en bonne compagnie, un peu dangereuse à la vérité" (p. 84); Mme de Miran: "Quelle dangereuse petite fille tu es, Marianne" (p. 200).

sortie d'une éducation de village, et qui se tient mal, mais dont les *grâces* encore captives ne demandent qu'à *se montrer*" (p. 52). Modesty of course does not totally inhibit sexuality, and Marianne is only too willing to *montrer* in the infinite little breathtaking ways it will permit. Her movements in the church are executed with all the calculated finesse of a strip-tease, which they simulate:

> De temps en temps, *pour les tenir en haleine,* je les *régalais* d'une petite *découverte sur mes charmes;* je leur en apprenais *quelque chose de nouveau,* sans me mettre pourtant en grande dépense.... C'était ma coiffe à qui j'avais recours; elle allait à merveille, mais je voulais bien qu'elle allât mal, en faveur d'*une main nue* qui *se montrait* en y retouchant, et qui amenait nécessairement avec elle *un bras rond,* qu'on voyait pour le moins *à demi,* dans l'attitude où je le tenais alors. [p. 62]

The "nudity" of the hand is hardly a merely accessory allusion, as Marianne makes clear: "C'est que ce n'est point une *nudité* qu'un visage, quelque aimable qu'il soit; nos yeux ne l'entendent pas ainsi: mais une belle main commence à *en devenir une;* et pour fixer de certaines gens, il est bien aussi sûr de les *tenter* que de leur plaire" (p. 63).

That much is intentional. The ankle is then sent by chance to continue the strip act, which although causally involuntary is nonetheless willed; for as the surgeon says he must see the ankle (she requires the help of a chambermaid to *undress* for this occasion!): "A cette proposition, je rougis d'abord par un sentiment de pudeur; et puis, en rougissant pourtant, je songeai que j'avais le plus joli petit pied du monde; que Valville allait le voir... et j'allais en avoir le profit immodeste, en conservant tout le mérite de la modestie" (p. 67). This ironic commentary encompasses Valville as well, as sexual magnetism draws him to the point of symbolic but unmistakable phallic contact:

> Le bon homme, pour mieux juger du mal, se baissait beaucoup, parce qu'il était vieux, et Valville en conformité de geste, prenait insensiblement la même attitude, et se baissait beaucoup aussi, parce qu'il était jeune; car il ne connaissait rien à mon mal, mais il se connaissait à mon pied, et m'en paraissait aussi content que je l'avais espéré.... Aussi est-il

un peu enflé, ajoutait Valville en y mettant le doigt d'un air de bonne foi. [pp. 68-69] [58]

There is also an irony of plot, of symbolic value too, in that Climal has so well clothed Marianne (paying special attention to her underwear) only to have Valville replace him at the unveiling.[59] It is equally essential, to be sure, that Valville be restrained by a timidity or "respect" by virtue of which Marianne qualifies him as "tendre" rather than "amoureux" (p. 74). Everything is very restrained ("je ne courais alors aucun risque avec Valville"), and for that matter Marianne rarely even hints at her own sexual excitement.[60]

Marianne also seduces with sentiment, and this — unlike sex, which attracted Climal like a bumblebee — affects only the good, like-minded souls. Mme de Miran immediately responds to Marianne's sadness, and even more to her story, whereas the abbess is as if frozen on the spot, emitting only minimally polite gestures: "il ne me parut pas que son cœur eût donné aucun signe de vie" (p. 153). Signs of life are defined as the teary sort of reciprocity marking the relations between Mme de Miran and Marianne, in which even the tainted *charité* can take on positive connotations (p. 185).[61] If Marianne is sensitive to the point of touchiness about references to herself, she is equally sensitive to the feelings of others: it is because she remarks on Mme de Miran's sadness that the story of Valville comes spilling out, and Climal's very humiliation as he lies dying embarrasses her (p. 244). Indeed it is characteristic, in situations which do not bring into play her visceral struggle for status, for her to be unvengeful and even compassionate.

---

[58] Valville's sexual curiosity is once more in play when a similar accident befalls Varthon and occasions some exposure: "nous la délacions ...; un de ses bras pendait hors du lit, et l'autre était étendu sur elle, ... tous deux d'une forme admirable" (p. 350); "La demoiselle ... s'apercevant du petit désordre où elle était, ce qui venait de ce qu'on l'avait délacée, elle en parut un peu confuse, et porta sa main sur son sein" (p. 352).

[59] She seems to taunt Climal later when she sketches an undressing as an expression of defiance: see pp. 123-24.

[60] Only, for instance, by a certain thrill: "Imaginez-vous ce que je deviens quand je pense que j'épouserai Valville, et combien de fois mon âme tressaille; et si, avec tant de tressaillement, j'avais le sang bien reposé" (p. 207).

[61] Tears alone do not suffice, nonetheless, to guarantee sincerity: indeed Tervire cites, as a symptom of Mme Dursan (the younger)'s ungratefulness, "beaucoup de facilité de pleurer" combined with an insufficient degree of real affliction (p. 532).

There is no doubt that the text contains an abundant discourse on the fine points of sensibility as something fragile, ultimately ineffable, which cannot be possessed and described but only intuited.[62] And it is doubtless accurate to say that *sentiment* here in large measure means what we would call intuition. But it also means sentiment, and it is futile to argue, as Deloffre has, that the novel is not sentimental by virtue of the fact that *langage entrecoupé* is absent.[63] All the "tendres et délicieuses larmes" (p. 155) are not there for nothing, and the fact that they do not in the style of this text interrupt sentences syntactically does not obviate their objective textual presence. The "entrecoupé" style is here represented diegetically rather than imitated: "Je me reculais honteuse, et avec des *paroles entrecoupées* de sanglots" (p. 179); "[j'étais] si attendrie moi-même, que j'étais *comme suffoquée*" (p. 181); "Mes pleurs ici me *coupèrent la parole*" (p. 251); "Helas! c'est elle [ma mère] que je regrette, répondis-je je ne sais comment, et *d'une parole entrecoupée*" (p. 412).

The priority of sentiment over sexuality preserves Marianne from succumbing to the principle of exchange represented, in Sylvère Lotringer's formulation, by sexual commerce (libertinage) on the aristocratic level and by money on the popular level: Climal, playing on both (since he offers money), is the mediator of exchange.[64] There

---

[62] "Ce sont des objets de sentiment si compliqués et d'une netteté si délicate qu'ils se brouillent dès que ma réflexion s'en mêle; je ne sais plus par où les prendre pour les exprimer: de sorte qu'ils sont en moi, et non pas à moi" (p. 166).

[63] There is an abashing degree of subjectivity in Deloffre's remark, on the tearful scene between Marianne, Valville, and Mme de Miran, "Il ne nous paraît pourtant pas qu'il y ait ici plus de larmes que n'en comporte la situation, qui est réellement attendrissante" (p. 198, n. 1): what does *réellement* mean?

[64] "Le libertinage, autrement dit *l'échange des corps,* recoupe et recouvre ... le mécanisme de l'argent, leur action conjuguée devant avoir pour effet de dissiper graduellement les prétentions du Message [vertu] à la différence [par rapport à la norme]" ("Le Roman impossible," p. 304). Lotringer speaks elsewhere of an "alliance ... de l'argent (Mme Dutour) et du libertinage (M. de Climal) en vue d'intégrer malgré elle Marianne au secteur non-marqué [= non-noble]" ("Manon l'écho," p. 106). Saint-Vincent's naïveté provides particular situational irony in this context when he advises Marianne, "comportez-vous d'une manière qui *récompense* monsieur des soins où sa piété l'engage pour vous" (p. 28).

are other "economic" expressions such as those designating the envy of Marianne's supposed inferiors,[65] but they excite little response in her. The real dilemma is presented by Climal, for several reasons. The first is that charity creates a debt: moral, inducing resentment in the heart of the beneficiary,[66] especially when juxtaposed with a pious motive (p. 38); and practical, in that the benefactor is enabled if not entitled to exact some quid pro quo. Even before he ups the ante with clothes and cash, Climal emphasizes the cost of his aid in order to underwrite obligation as exchange value; what is added subsequently serves only to make the proposition more concrete. Not that Marianne ever shows any evident temptation to yield to him in the area of sexual favors, but she is all the same drawn into complicity by the desire of gain, and finds herself involved in exploring the proposition that the exchange principle can be exploited without reciprocity, or with only token return such as expressions of gratitude.

It is clear enough that she recognizes Climal's bid and down payment for what they are: an offer to buy. And she, cheating a bit in terms of her bona fide intentions (the foundation of a solid contract, the bourgeois ethic), has tacitly accepted: "il espérait de me gagner par là, et qu'en prenant ce qu'il me donnait, moi *je rendais ses espérances assez bien fondées*" (p. 39). This defers the moment of truth and temporarily makes exchange a one-way proposition: "Par là je reculais une rupture avec M. de Climal, et je gardais ce qu'il me donnait." Despite her indigence, the constraint of Climal's dual role, by imposing a degree of indirection on his negotiations, puts him in the weaker position — "c'était lui qui était dans l'embarras, et non pas moi" (p. 37) — for while the licit (charity) can be explicit, the illicit (sex) must be only implied.

The rawest symbol of exchange is of course money, and this Marianne wants to refuse, preferring the clean money she already has; but her resistance to his *louis d'or* is not adamant enough not to compromise her purity of morality and nobility: "Je les pris donc

---

[65] "[Toinon] aurait bien *troqué* son père et sa mère contre le plaisir d'être orpheline *au même prix* que moi" (p. 49); Cathos: "je voudrais bien être à votre place, moi qui vous parle" (p. 305).

[66] Cf., pp. 220-22, three intense pages devoted to exploration of the psychology of obligation and ingratitude; Marianne does affirm, nonetheless, that gratitude can be sweet when pride is not made to suffer (p. 38).

avec honte, car cela m'humiliait" (p. 35). Marianne plays with implications while hoping to evade specific consequences, which, like Marianne I's rationalizations, Marianne II's irony helps keep in abeyance: "il était arrêté que je ne verrais rien" (p. 40).[67] Climal of course responds first by threats to drop his support (p. 114), then with gradually increasing explicitness: "Petite ingrate que vous êtes, ...est-ce là comme vous *payez* mes bienfaits?" (p. 122), still maintaining a terminology, though, which thanks to its fundamental ambiguity ("un peu de reconnaissance") permits some backtracking.[68]

Once Marianne moves on to a new base of support, she discharges everything received as a signal of final refusal and purgation: nothing gained, nothing conceded.[69] As she suggests just before this point, she is redefining her "economic" strategy: the "moi qui suis sage, qui aimerais mieux mourir que de ne pas l'être, qui ne possède rien que ma sagesse" (p. 121) is going to turn her virtue into a capital to be invested for future dividends rather than a currency for present gains. This better suits her noble consciousness because it deals exclusively in abstracts, and in consequence there is a pretention that nothing is tallied — that all takes place in the quasi-Corneillian domain of pure *grandeur d'âme*.[70] Delicacy edulcorates all the tokens of exchange, as is shown by the way Marianne phrases her remarks on Mme de Miran's fine sense of tact:

---

[67] Cf. the irony with which Tervire describes the offer of the *dévot* baron who, like Climal, wants to hoard sex with money (cf. Lotringer, "Le Roman impossible," p. 308): "il se persuada, puisque je manquais de bien, que ce serait une bonne œuvre que de m'aimer jusqu'à m'épouser, qu'il y aurait de la piété à se charger de ma jeunesse et de mes agréments, et à les retirer, pour ainsi dire, dans le mariage" (pp. 467-68). But there it is a question of marriage, even if with a lecher — and Tervire accepts.

[68] He illustrates a more general rule of sexual negotiations which I have studied earlier in *Le Masque et la parole* (Paris: José Corti, 1973): indirection allows for tactical retreat up to the time the pact is sealed.

[69] "...les louis d'or qu'il m'a donnés, que je lui rendrai, et ces hardes que je suis honteuse d'avoir sur moi, et dont je ne veux *pas profiter,* Dieu m'en préserve!" (pp. 142-43).

[70] One of the implicit reasons why Marianne compares her departure from a bourgeois milieu to a voyage in a foreign land (p. 158) is that the systems of exchange operating in the new domain are still unfamiliar. But all sense of quantification is not lost there; on the contrary, Marianne expresses a sort of theory of maximum interest which combines old and new (bourgeois and noble) terminology: cf. above, n. 50.

> On ne saurait *payer* ces traits de bonté-là. De toutes les *obligations* qu'on peut avoir à une belle âme, ces tendres attentions, ces secrètes politesses de sentiment sont les plus touchantes. Je les appelle secrètes, parce que le cœur qui les a pour vous ne vous *les compte point,* ne veut point en *charger* votre reconnaissance. [p. 154]
>
> La dame rougit à cette indiscrétion ... et cette rougeur fut une nouvelle bonté dont je lui tins *compte.* [p. 156]

Counting has no rigorous mathematical sense here; contracts are informal, and generous; such finesse is an attribute of class and *hors commerce.* "Il y a des degrés de générosité supérieurs à des âmes très généreuses" (p. 240); even vengeance for Marianne is "generous" (p. 407). Note also the terms in which Mme Dorsin "borrows" Marianne from her friend: "Voulez-vous me la *laisser?* Je *me charge* d'elle en attendant que tout ceci se passe. Je ne prétends pas vous *l'ôter,* elle y *perdrait* trop; et je vous *la rendrai* dès que le mariage de votre fils sera conclu, et que vous me la *redemanderez*" (p. 180). Indeed the temptation, in this kind of euphoric climate, is to give everything, assuming that everything is in turn liberally returned; but this can be a dangerous fallacy, as the story of Tervire repeatedly illustrates.[71]

Something goes awry with this system too when Valville apparently derogates from the generous cycle by withdrawing his love and hand. There is a contamination by the exchange principle: the whole last part of the novel, with the Varthon episode and then Tervire, takes place in a mode of *substitution* — of, so to speak, bad money for good. The scene where Valville remains obstinately kneeling before the supine Varthon and holding her hand is an obvious réplique for the earlier one where he knelt before Marianne, just as that scene had initiated the apparent liberation from exchange by an

---

[71] Tervire suffers twice from the total gift: once as an infant, when her grandfather gives everything to his younger son, leaving her father destitute, and once by her own act, when she diverts Mme Dursan's legacy from herself to a daughter-in-law who has no inclination to share it; in addition, Tervire's mother, the Marquise de ..., is turned out of her son's house and deprived of support after signing over everything in his marriage contract. Less worthy characters are incapable of such high-mindedness: "les petites âmes ne se fient à rien.... Ce neveu, par pure avarice, oublia les intérêts de son avarice même" (p. 486).

ironic substitution of Valville for Climal. Marianne reacts with obvious pique, although she never sorts out well the feelings about Varthon which this inspires in her. She has been traded for someone who has many of the same attractions she offered herself: the erotic accident, the exotic (foreign) birthright, perhaps even orphanhood; Marianne herself details these parallels (p. 355) without seeming to grasp that they explain an operation of the same mechanism of response in Valville in each instance.[72] Mme de Miran's "vous n'êtes pour rien dans tout cela" (p. 417) is a gracious way of accepting Varthon's excuses, yet has sarcastic overtones of her utter insignificance as a kind of substitute and inauthentic coinage. And the economic principle is implicated also in a more direct way: according to Valville's explanations to Varthon, which she repeats to Marianne, he has yielded to the noble equivalent of the mercantile ethic, which is the doctrine of *alliance*. After failing to force a capitulation at the family council, a subterranean barrage of criticism has now evidently taken its toll and restored social "reason" to Valville; and Varthon, reflecting this same mentality foreign to the generous ethic, has every reason to consider herself a more appropriate match for Valville than is Marianne.

Marianne II seems to realize at the beginning of part eight a tendency to present Valville's role too melodramatically, and strives for a sharp break in tone: "J'ai ri de tout mon cœur, madame, de votre colère contre mon infidèle" (p. 375). His defection is not to be classed among the afflictions which have punctuated her life's story; the sufferings of jealous love, though obviously important, are not *malheurs* but *chagrins*: "les plus grands chagrins que j'aie eus de ma vie" (p. 348). She further depreciates his thematic centrality by announcing his eventual return — in circumstances we will never know — and in relating the scene where Marianne I reduces him, by

---

[72] Varthon expresses her own awareness of the exotic features which have attracted Valville to each of them: "c'est mon évanouissement qui en a fait un infidèle. Et ... peut-être avez-vous eu besoin d'être infortunée, et d'être dangereusement tombée à sa porte, pour le fixer quelques mois" (p. 378). As if to recognize his return to the exchange principle, Varthon denies his intrinsic worth and reduces him to a free-floating cipher: "c'est comme si vous n'aviez point eu d'amant.... Valville était hier le vôtre; il est aujourd'hui le mien, à ce qu'il dit; il sera demain celui d'une autre, et ne sera jamais celui de personne" (p. 379).

another of her great performances, to such confusion in the presence of all the key witnesses that his only possible way out, even though it is a totally inadmissible one, is to depart without a word (p. 411).

It is obviously, however, a major transition in terms of the plot. When Marianne renounces hope, the perspective rather suddenly shifts; a certain Valville has disappeared: "je ne le reconnus plus; ce n'était plus le même homme" (p. 397). There is no telling whether the change is in him, on this occasion, or in her. And perhaps a certain Marianne has died too, as her near-death suggests, the Marianne who was Valville's fiancée; while she is "dying" of love,[73] he is replacing her with Varthon in his affection. Various factors, including perhaps a fear that her chances for advantageous marriage have been significantly reduced, lead her to the idea of another form of burial, the taking of religious vows, which sets the stage for Tervire.[74] In any case we know that Tervire's story has a dissuasive function, and that the "new" Marianne will not in fact wear a habit.

For quite aside from the convent question in itself, Tervire imposes on Marianne the necessity of a renewed vision, additive and not substractive in gist — "tâchez de vous dire: Les autres ont un avantage qui me manque, et ne vous dites point: J'ai une affliction de plus qu'eux" (p. 429) — in which Valville will no longer be a goal but rather replaceable himself, a sort of way-station. In other words, Marianne can substitute something better for Valville (p. 382), and there is a new suggestion that Mme Dorsin, whose salon has already provided the occasion for a homily on the equality of minds (p. 227), will take over from Mme de Miran.[75] With the officer's proposal to her, this Dorsin principle is sealed, since he rejects outright any inspection of birth credentials, thus offering Marianne

---

[73] "Ah! je ne survivrai pas à ce tourment-là, j'espère; Dieu m'en fera la grâce, et je sens que je me meurs" (p. 367). There will later be a new Marianne to entice Valville through a renewed form of exoticism: "il me reverra, pour ainsi dire, sous une figure qu'il ne connaît pas encore.... Ce ne sera plus la même Marianne" (p. 377).

[74] "La tentation de la démission, de la retraite, de la mort même par laquelle a commencé sa vie, est très forte chez elle," argues Henri Coulet (p. 208). There may be truth in this, but adequate emphasis must also be given the subtly aggressive force in Marianne which I have discussed earlier.

[75] "Mme Dorsin, dont vous m'avez parlé, et qui passe pour si bon juge du mérite, serait une autre Mme de Miran pour vous, si vous vouliez" (p. 383).

a definitive exit from the terrorism of labels.[76] Curiously enough, except for the fact that he does not abuse the word "love," his discourse is the honorable pendant of Climal's, which it otherwise resembles: "Vous ne risquez avec moi rien de pareil à ce qui vous est arrivé avec [Valville]; ... car qu'est-ce que c'est qu'un amant? C'est bien à l'amour à qui il appartient de vous offrir un cœur! Est-ce qu'une personne comme vous est faite pour être le jouet d'une passion aussi folle, aussi inconstante?" (p. 422; cf. p. 110). There is no indication in the text as to whether Marianne is to accept. According to Lotringer's argument, the real matter does not lie there but in the impossibility for the text to realize such a marriage, which has the same bases as the "impossible" chronological joining of Marianne I and II: the point then is not that Marianne's story is incomplete but that for reasons of structure it *cannot* be complete.[77]

Even before Tervire's story utterly supplants Marianne's, her earlier intervention on the subject of love performs a duplicative and substitutive function. There she sets herself up as the double of Marianne, with another friend playing her own role, creating a situation which parallels her present narrative instance and is meant to apply directly to it:

---

[76] Marrying Valville, according to Lotringer, would still make of Marianne a *parvenue* because she would owe both "naissance" and marriage to the same Mme de Miran, whereas the free offer of the officer provides a clear path to respectable status ("Le Roman impossible," pp. 311-15).

[77] "L'oubli de la naissance doit être général pour que l'adéquation du mérite et de la noblesse puisse se réaliser. Or il n'en est rien car la société tout entière, Marianne comprise, est ici fondée sur la différence des conditions. La marge ne cesse, tout au long, de se réduire en faveur de l'héroïne, mais si minime qu'elle puisse être, elle interdit toute égalité spirituelle. Le mariage de l'orpheline est donc voué à rester une aspiration dont l'actualisation est reportée à l'infini.... C'est en ce sens que l'on peut considérer la *Marianne* comme terminée: l'interruption y est inscrite dans sa forme.... Si le syntagme narratif tolère ainsi d'être tronqué, ce n'est pas qu'en fait il l'est déjà et qu'un degré de plus ou de moins n'importe guère devant l'absence de tout 'dénouement', c'est que *celui-ci est à chaque instant présent dans la forme*" (ibid., pp. 315-16). The only objection this brilliant argument is exposed to is that the critic who proves that the novel "had to" remain uncompleted already holds the privileged information that it *is,* and one wonders whether there is not some conflict-of-interest as it were, some tautological feedback of this a priori knowledge. It is thus all the same somewhat gratuitous to call the conclusion "impossible," unless one assumes that the text was writing itself.

> Moi qui vous parle, je connais votre situation, je l'ai éprouvée, je m'y suis vue, et je fus d'abord aussi affligée que vous; mais une amie que j'avais, qui était à peu près de l'âge que j'ai à présent, et qui me surprit dans l'état où je vous vois, entreprit de me consoler; elle me parla raison, me dit des choses sensibles.... Ces motifs de consolation *me touchèrent*, me dit-elle tout de suite, et ils doivent *vous toucher* encore davantage, ils *vous conviennent plus* qu'ils ne me convenaient. [pp. 381-83]

In substance, the process consists in beginning with the private suffering as an acute singular instance, and extrapolating it to a more general, iterative level of experience: "Voyons, me dit cette amie, de quoi vous désespérez-vous? de l'accident du monde *le plus fréquent*"; and in boosting Marianne's spirits, she stresses via this adopted voice the parallel lesson for the two (three) of them, thus preparing the way for her full-scale narration soon to begin:

> Il est très possible que vous y gagniez, comme j'y ai gagné moi-même, ajouta-t-elle, à ne pas épouser un jeune homme riche, à qui j'étais chère, qui me l'était, et qui me laissa aussi pour en aimer une autre qui est devenue sa femme, qui est malheureuse à ma place, et qui, avant que d'être à lui, aurait eu l'aveugle folie de se consumer en regrets, s'il l'avait quittée à son tour. [p. 382]

Nothing flies more flagrantly in the face of romantic love than such substitutive language. The multiple levels of substitution figure the symbolic process of widening the significance from the individual and unique to the general and frequent — even if some of these are purely discursive, with the "friend" just an invention of Tervire's. Although the swain could correspond to her cousin Dursan, there is no way to know, really, whether this whole passage is just a parable or not.

Certainly her long story occupying books nine through eleven is not presented as such, yet it abounds in echoes and parallels with relation to much that has preceded in Marianne's: a social flaw weighing on her parentage (secret marriage, disinheritance), hidden identity, the vagaries of orphanhood,[78] a precocious sensitivity arising

---

[78] "Elle vous [ferait pitié] encore bien davantage, si vous saviez *qui elle est*, monsieur" (p. 434); "Mlle de Tervire n'est point une *orpheline* comme vous le pensez" (p. 444); "je n'étais *plus rien pour qui que ce soit*" (p. 446); etc.

from concentrated experience,[79] a narrow escape from the convent reaching out to absorb her and remove her from the world,[80] the dissuasive function of a nun's story, a nearly ruinous scrape with a *faux dévot*.[81] Further duplications, with their attendant ironies,[82] appear in the final episode leading to the reunion of Tervire with her mother (figuring too the discovery Marianne will make some twenty years hence of her parents' identity). The search for Tervire's mother is automatically fraught with numerous overtones, all the more since her poverty — which is what makes her so difficult to find and identify — repeats the poor/rich cycle once more, in reverse, and the adoptive idea returns when the Marquise de . . . remarks, "Je voudrais bien être cette mère-là" (p. 542).[83] The *reconnaissance* or recognition scene imitates the one between Marianne and Mmes Dorsin and Miran where the relationship between Valville and Marianne is progressively discovered. And finally, the Marquise also tells her story (p. 569). There are, moreover, similarities between Marianne's and Tervire's discourse. The *vous* in the second narrative situation is Marianne; but because of the substitutive mechanism (parallel to the substitution of Tervire's story for Marianne's), and the "shifter" function of the pronoun, it reads in exactly the same way. And despite great differences in rhythm and even style, Tervire manifests much the same kind of sensitivity (indicative again of their proximity in true birth) and even narrative irony as Marianne, factors recognizable in such passages as:

---

[79] "Quatre jours d'une situation comme était la mienne avancent bien le sentiment; ils valent des années" (p. 450).

[80] She like Marianne is called a "prédestinée" (p. 454).

[81] Henri Coulet compares the structure of each experience (and of Jacob's in *Le Paysan parvenu*) in terms of four main stages: a transplantation; the acquisition of an identity, but alienating and false; a sudden change of vision provoking a break with what preceded; a public act forcing recognition of the hero (this act is fragmented in Tervire's case). The second stage is not entirely negative: Marianne's dress provides the transition to the third, and Tervire, turned away from the convent, will eventually return there (Coulet, pp. 395-98).

[82] "Je ne pensai point à elle; je n'étais occupée que de ma mère" (p. 550); "cette inconnue, dont l'infortune me fit encore songer à ma mère" (p. 559); "où est cette mère que vous êtes venue retrouver . . . ?" (p. 564); "que votre mère a de reproches à se faire, aussi bien que moi!" (p. 565).

[83] The parallel constitutes just a hint, although no more, that by some mysterious route Mme de Miran could be Marianne's true mother.

> Cette idée-là [that the baron might soon leave her a widow] ne fit qu'une apparition légère dans mon esprit; mais elle en fit une dont je ne voulus point m'apercevoir, et qui cependant contribua sans doute à me déterminer. [p. 470]
>
> Je n'étais plus la même.... Ce n'était plus eux, ce n'était plus moi. [pp. 462, 466]
>
> Mes façons ingénues réussissaient auprès de Mme Dursan. [p. 487]
>
> Oui, ma fille, tu as raison, me dit-elle; ... ton action est très louable. (Pas si louable qu'elle se l'imaginait, ni que je le croyais moi-même; ce n'était pas là le mot qu'il eût fallu dire.) [p. 503]
>
> ... les grâces qu'il avait, ou que je lui croyais ... [p. 505]
>
> J'aimais à me sentir un si bon cœur. [p. 508]
>
> Malgré mon peu d'usage, je démêlai, à sa contenance paresseuse et hautaine, toutes ces petites fiertés qu'elle avait dans l'esprit. Notre orgueil nous met si vite au fait de celui des autres, et en général les finesses de l'orgueil sont toujours si grossières! [p. 575]

The point is not that Tervire is just a pale redundancy of Marianne, for she is also in important ways her opposite number, but that the themes and lexemes of her story often rejoin and reinforce those of Marianne's, just as the notion of conclusion — to either — recedes further and further from grasp.

One too easily reacts with a regret that the author does not tell "how the story ends," a natural projection of the referential illusion that narrative spins. Some uncompleted works produce less feeling of dissatisfaction in this respect than others, but there is nothing subjective about the matter of incompletion itself: even a plot summary, which would reduce to a minimum the rhetorical controls brought to bear on the reader, would manifest the incompletion; something does not come full circle, as it does in a completed plot, and any reader will recognize that. In the case of *La Vie de Marianne*, it appears quite possible to assert that that open-ended status is consistent with the structure of the rest of the novel, which operates, in the manner of the fugue or theme and variations (like running in place, in Grimm's view), on a single figure.[84] Marianne and her allies recount and re-recount; besides the repetitions in various guises of "the" original story, there are the numerous recitations, by both Marianne and others, of what has befallen her since her arrival in Paris — to Mme Dutour, to Saint-Vincent, to Mme de Miran, to Valville, implicitly to Tervire, and so on. Marianne also re-imagines in order to re-tell: "Il me sembla que je sortais de l'église, que je me voyais encore dans cette rue où je tombai avec ces maudits habits que Climal m'avait donnés, avec toutes ces parures qui me valaient le titre de grisette en ses beaux atours des jours de fête" (p. 177). Besides Marianne II's meta-commentary on her writing enterprise, we have a meta-narration; and on this level the conclusion is quite remarkable: after toying for chapter after chapter with the question of how industrious or indolent she is in her writing, Marianne pretends to resolve the matter in the final book: "ma diligence vient de ce que je me corrige, voilà tout le mystère; vous ne m'en croirez pas, mais vous le verrez, madame, vous le verrez" (p. 539) — just at the point where *nothing* further will be forthcoming. The *last* line of part eleven (and of *La Vie de Marianne*) caps this compositional irony: "je vous enverrai *incessamment la fin*, avec la continuation de mes propres aventures" (p. 580).

The novel is structurally coherent, however, in ways that it has not always been given credit for. The chronology, in particular, seems at first somewhat vague, but can be quite well accounted for: between the death of the curé's sister and the point where Tervire preëmpts the primary narrative, there elapse between seventeen and twenty weeks, focalized around the Sunday of Saint-Mathieu (21 September) which includes all of parts two and three, in about the year 1655.[85] The only incoherence I find anywhere is a reference

---

[84] Comparisons used by Annick Jugan, No. 2, pp. 87 and 95. Or as Michel Gilot puts it, Marianne's life "est un parcours de figure en figure" (introduction to the Garnier-Flammarion edition, 1978, p. 24).

[85] Henri Coulet too counts at most twenty weeks (p. 455). The only disconsonant note in the text is Marianne's allusion to "une âme de dix-huit ans" (p. 145) in the same day where she has said she had "une tête de quinze ou seize ans" (p. 80; cf. Coulet): everything else concords for an (uncertain, naturally) age of fifteen to sixteen. Frédéric Deloffre, in his Garnier edition,

to "la dernière fois [que Mme de Miran] me ramenait à mon couvent" (p. 348), which cannot be situated as *dernière* either in reference to what preceeds or to what follows; and, in the same general sequence, a mention of Marianne's "return" to the convent (p. 355), probably after the eight or ten days in the country (p. 347), which does not square with the neighboring passages. But since she has said at this point that, after said return, she will remain only somewhat more than one more month at the convent, this does not leave much margin for chronological uncertainty, and one can well suppose that at the point of Tervire's tripartite narration she is near the point of leaving.[86] It is true, of course, that these few crucial months in Marianne's story occupy a great extent of text, but this does not create implausibility in itself unless one expects the tale to encompass the full cycle of a life.[87]

It is obvious that long-range evolution is lost in the intensity of this analysis of the moment; diegetic action must be held almost to slow-motion in order for narrative discourse to keep up with it. The result, in terms of comparison with the general world of fiction, is a pronounced disproportion of length of narrative time with length of narrated time, or what Genette terms anisochrony. "Ceci, au reste, se passe plus vite que je ne puis le raconter" (p. 264): thought and action can concentrate in energetic bursts which words and narrative syntagms cannot duplicate. Ultimately there are instances, not just in the portraits but also in fully diegetic passages, where a stasis occurs, as if to allow time for the narrative fully to

---

seizes on a very slight allusion with no detail whatever to pretend that one reference to English history sounds more like 1688 than the Protectorate of 1655, and this he calls a "difficulté de chronologie" (p. 349, n. 1); but this seems to me completely meaningless.

[86] Tervire's story too keeps pretty good track of time: she is seventeen when the Sainte-Hermière affair begins; some ten months later she is seventeen-and-a-half (p. 483), which is a usual round way of counting; she then lives five or six years with Mme Duran (p. 495) — later she says six or seven (p. 565) — and three months after her death leaves for Paris. Since she has not seen this aunt of hers for nearly twenty years (p. 564), she must be about forty-four when Marianne knows her.

[87] Cf. again Lotringer's argument: "L'ouvrage n'est pas resté inachevé parce que Marivaux a, comme on l'a dit, décrit quelques jours en quelques centaines de pages. Ce rythme dément n'a au contraire pour but que *d'empêcher la sphère du présent et celle du passé de coïncider*, donc le fossé qui les sépare d'être comblé par la narration" ("Le Roman impossible," p. 315, n. 29).

take account of all that is going on. They are motivated on the level of the diegesis and produce what in the eighteenth century came to be known as *tableaux*, theatrical combinations of visually oriented drama and slow or arrested action. There are a number of such in *La Vie de Marianne,* each marked by immobility and silence; one might say they comprise Marianne's snapshot album:

1) Climal surprises Valville on his knees before Marianne: "N'était-ce pas là un *tableau* bien amusant pour M. de Climal? ... Nous étions trois figures *très interdites*" (pp. 83-84).

2) Valville in turn catches Climal on his knees before Marianne: "Jugez de ce qu'il devint à cette vision [i.e., Climal when he spies Valville]; elle le *pétrifia,* la bouche ouverte; elle le *fixa* dans son attitude. Il était à genoux, il y *resta; plus d'action,* plus de présence d'esprit, *plus de paroles;* jamais hypocrite confondu ne fit moins de mystère de sa honte, ne la laissa contempler plus à l'aise" (p. 120).

3) Marianne's explanation regarding Valville with Mmes de Miran and Dorsin: "Ici mes pleurs coulèrent avec tant d'abondance que je restai quelque temps *sans pouvoir prononcer un mot....* Mes pleurs continuaient; ma bienfaitrice *ne me répondait point,* mais elle me regardait d'un air attendri, et presque la larme à l'œil elle-même" (p. 179). Extension of the same scene: "je baisai [sa main] mille fois à genoux, si attendrie moi-même que j'en étais comme suffoquée. Il se passa en même temps un *moment de silence* qui fut si touchant, que je ne saurais encore y penser sans me sentir remuée jusqu'au fond de l'âme. Ce fut Mme Dorsin qui le rompit la première" (p. 181).

4) Mme de Miran blesses Valville's and Marianne's love: "Je *m'arrêtai* alors, et me mis à essuyer les pleurs que je versais. Valville, toujours sa tête baissée, et plongé dans une profonde rêverie, fut quelque temps *sans répondre.* Mme de Miran le regardait, et *attendait,* la larme à l'œil, qu'il parlât. Enfin il rompit *le silence*" (p. 197). Extension: "Ses pleurs coulèrent après ce peu de mots; il ne les retint plus: ils attendrirent Mme de Miran, qui pleura comme lui et qui ne sut que dire; *nous nous taisions tous trois,* on n'entendait que des soupirs" (p. 198). Second extension: "Valville, à ce discours, pleurant de joie et de reconnaissance, embrassa ses genoux. Pour moi, je fus si touchée, si pénétrée, si *saisie,* qu'il ne me fut *pas possible d'articuler un mot;* j'avais les mains tremblantes, et je

n'exprimai ce que je sentais que par de courts et fréquents soupirs. Tu ne me dis rien, Marianne, me dit ma bienfaitrice, mais j'entends *ton silence*" (p. 206).

5) Climal's deathbed: "Il se fit un moment de *silence* après que Mme de Miran fut sortie; nous entendîmes soupirer M. de Climal" (p. 246). Extension: "Pleurez [says Saint-Vincent to Climal] ... Et ce bon religieux en versait [= des pleurs] lui-même en tenant ce discours, et nous pleurions aussi, Valville et moi" (p. 248). Second extension: "Je fondais en larmes pendant qu'il me faisait cette satisfaction si généreuse et si chrétienne; elle m'attendrit au point qu'elle m'arracha des *soupirs*. Valville et le père Saint-Vincent s'essuyaient les yeux et *gardaient le silence*" (p. 250).

6) The climax of the family council: "Ici, à travers les larmes que je versais, j'aperçus plusieurs personnes de la compagnie qui détournaient la tête pour s'essuyer les yeux. Le ministre baissait les siens, et voulait cacher qu'il était ému. Valville restait comme *immobile,* en me regardant d'un air passionné, et dans un parfait *oubli* de tout ce qui l'environnait; et ma mère laissait bien franchement couler ses pleurs, sans s'embarrasser qu'on les vît" (p. 335).

7) The confrontation between Marianne and Valville: "Et puis nous fûmes l'un et l'autre un petit intervalle de temps *sans rien dire;* ce qui arriva plus d'une fois" (p. 397). Extension: "Ainsi il se passa un petit intervalle de temps sans que nous ouvrissions la bouche, Valville et moi.... Il fallait bien un peu remplir *ce vide étonnant* que faisait notre *silence*" (p. 409).

8) Marianne explains everything to Mme de Miran: "De son côté, Mme de Miran était restée comme *immobile*. Mme Dorsin, morne et pensive, regardait à terre. Mlle Varthon, plus inquiète que jamais de ce que je pourrais dire, ne songeait qu'à prendre une contenance qui ne l'accusât de rien; de sorte que nous étions toutes, chacune à notre façon, *hors d'état de parler*" (p. 411).

These all are syncopes in the middle of scenes which are already long in their own right, and from a visual standpoint are an obvious invitation to engravers. There is always a dynamic tension; the word-void is full, for much is happening — too much, in effect, for action itself (like narrative's relation to action) to keep pace with it, and it takes a moment afterward for it to start moving again. Thought does not go numb, but language does, leaving only sighs. This list does not, however, include all the most important events in the novel, some of which, like the Dorsin dinner in parts four and five, have no such snapshot effect.[88] Others are marked by a subtle sense of continuous motion: the church scene (pp. 60-64) is intense with looks and thoughts animating the silence; the Varthon fainting incident is posed like a tableau but again is forever stirring.[89] Analogous passages exist too in Tervire's story, but in its much more rapid rhythm they produce nowhere near the same effect of gradual slowing to a stop with equally gradual reprise.

On the other hand, there are a series of moments which resemble the snapshots in their silence and stillness, but where an aphasia or paralysis obliterates the dynamism of interplay. Marianne I then becomes completely passive:

1) Marianne returning to Mme Dutour's after the Valville/Climal scene: "On me menait, et j'allais. Qu'est-ce que tout cela deviendra? Que vient-il de se passer? Voilà tout ce que je me disais dans un *étonnement* qui ne me laissait *nul exercice d'esprit,* et pendant lequel je jetai pourtant un grand soupir qui échappa plus à mon instinct qu'à ma pensée" (p. 90).

2) Mme Dutour at the La Fare's: "Mme Dutour venait de frapper mes yeux, et elle n'embrassa *qu'une statue:* je restai *sans mouvement,* plus pâle que la mort, et *ne sachant plus où j'étais.* . . . A ce discours, pas un mot de ma part; j'étais *anéantie.* Là-dessus, Valville arrive d'un air riant; mais, à l'aspect de Mme Dutour, le voici qui rougit, qui perd contenance, et qui reste *immobile à son tour.* . . . Pour moi, qui me sentais faible et les genoux tremblants, je me *laissai tomber* dans un fauteuil qui était à côté de moi, où je ne fis que pleurer et jeter des soupirs" (pp. 263-65). Although Val-

---

[88] Coulet points out that "un personnage peut avoir une grande place dans l'intrigue et n'avoir aucune importance pour l'histoire intérieure du narrateur . . ., inversement un personnage peut ne jouer presque aucun rôle dans l'action et représenter une des rencontres les plus importantes dans l'histoire intérieure du narrateur, c'est le cas de Mme Dorsin" (op. cit., p. 409). Michel Gilot labels "jalons" the 165 (in his count) "indices" controlling the rhythm of the narrative, and notes that "ils sont loin de toujours correspondre au découpage des scènes ou des paragraphes" (ed. cit., p. 20).

[89] "[Les] *mouvements* que nous lui donnions"; "il ne faut pas l'*agiter* tant"; "[elle] entr'ouvrit les yeux, qu'elle *promena* languissamment sur Valville" (p. 351), etc. There is an intense silence in the scene where the two women drive Marianne and Varthon back to the convent (p. 414) but, besides the fact that nothing more is really happening during this interval, there is of course the implicit movement of the carriage.

ville and Marianne are both frozen to the spot, the unfailing energy of Mme Dutour keeps the scene going.

3) Marianne's kidnapping: "J'avais l'esprit bouleversé, c'était de ces accablements où l'on est *comme imbécile*" (p. 302).

4) Marianne reading Valville's letter to Varthon: "j'achevais malgré les soupirs qui me suffoquaient. Mlle Varthon avait les yeux fixés à terre, et paraissait rêver profondément en pleurant. Pour moi, la tête renversée dans mon fauteuil, je restai presque *sans sentiment*" (p. 377). Extension: "Me voilà seule, immobile, et toujours renversée dans mon fauteuil, où je restai bien encore une demi-heure dans une si grande confusion de pensée et de mouvement, que j'en étais *comme stupide*. ... [Tervire] ne savait que penser de mes monosyllabes et de l'*air imbécile* dont je les prononçais" (p. 380). [90]

None of these instances seems to have any relation to the moment of total "surprise," an instantaneous kind of intuitive discovery only later to be fully apprehended, [91] for here no new awareness emerges; they are instead a pure effect of annihilation due to a different kind of utter surprise where what has been thought a firm expectation is suddenly undermined from without. Its intense disappointment usually just precedes a great victory.

There is of course no such aphasia on the plane of enunciation, for narrative cannot but go on. Marianne is wordy, not just in her prolixity but in her sensitivity to words and her implicit confidence that it is the nature of knowledge to be verbal, in a very broad sense. Not that an important role is not ascribed to intuition, [92] and even to non-verbal forms of communication; but these can only be realized,

---

[90] Cf., in Tervire's story: the nun, "une spectatrice stupide de l'engagement éternel que je pris" (p. 459); Tervire after recognizing her mother: "j'avais perdu la force de parler, ... j'étais faible, pâle, et comme dans un état de stupidité" (p. 567).

[91] See Georges Poulet, *La Distance intérieure* (Paris: Plon, 1952), ch. 1; cf. also Jean Rousset, p. 112. Virtually nothing in Poulet's analysis of Marivaux's "human time" seems to me applicable to *La Vie de Marianne;* Leo Spitzer politely made much the same remark in a well-known rejoinder entitled "À propos de *La Vie de Marianne,*" *Romanic Review*, 44 (1953), 102-26.

[92] Peter Brooks speaks of Marianne's "faith in intuitive knowledge, knowledge at a pre-logical and pre-verbal stage, her assertion that there are things she feels but cannot conceptualize and express" (p. 106): there is doubtless a good point in this, but attention must be given also to the resolving power of words: all of these presumably non-verbal things, after all, are *said*.

published, in language. All awareness takes a verbal form; indeed the *word* becomes a metaphor for thought: "Je ne m'étais amusée qu'à mépriser Climal, qu'à ... regretter mes hardes; et de mon état, *pas un mot:* il n'en avait pas été question, je n'y avais pas pris garde" (p. 134).[93] Language has a flexible, metamorphosing quality in *Marianne* that is quite different from its fixating function in, for example, *La Princesse de Clèves*. When Marianne seeks to avoid an assertion of value preference after describing Mme de Miran as "la meilleure personne du monde," she must introduce Mme Dorsin as "un autre portrait de la meilleure personne du monde aussi" (p. 222): such an expression has none of the absolute, pregnant value it would have had in the earlier novel, but is instead a mere skeleton on which to hang a fleshed-out commentary.

There are constant interferences between the written and the spoken, especially since Marianne ostensibly can write only the way she speaks. Her *histoire* implies an oral quality,[94] which "Marivaux" corroborates: "Figurez-vous qu'elle n'écrit point, mais qu'elle parle" (p. 56). But how can one write the spoken? Her model is conversation, but that hardly defines a specific style, nor is it a one-way street: she must appeal to the written after all, and imitate the style of (her own) letters (p. 9). The intervention of Tervire, however, raises the opposite question, a swing in polarity from suppositions of the non-written to the written: "Ne serait-ce pas que la religieuse aurait elle-même écrit [son histoire], qu'elle vous aurait laissé son manuscrit, et que vous le copiez?" (p. 539). One pre-existent manuscript seems to imply the existence of another; not just the story but the text apparently pre-exists — if only by way of denial. Marianne's writing, like Mme Dutour's speech (pp. 98-

---

[93] If one thinks of the classical definition of metaphor as the displacement of the proper word by an analogical one, then the word as metaphor itself appears all the more striking. There is also a hesitation between a literal and a figurative sense ('hear'/'understand') of *entendre* when Marianne says: "Je ne laissai pas ... de *dire* en moi-même (mais si bas, qu'à peine m'*entendis-je*): [le linge] est pourtant bien choisi..." (p. 131). Cf. the correlation between thought and word in: "Je le laissai achever tout ce discours, qui n'avait ni suite ni raison, et qui marquait si bien le désordre de son esprit" (p. 403).

[94] "Il est vrai que l'*histoire* [de ma vie] est particulière, mais je la gâterai, si je l'écris; car où voulez-vous que je prenne un style?" (p. 8).

99), rides on its own inertia, is propelled like a jet by its own exhaust.[95]

Gestures as well talk, especially the *regard,* which would seem to include overall facial expression and perhaps more. Marianne often furnishes its at least approximate verbal equivalent:

> [Valville] répondit ... par une révérence qu'il accompagna d'un coup d'œil où il y avait bien des choses que j'*entendis* toutes, mais que je ne saurais rendre, et dont la principale signifiait: Que faut-il que je pense? [p. 90]

> Je le regardai alors en prenant sa lettre, je lui trouvai les yeux sur moi; quels yeux, madame! les miens se fixèrent sur lui; nous restâmes quelque temps sans nous rien dire; et il n'y avait encore que *nos cœurs qui se parlaient.* [p. 161]

> Il me parlait, et moi je le regardais, et ses *discours* n'étaient pas plus tendres que mes *regards.* Il le sentait bien: ses expressions en devenaient plus passionnées, et le *langage* de mes yeux encore plus doux. [p. 261]

Indeed one cannot even look without signifying, and expression on occasion, ocular as well as verbal, equivocates: "il [ne] jetait pas un [regard] sur moi qui ne signifiât: *Je vous aime;* et moi, je ne savais que faire des miens, parce qu'ils lui en auraient dit autant" (p. 67, italics in the text). Tacit convention permits a ritual of mutual inspection which Marianne voyeuristically refers to as "observations clandestines." But not to look also may signify a look: "Il le faut bien, repris-je en baissant les yeux d'un air triste (ce qui valait bien le regarder moi-même)" (p. 72). *Regard* itself has no signified, but takes one on in context.

Similarly, the sigh, one of the most flexible non-verbal notations, occupies an ambiguous middle ground between verbal and non-verbal discourse which on occasion is reflected by a syntactic ambiguity in Marianne's description: "Un petit soupir naïf précéda ma réponse, ou plutôt la commença" (p. 76). But, like tears, it pretends to be a spontaneous (and therefore full) signifier, erupting like a natural force beneath every effort to contain it: "Je sentis que les larmes

---

[95] "Cette réflexion a coulé de ma plume sans que j'y prisse garde; heureusement elle est courte, et j'espère qu'elle ne vous ennuiera pas. Continuons" (p. 209).

m'en venaient aux yeux; je crois même que je soupirai, il n'y eut *pas moyen de m'en empêcher;* mais je soupirai le plus bas qu'il me fut possible" (p. 193). Occasionally, other gestures are similarly interpreted: "je laissai même tomber amicalement mon bras sur [Tervire], d'un air qui signifiait: Je vous remercie, il est bien doux d'être entre vos mains" (p. 384); the amusingly awkward greeting of Marianne to Climal is articulated like a (contradictory) sentence: "En un mot, j'en fis trop et pas assez. Dans la moitié de mon salut, il semblait que je le connaissais; dans l'autre moitié, je ne le connaissais plus; c'était oui, c'était non, et tous les deux manqués" (p. 84).

Qu'est-ce que cela signifie? The cry goes up from one end of the novel to the other,[96] provoked not by the unknown feeling within but by the perplexity of the ambiguous world without. Meaning-making is threatened by the empty signifiers, like the abbess's compassionate face (p. 149) or Varthon's noble procedures ("une vaine démonstration qui ne signifiait rien" [p. 418]); the world is full of appearances from which one can draw misleading inferences. Even the demand for meaning — "qu'est-ce que cela signifie?" — can be an empty signifier: "quelques mots qui ne mettaient ordre à rien, de ces mots qui diminuent la confusion qu'on a de se taire, qui tiennent la place de quelque chose qu'on ne dit pas et qu'on devrait dire" (p. 73). Marianne refers later to a reply of Valville's as a stab at "quelques mots qui figurassent, qui tinssent lieu d'une réponse" (p. 409). A character like Saint-Vincent, although never dealt with harshly, is caricatural in this regard, for he would prefer to void all signifiers except those whose stability is guaranteed in advance by a closed system: "Ah! Seigneur, où en sommes-nous! Ce qu'il disait joignant les mains, en homme épouvanté de mon discours, et qui éloignait tant qu'il pouvait une pareille *idée,* dans la crainte d'être tenté d'examiner *la chose*" (p. 141).

The lie prowls and preys in a hostile world. It is all but structurally impossible to disbelieve a narrator, at least for very long, but as insurance there are still many confidence-sustaining phrases such as "je ne sais point mentir" (p. 188). But untruth insinuates itself into all discourse, threatening, as it does, the authenticity of

---

[96] See pp. 139, 263, 266, 276, 289, 307, 327, 361, 410, 473.

even the first person, who must hedge ("je ne mentais presque pas" [p. 133]), tell half-truths (pp. 181-82), and lie in ways proposed by Mme de Miran (pp. 184, 211, 285; cf. p. 513). Mme de Miran's rationalization concerning her phrase "ce que je dirai est presque vrai" (p. 211) can only be taken humoristically, but even her irony recognizes a slight disquiet at the adoption of procedures worthy only of the (evil) adversary. Detachment from one's own untruths comes, in effect, by way of playing or becoming a writer. "En un mot, je ne mentis en rien, je n'en étais *pas capable;* mais je *peignis dans le grand:* mon sentiment me menait ainsi sans que j'y pensasse" (p. 356): the integrity of the self is preserved by its story; "ce n'est pas mensonge," says Rousseau, "c'est fiction." [97]

This context lends additional value to the constant effort of Marianne to nuance. Over against the fleeing signifier she opposes, centripetally, her incessant *distinguo,* as in the epigrammatic: "il ne me disait de si *jolies* choses qu'à cause qu'il commençait à n'en plus sentir de si *tendres*" (p. 348).[98] By creating a tension between the connotations of two usually synonymous adjectives or nouns, she draws attention to a fundamentally asynonymic theory, enunciated for example in the course of a description of Varthon: "En voyant cette jeune personne, on eût plutôt dit: Elle ne vit plus, qu'on n'eût dit: Elle est morte. Je ne puis vous représenter l'impression qu'elle faisait, qu'en vous priant de distinguer ces deux façons de parler, qui paraissent signifier la même chose, et qui dans le sentiment pourtant en signifient de différentes" (p. 350). Although reality cannot be captured by language, it can be confined, delimited on either side by two terms calipered to the minimum possible distance.

A passage like this, with its "on eût plutôt dit..." also typifies the manner in which, for Marianne, all sense-making must pass via the general truth, sometimes delivered in lapidary form ("Le mauvais exemple débauche" [p. 93] reminiscent of Mme Dutour's endless proverbs, but more often approaching the totalizing psychologism of seventeenth-century maxims:

---

[97] *Rêveries du promeneur solitaire,* 4e promenade.
[98] Cf.: "Mme Dutour ... *se fâchant* souvent au delà de ce qu'elle était *fâchée* ..." (p. 98).

> La charité n'est pas galante dans ses présents; l'amitié même, si secourable, donne du bon et ne songe point au magnifique. [p. 39]
>
> Notre orgueil et nous, ce n'est qu'un, au lieu que nous et notre vertu, c'est deux. [p. 86]
>
> Dans la vie, nous sommes plus jaloux de la considération des autres que de leur estime. [p. 87]
>
> On fait des lâchetés qu'on ne veut pas savoir, et qu'on se déguise sous d'autres noms. [p. 132]
>
> Il est bon en pareille occasion de plaire un peu aux yeux, ils vous recommandent au cœur. [p. 146]
>
> Ce qui [aide le cœur] à être ferme, dans un cas comme le mien, c'est la liberté d'être faible. [p. 159]
>
> Nous avons tous besoin les uns des autres; nous naissons dans cette dépendance, et nous ne changerons rien à cela. [p. 221]
>
> Nous sommes bien près de nous consoler quand nous nous affectionnons aux gens qui nous consolent. [p. 384]

For that matter, the "Avertissement" to part two assimilates *Marianne* to an hypothetical work entitled *Réflexions sur l'homme*, which could be the title of a book of maxims or of the less formal but still generalized observations so congenial to Marianne. In these, the "knowledge" invoked appears less to be borrowed from outside, mundane discourse than distilled from her own experience, and is expressed in a more flexible and often slightly attenuated style:

> Quand un malheur, qu'on a cru extrême, et qui nous désespère, devient encore plus grand, *il semble que* notre âme renonce à s'en affliger; l'excès qu'elle y voit la met à la raison, ce n'est plus la peine qu'elle s'en désole; elle lui cède et se tait. [p. 394]
>
> Les grandes actions sont difficiles; quelque plaisir qu'on y prenne, on se passerait bien de les faire: ... mais *en général*, il faut se redresser pour être grand: il n'y a qu'à rester comme on est pour être petit. [p. 131]

> *Il y a des* afflictions où l'on s'oublie, où l'âme n'a plus la discrétion de faire aucun mystère de l'état où elle est. Vienne qui voudra, on ne s'embarrasse guère de servir de spectacle, on est dans un entier abandon de soi-même; et c'est ainsi que j'étais. [p. 380]

The syntax of this last example, landing only at the end on Marianne as referent, figures the whole epistemological process which filters all observation through the general rule; but Marianne likes to emphasize the personal aspect too through first- and second-person forms which have a more familiar tone although they lead in the same direction:

> Si vous me laissez là, si vous négligez ma personne, je ne suis pas content, vous prenez à gauche.... C'est que pour parvenir à être honoré, je saurai bien cesser d'être honorable; et en effet, c'est assez là le chemin des honneurs: qui les mérite n'y arrive guère. [p. 87]

> Vous dites que celui qui vous oblige a de l'avantage sur vous. Eh bien! voulez-vous lui conserver cet avantage, ... vous n'avez qu'à être ingrat [etc.]. [pp. 221-22] [99]

The *je* and *vous* are neutral here (as the masculine adjectives show), which connects the discourse not to Marianne II and the Marquise but as before to the realm of universal information. Despite the personal flavor, the sense and shape of such passages assimilates them to the "known," that is, to the *vraisemblable*.

---

[99] Tervire furnishes some similar instances: "c'était un de ces hommes ordinaires, qui sont incapables de s'élever à rien de généreux, qui ne sont ni bons ni méchants, de ces petites âmes..." (p. 436); "ce sont des affronts qui ne corrigent personne, et nos torts disparaissent dès qu'on nous offense" (p. 440); "ce sont de ces tristesses retirées dans le fond de l'âme, qui la flétrissent, et qui la laissent comme morte" (p. 447); "On est tout d'un coup lié avec les gens qui ont le cœur bon, quels qu'ils soient; ce sont comme des amis que vous avez dans tous les états" (p. 450). René Démoris has remarqué in this way on the function of the general truth in this text: "on voit quelle est la fonction des réflexions du narrateur: elles permettent de tisser entre lui et le lecteur tout un réseau de maximes admises, qui justifient la démarche souvent paradoxale des héros. Elles tendent à faire passer leur conduite comme la plus naturelle et la plus vraisemblable, selon les lois générales que reconnaît la société honnête" (op. cit., p. 411).

Besides the code of nobility, which is diffused throughout, another code exercises particular force, that of femininity. The social world of *Marianne* is strongly matriarchal; we never see MM. de Fare, Dorsin, or de Miran (there is only one allusion to Valville's dead father), and the men present at the family council — with exception of the minister, who represents authority — play no role. But a whole stereotyped discourse about women associates their temperament with vanity, beauty, and so forth, while men are characterized by science and philosophy. It is true that irony undermines their pretensions, but it affects the feminine domain as well: "Les hommes parlent de science et de philosophie; voilà quelque chose de beau, en comparaison de la science de bien placer un ruban, ou de décider de quelle couleur on le mettra!" (p. 50; cf. pp. 22-23). Indeed, this feministic irony is generally the more insistent:

> Du côté de la vanité, je menaçais déjà d'être furieusement femme. [p. 49]

> Il n'y a point de jolie femme qui n'ait un peu trop envie de plaire. [p. 215]

> La plupart des femmes qui ont beaucoup d'esprit ont une certaine façon d'en avoir qu'elles n'ont pas naturellement, mais qu'elles se donnent. [p. 215]

> Nous autres filles, ou nous autres femmes, nous pleurons volontiers dès qu'on nous dit: Vous venez de pleurer; c'est une enfance et comme une mignardise que nous avons et dont nous ne pouvons presque pas nous défendre. [p. 147]

Even in the absence of coquetry, there is another coquetry (p. 216). These categories do not seem to be much challenged by Marianne in either of her incarnations. What must perhaps be said, though, is that, first of all, within them (and their limitations), women exercise a form of genius that is not to be denied because it operates in infinitesimal subtleties and at lightening speed; and secondly, that it exercises a levelling effect denying male superiority as such: "Est-ce à cause que je ne suis qu'une femme, et que je ne sais rien? Le bon sens est de tout sexe" (p. 225). And although she distinguishes between the masculine and feminine forms of *esprit*, she calls that of Mme Dorsin sexless and even "mâle" (p. 225) while at the same time asserting its capacities as "de tous les esprits de femme le plus aimable" (p. 215).

Yet there is a kind of reinvention of the referent by which it is not merely recalled or alluded to but reshaped; a certain violence is done to the *on dit*. This happens precisely through such devices as the word plays based on apparent synonymity such as: "il est vrai que la vertu s'en scandalise; mais la vertueuse n'est pas fâchée du scandale" (p. 70). The unexpected opposition of abstract to concrete permits margin for experimentation on the validity of the general precept; "la vertu s'en scandalise" turns out to be only a half-truth, and the "virtue" code fails in fact, in this sentence, to meet a certain test of viability in lived experience.

Similar distinctions are in order for Marianne's use of metaphor. There are a certain number of simple and straightforward ones — "tout l'univers était un désert" (p. 21; cf. p. 134); "la harpie ... la parente pie-grièche" (pp. 330-31); "ce grand spectre" (p. 289) — and rarely a somewhat precious and extended metaphor.[100] They do not seem to be the idiom most congenial to her, however; she tends toward similes instead, and tends to accompany them with a *clause de style* indicating their self-conscious nature:

> J'étais, *comme on dit,* la fable de l'armée; mon histoire courut tout le couvent. [p. 232]

> Valville, qui m'aime dès le premier instant avec une tendresse aussi vive que subite (tendresse ordinairement de peu de durée; *il en est comme* de ces fruits qui passent vite, à cause qu'ils ont été mûrs de trop bonne heure) ... [p. 376]

> On disait l'autre jour à une dame qu'elle était au printemps de son âge: *ce terme de printemps me fit ressouvenir* de la jeune demoiselle dont je parle, et je gagerais que c'est

---

[100] Coquetry is called "un enfant de l'orgueil qui naît tout élevé, qui manque d'abord d'audace, mais qui n'en pense pas moins" (p. 59); cf. the heart/money analogy when Mme de Miran gives Marianne a purse: "Je vous remercie, ma mère, lui repartis-je: mais où mettrai-je tout l'amour, tout le respect et toute la reconnaissance que j'ai pour ma mère? Il me semble que j'en ai plus qu'il n'en peut tenir dans mon cœur" (p. 344); and the flower simile p. 313. Note one example too of a "diegetic" metaphor, when Marianne worries about what Valville will come to think of her: "et quelle *chute* n'était-ce pas faire là dans son esprit?" (p. 70).

quelque figure comme la sienne, qui a fait imaginer cette expression-là. [p. 256]

D'abord ses yeux se jetèrent sur moi, et me parcoururent; *je dis se jetèrent,* au hasard de mal parler, mais c'est pour vous peindre l'avidité curieuse avec laquelle elle se mit à me regarder. [p. 254]

Such passages are operational in that they work on the metaphor before our eyes, rationalizing it or creating it as a distinct rhetorical entity; to describe Mme Dorsin's beauty, Marianne begins: "*Personnifions* la beauté, et supposons..." (p. 214). They have to do with expectations of the written style, and it is part of her stance to be a stranger to it. Her reservation about Climal: "je devrais rayer l'épithète de tartufe que je viens de lui donner" (p. 88) is an ostensibly "oral" form of reverse preterition, objectively false in a written text, where the act *rayer,* which is here the "metaphor," is literally possible: *rayer* is written instead of being performed, which would remove it and its object from the text.

These remarks necessarily lead us to at least touch on irony, the ubiquitous doubter of Marianne's discourse. For if metaphor to her is in dubious status, so is everything else which her gentle but pervasive irony attacks. "Ce discours était assez net, et il était difficile de parler plus français": this remark appears, of all places, immediately following a metaphor, Climal's lecherously gallant "Allez, friponne, allez rendre votre cœur plus traitable et moins *sourd,* je vous laisse le mien pour vous y aider" (p. 41). And she follows it up with another, which coheres only thanks to the metonymic contagion of *oreille:* "je fis semblant d'être distraite pour me dispenser d'y répondre; mais un baiser qu'il m'appuyait sur *l'oreille* en me parlant s'attirait mon attention malgré que j'en eusse, et il n'y avait pas moyen *d'être sourde à cela.*"

One of the most evident aspects of Marianne's irony is her use of epithets — "ces maudits habits," "une physionomie friponne," "ma misérable vanité," "cette fâcheuse boutique," "cette malheureuse boutique" — which contribute greatly to maintaining distance of perspective between Mariannes I and II (although Marianne I also, from all appearances, possesses a sense of irony). Especially insistent is Marianne's use of *petit(e).* It can have a non-humorous function, of course, especially when applied to Marianne by someone else —

"votre petite tête," "petite langue de serpent," "la dangereuse petite créature," "aimable petite personne," "petite aventurière" — as a part of a generally deprecatory insinuation proffered to a social or moral inferior; Mme de Miran calls Mme de Fare "une bien petite femme." [101] There is also Tervire's tender teasing over Marianne's lovesickness: "je prétends vous appeler petite fille encore longtemps à cause de cela" (p. 384). Marianne herself uses the adjective both as an affectionate diminutive of this sort, and as ironic self-depreciation (or disparagement of Marianne I by II). But these two manners are complementary, simultaneously present in almost every utterance:

de petites façons	ma petite figure
mon petit amour-propre	mes petites affaires
ce petit cas de conscience	le plus joli petit pied du monde
un petit raisonnement	un jeune petit cœur fier
mon petit arrangement	mon petit discours ou ma petite harangue
un petit miroir ingrat	
un petit minois	mon petit plan généreux
ces petits égards	ma petite expédition

There is both self-indulgence and ironic distance in numerous such expressions,[102] of which many more examples could be cited.

In both the relationships these ironies suggest between the two Mariannes [103] and their effects on the effective value structures functioning in Marianne II's discourse there are many gradations. When she prefaces a decision with: "vous allez être édifiée du parti que je pris: oui, vous allez voir une action qui prouva que Valville avait eu raison de me respecter" (p. 178), the insistance on edification supposes an ironic distance with regard to her heroic image, yet the affirmation of merit in the action is not for all that completely

---

[101] Cf. the "mon petit cousin" addressed to Valville at the family council, and his sarcastic "ma grande cousine" in reply (p. 327).

[102] Climal, for comparison, adds the diminutive to his speech as a means of lessening the implied guilt (and violence): "ma petite faiblesse" (p. 114); "vous assurer une petite fortune" (p. 115); "je subis humblement la petite humiliation" (p. 117): but at the same time a social condescension is implied.

[103] "L'art imperceptible de mes petits raisonnements" (p. 133), for example, seems to make Marianne I the target of Marianne II's irony; but "je pourrai encore me soutenir, me disais-je bien secrètement en moi-même, et si secrètement que je n'y faisais pas d'attention" (p. 191) implies a complicity latent in Marianne I.

undermined. Is "Je venais de m'épuiser en générosité" (p. 200) ironic? It is difficult to so assert, though it obviously contains ironic potential — in other words, it is subject to an ironic reading to which no objection can be raised. Or consider the sense of good faith in the following passage:

> Et remarquez que, pendant ce discours, [Valville] avançait sa main pour ravoir la mienne, que je lui laissais prendre, et qu'il baisait encore en me demandant pardon de l'avoir baisée; et ce qui est de plaisant, c'est que je trouvais la réparation fort bonne, et que je la recevais de la meilleure foi du monde, sans m'apercevoir qu'elle n'était qu'une répétition de la faute. [p. 75]

This might be styled an (ironic) figure of thought; the affirmation of "la meilleure foi du monde" suffices to deny its own candor, in a discourse which speaks of a (gallant) crime that can only be atoned for by being repeated. The passage figures repetition, which is a figure of desire. But then Marianne II is capable, even explicitly, of taking distance from one sentence to the next: "je suis toute honteuse du raisonnement que je viens de faire, et j'étais toute glorieuse en le faisant" (p. 22). In an ironic medium, there is no intact, unvulnerable self; on its every manifestation falls the shadow.

There is a similar ambiguity governing the status of the text as fiction. Marianne both affirms and refutes that she is an *héroïne de roman,* but she and other characters alike subscribe generally to the rules governing romance. It makes no sense whatever, in relation to a *real* claim to noble treatment, to assert that for people like Marianne "leur infortune leur tient lieu de rang auprès des cœurs bien faits" (p. 328), yet Mme de Miran says this to her family assembled. Marianne too, in flagrant disregard for the kind of credentials the world demands, lists the following among her "titres pour être respectée": "Premièrement, j'avais mon infortune qui était unique; avec cette infortune, j'avais de la vertu, et elles allaient si bien ensemble! Et puis j'étais jeune, et puis j'étais belle; que voulez-vous de plus?" (p. 131). A language of this sort lulls the reader into accepting as valid, for the purposes of his reading, romantic suppositions which have no currency in real situations.[104]

---

[104] "Sous le ciel romanesque, l'infortune est signe d'élection," writes Jugan (No. 2, p. 68). This promotion of *infortune* is only the most obvious example,

Marianne's "harpie" is therefore not objectively mistaken in labelling Marianne's assets "vertus romanesques," nor in linking them to an archetypical happy end: "Adieu, la petite aventurière, vous n'êtes encore qu'une fille de condition, nous dit-on; mais vous n'en demeurerez pas là, et nous serons bien heureuses, si au premier jour vous ne vous trouvez pas une princesse" (p. 338). She has sensed, indeed, how much Marianne's "story" is set up similarly to that of a Cinderella. The collateral plots in Tervire's story contain numerous stock romance elements, such as the hidden stairway which costs Tervire her reputation and the elopement of Mme Dursan's son with a poor artisan's daughter. The subtitle, *Les Aventures de Madame la comtesse de ****, is amply justified by the number of times Marianne herself makes use in both singular and plural of the term *aventure* which, despite its everyday sense, carries romantic connotations which she does not deny: "Je suis née pour avoir des aventures," she remarks, "et mon étoile ne m'en laissera pas manquer" (p. 418). The characters rather neatly divide, as we have seen, into simplistic romantic categories, good and bad by virtue of their stance concerning the love interest and Marianne's right of place. And whatever the other disclaimers of the text, when Marianne avows that she is writing only "pour vous amuser seulement" (p. 345), she is playing the standard role of an *auteur de roman*.

Besides, the text is forever, and from the start, referring to the institutional novel as a counterpoint. The first "Avertissement" states that *La Vie de Marianne* does not conform to current tastes — for novels — which "ne veut dans des aventures que les aventures mêmes," and the second reconfirms that "ce n'est pas là la forme ordinaire des romans, ... Marianne n'a aucune forme d'ouvrage présente à l'esprit" (p. 55). In the context of the contemporary novel, where protestations of veracity were routine, it would have been normal to read these assertions more as a claim to something original with respect to the novel as usually practiced than as an effort to make it pass for something not a novel in any sense — as if, in other words, the second passage had actually said: "Marianne n'a aucune forme de *roman* présente à l'esprit." Indeed one cannot write with "aucune forme d'ouvrage" in mind. *Roman* is a referent

---

but there are many other "rules" of fiction invoked, such as: "je comptais sur sa tendresse à cause de son malheur" (p. 553).

whose definition can in effect be modified by the very work which defines itself in opposition to it. Marianne adds her own voice at the beginning of part two in self-defense against the expectations of a certain kind of conventional reader accustomed to more heroic forms of romance.

Her position is thus itself ambiguous. Is it only by way of metaphor, and thus an ironic allusion to the fact she is not an "author," that she begins her first letter to the Marquise: "Quand je vous ai fait le récit de quelques accidents de ma vie, je ne m'attendais pas, ma chère amie, que vous me prieriez de vous la donner toute entière, et d'*en faire un livre à imprimer*"? Or is there an allusion to some intention to "publish" which in fact makes an author of her? Any mention of a "book" can only be equivocal in this way: "je n'ai garde de songer que *je vous fais un livre*" (p. 36); "aventures dont le caractère paraîtrait bas et trivial à beaucoup de *lecteurs, si je les faisais imprimer*" (p. 57). It is easier to define the function of such asides in terms of the real, extradiegetic author and reader (Marivaux and ourselves) than of Marianne and the Marquise. What is going on in this (non)novel written by a non-author? When Marianne returns to this subject much further on, again to affirm: "C'est qu'au lieu d'une histoire véritable, vous avez cru *lire un roman*. Vous avez oublié que c'était ma vie que je vous racontais" (p. 375), the denial is tantamount to an admission. Literally, how could her fictional reader (the Marquise and friends) have "cru lire un roman"? There is an incongruity in the protestation which extrapolates the message in fact to another level, and to another "reader": read the text, it says in sum, *as if* it were the personal story of a friend, and not a novel as you know them. It is in the category of *mode d'emploi* rather than objective claim.[105]

Marianne's own narrative shows ample awareness of romantic models on various levels. In the first place, Marianne I has read novels, and they have filled her thoughts with exotic (and erotic) imaginations:

---

[105] On this notion see Ronald Rosbottom's article entitled "A Matter of Competence: The Relationship between Reading and Novel-Making in Eighteenth-Century France," in *Studies in Eighteenth-Century Culture*, 6 (1977), 245-63.

> Enfin tous ces visages [de l'auberge] me faisaient frémir, je n'y pouvais tenir; je voyais des épées, des poignards, des assassinats, des vols, des insultes; mon sang se glaçait aux périls que je me figurais: car quand une fois l'imagination est en train, malheur à l'esprit qu'elle gouverne. [p. 26]
>
> J'en avais vu, des amants, dans mon village, j'avais entendu parler d'amour, j'avais même déjà lu quelques romans à la dérobée; et tout cela, joint aux leçons que la nature nous donne, m'avait du moins fait sentir qu'un amant était bien différent d'un ami. [p. 37]

This last example perches her formation, appropriately, half-way between nature and literature; the worldly-wise character in the novel is not just Marianne II but her earlier avatar as well, who has imagined her "roman" in advance even though — like us — she does not know how it will "end." As it approaches its eclipse, Marianne adopts a frequently melodramatic tone, scolding Varthon and especially Valville for their crime against love ("un héros de roman infidèle!" [p. 375]):

> Il me regrettera, mais je n'y serai plus, il se ressouviendra combien je l'aimais, il pleurera ma mort. Vous aurez la douleur de le voir; vous vous reprocherez de m'avoir trahie, et jamais vous ne serez heureuse! [p. 368]
>
> Ah! c'en est trop, vous dis-je, et Dieu me vengera, mademoiselle, vous le verrez. [p. 393] [106]

This is either the fantasy of a child hoping to punish through her own death, or the malediction of a wounded heroine.

Marianne's own terms assimilate her story to a novel, and her qualities to the "vertus romanesques" her enemy alludes to, when she makes herself into the "illustre infortunée" ennobled by tears who appeals precisely to the romantic in Valville:

---

[106] It is worth noting that in at least one passage such melodramatic diction releases a chain-reaction: first Valville invokes a rhetorical "death": "je serai malheureux ... mais je ne le serai pas longtemps"; then Marianne follows: "Je suis au désespoir d'être au monde, et je prie le ciel de m'en retirer"; and finally Mme de Miran likewise is implicated in death by Marianne: "vous désolez ma mère, vous la faites mourir" (p. 198). The rhetoric (of fiction) is contagious.

> C'est que cet abattement et ces pleurs me donnèrent, aux yeux de ce jeune homme, je ne sais quel air de *dignité romanesque* qui lui en imposa, qui corrigea d'avance la médiocrité de mon état.... Il y a de certaines *infortunes* qui *embellissent* la beauté même, qui lui prêtent de la *majesté*. Vous avez alors, avec vos grâces, celles que *votre histoire, faite comme un roman,* vous donne encore. Et ne vous embarrassez pas d'ignorer ce que vous êtes née; laissez travailler les chimères de l'amour là-dessus; elles sauront bien vous faire un rang distingué, et tirer bon parti des ténèbres qui cacheront votre naissance. Si une femme pouvait être prise pour une *divinité,* ce serait en pareil cas que son amant l'en croirait une. [pp. 80-81]

It is one thing for Marianne to stake a claim to nobility; but when she speaks of majesty and divinity she is in the realm of the "princess" her "harpy" invokes: that of fairy tales. Correspondingly, Marianne I indulges herself in playing rather egregiously the heroine — trying out already, in effect, the role of Marianne II:

> Mon *récit* devint intéressant; je le fis, de la meilleure foi du monde, dans un goût aussi *noble* que *tragique;* je parlai *en déplorable victime du sort, en héroïne de roman,* qui ne disait pourtant rien que de vrai, mais qui *ornait la vérité* de tout ce qui pouvait la rendre touchante, et me rendre moi-même *une infortunée* respectable.... Tout vint à sa place, aussi bien que Mme de Miran, ... sauf à la nommer après, quand je serais hors de ce *ton romanesque* que j'avais pris. [p. 356]

Even without notation of all the mutual tears between her and Varthon punctuating this episode, it is an unmistakable comment of *La Vie de Marianne* on itself, and falling within the ever-inclusive compass of its own irony. Marianne deromanticizes Valville at the beginning of part eight; "bientôt vous ne saurez plus comment le trouver" means that he is neither hero nor villain, that the "truth" about him is middling; but there is no "truth" in a story, and as soon as she returns from him to it the romantic returns full force: "Continuons, et rentrons dans tout *le pathétique de mon aventure*" (p. 377). With irony, of course.

Or we can take the dramatization through theatrical terms: "J'allais soutenir une terrible *scène*" (p. 191); the many scenes and many masks which make of Marianne the consummate comedienne.¹⁰⁷ The asides of Marianne II in certain situations, commenting on what Marianne I hears almost as if she "overheard," function exactly like *apartés* in comedy, and like them reveal the thoughts of the character in complicity with the audience; Marianne I can play a similar function. Mme Dorsin: "Car il n'est question que d'une grisette, ou tout au plus de la fille de quelque petit bourgeois, qui s'était mise dans ses beaux atours à cause du jour de fête"; Marianne: "Un jour de fête! Ah! Seigneur, quelle date!; est-ce que ce serait moi? dis-je encore en moi-même toute tremblante, et n'osant plus faire de questions" (p. 175). Her "Ahi! ahi!" when all doubt is finally dispelled is an exclamation of farce, emphasizing even more the stock "reconnaissance" function of the preceding dialogue. Valville's disguising himself as a valet in order to deliver his letter to Marianne is shocking in terms of social codes ("et quelle démarche: prendre une livrée!" [p. 183]), but perfectly standard comic fare. The literary reference of the role of Climal would be evident even if Marianne did not refer to him as "mon tartufe" (p. 88) both because of the similarity of certain lines to those of Tartuffe ¹⁰⁸ and because Marianne later recalls Orgon by referring to Climal twice in succession as "ce pauvre homme" (p. 203). And of course the scene of Climal caught in Valville's earlier posture is a classic case of comic reversal: "La revanche était complète" (p. 120).

More fundamental are references of a structural nature — structural, that is, principally in terms of comedy as genre. The adoptive-father role of Climal, "qui paraissait vouloir me tenir lieu de père" (p. 35), assimilates him to the traditional *barbon* or *senex* of comedy, the "uncle" or guardian ¹⁰⁹ who by implication seduces his own daughter. And like the senex, he is obsessed with the competition

---

¹⁰⁷ The point is not the inauthenticity of the masks but the register of reference involved. As Coulet says, the various images of Marianne "sont toutes également vraies, quand l'une prédomine, les autres ne sont pas totalement absentes" (p. 212).

¹⁰⁸ "C'est de la prudence que j'entends, et non pas une certaine austérité de mœurs.... La plupart des hommes ... sont indiscrets, ... et vous ne risquez rien de tout cela avec moi" (pp. 112-15); cf. *Tartuffe*, III.3.

¹⁰⁹ "C'est à moi désormais à vous tenir lieu de vos parents que vous n'avez plus" (p. 116); "vous y arriverez sous le titre d'une de mes parentes, qui n'a plus ni père ni mère, que j'ai retirée de la campagne et dont je veux prendre soin" (p. 118).

of the young, the "mille petits soupirants" (p. 31), whom he of course puts Marianne on guard against as much as possible: "mon neveu, qui est un étourdi"; [110] "ces jeunes fous-là savent-ils aimer?" (pp. 110-11); "vous ne voudriez pas perdre votre temps à être la maîtresse d'un jeune étourdi" (p. 112); "la plupart des hommes, et surtout des jeunes gens, ne ménagent pas une fille comme vous quand ils la quittent" (p. 114). He wants to sequester her, like Agnès in *L'École des femmes,* from the nephew whom he sees as being in direct competition with him. The nephew and son in comedy often occupy similar functions, and this father-daughter-nephew triangle, further complicated by the adoptive-mother role of Mme de Miran, sets off an endless reverberation of incestuous implications familiar to the world of comedy: "elle en agit avec moi comme si j'étais votre sœur" (p. 195); "nous aurons tous deux la même mère, vous serez mon frère" (p. 198). [111] And of course all such situations foreshadow an eventual recognition scene, such as the one played out in Tervire's story when the lost son is found, in a manner reminiscent of many comedies, through a ring, characteristic token of the hidden identity.

References to the love code are a bit more insidious than those to novel and comedy, which are not semi-sacred institutions. It is untarnished in the use Climal makes of it because, although he employs the traditional euphemisms with their attendant gradations ("Eh! ne changez point mes termes, reprit-il, je ne dis pas mon amitié, je parle de ma tendresse" [p. 41]), he is interested only in sex, and sentiment does not cloud the picture. Marianne's premonitions of sexuality in love are, however, brought into play in a more delicate fashion through the veiled manner in which she conceives her attraction to Valville: a girl in this situation "y trouve du plaisir,

---

[110] In contrast, Mme Dorsin affirms to Mme de Miran, "votre fils n'est point un étourdi" (p. 174). The version Climal has communicated to Saint-Vincent of his affair with Marianne, and which she hears from the latter (p. 138), fits perfectly in this pattern.

[111] Rotrou exploited such a situation in *La Sœur* with the grandiloquent rhetoric of the son who, in the belief he has unknowingly married his own sister, exclaims to his mother:

> Quoi! je puis être, ô tache à votre sang infâme!
> Et mari de ma sœur et frère de ma femme,
> Père de mes neveux, oncle de mes enfants?
> Et votre gendre enfin est sorti de vos flancs? [IV.4]

mais c'est un plaisir fait comme un danger, sa pudeur même en est effrayée" (p. 66); she does not quite know "où cela mène," and anticipates it as a sort of rape. Much attention is given to the awakening of these sensations, but in ways that are not rigidly conventional. The "je vous aime" is dramatized, to be sure (p. 67), but its grandiloquence is muted, and only rarely does one find such expressions as the "esclavage futur" (p. 66) which seems to await her.

Instead, Marianne tends to use a language which, while assuming the authenticity of love as a non-preconditioned response, evokes it without its usual gallant accoutrements: "Tout ce que je sais, c'est que ses regards m'embarrassaient, que j'hésitais de les lui rendre, et que je les lui rendais toujours; que je ne voulais pas qu'il me vît y répondre, et que je n'étais pas fâchée qu'il l'eût vu" (p. 64). The "tout ce que je sais" implies a freshness which makes the "muet entretien de nos cœurs" (p. 67), like coquetry, into something instinctual. Valville, on the other hand, seems determined by cookbook formulas: "pourriez-vous hésiter d'ouvrir votre cœur à qui vous a donné tout le sien, à qui vous jure qu'il sera toujours à vous, à qui vous aime plus que sa vie, à qui vous aime autant que vous méritez d'être aimée?" (p. 81). He dons the traditional attributes by which one signals "I am in love": "triste et méchante humeur," "mélancolie"; he is "sombre," "distrait," "rêveur" (pp. 177-78). Varthon, even in disparaging Valville's capacity for love, likewise uses a stock rhetoric; she will not even "flee" him (p. 379), for that would be too dignified a coded gesture. Marianne's irony, with those of the plot — notably Valville's "infidelity" — saps the substance of such signs, placing necessarily in doubt the possibility of the exclusive and eternal attachment which they constantly promise. Tervire's teaching in this regard, although gentle, is cynical and subversive: the love object is expendable, replaceable, and Marianne should look for better. Such talk is a violent affront to romantic conceptions of love, which Marianne nowhere espouses unambiguously. Although she never radically denies the sentiments it inspires, there is throughout a subtle undermining of its premises in the wry asides about its goals — "tous les jours, en fait d'amour, on fait très délicatement des choses fort grossières" (p. 41) — and its delusions — "les chimères de l'amour" (p. 81). The referent hardly emerges unscathed, although this destruction is so delicate as to be almost unnoticeable. The code both functions for the narrative and undergoes the relentless erosion of irony.

Much the same is true of a sacred code concerning God. Charity and piety are at once negatively marked through Climal. While mouthing his pious platitudes "Dieu est le maître" and "Que les desseins de Dieu sont impénétrables!" he not only hides his vice in sanctimonious language and makes it pass as a function of his virtues (p. 119), but sacrilegiously ascribes it to God's inspiration for Marianne's benefit.[112] Saint-Vincent beatifically causes plenty of problems with his naive benevolence. Religious irony is not heavy in *La Vie de Marianne,* but it is persistent, as in the humorous portrait of the abbess's *embonpoint:* "on sent qu'il faut, pour l'avoir acquis, s'en être saintement fait une tâche" (p. 148), or, more somberly, the words of the second abbess who exemplifies the Church's collusion with social prejudice. "Dieu n'est-il pas le maître?" (p. 293) is the byword of those proposing to do some violence to Marianne,[113] who claims to understand very little of how God really works. He is activated rhetorically, in ways that leave his status unclear. "Eh bien! vous ne m'épouserez pas; mais c'est Dieu qui ne l'a pas permis" (p. 198) — not to mention the "Dieu me vengera" thrown at Varthon, figment of a romantic imagination.

Marianne's theology does not have anything very Christian about it, in any event. She asserts that "dans la vie d'une femme comme moi, il faut bien parler du destin" (p. 17); that her protectress "me remit avec confiance entre les mains de celui qui dispose de tout" (p. 19); but she does not as she goes about her story give Providence much credit, or display any consciousness of divine agency.[114] God

---

[112] "Ne semble-t-il pas que c'est la Providence qui permet que je vous aime, et qui vous tire d'embarras à mes dépens?" (p. 114); "[ma] tendresse ... est un présent que le hasard vous fait; ... dont le ciel, qui se sert de tout, va se servir aujourd'hui pour changer votre sort!" (pp. 119-20).

[113] Mme de Saint-Hermières too uses the expression, ironically, to suggest to Tervire the hope that her baron will not long survive their marriage (p. 469).

[114] It is interesting to note too that, in terms of the topology of the novel, the convent where Marianne spends quite a few weeks has no existence except the way a theater wing does: there she disappears betimes from sight ("remettons-la dans son couvent" [p. 413]); it seems to have only a parlor, for relating to the outside world, and otherwise no information emits there-

helps vaguely explain her misfortunes: "Eh! mon Dieu! pourquoi m'avez-vous ôté mon père et ma mère?" (p. 132), but only in this way does she appeal to Him — as the author of fate; operations of His *will* are neither affirmed nor denied. She makes it clear that Marianne I had no great confidence in Him (or in His ministers, for that matter):

> Les saintes et pieuses consolations [que Saint-Vincent] venait de me donner me rendaient mon état encore plus effrayant qu'il ne me l'avait paru; c'est que je n'étais pas assez dévote, et qu'une âme de dix-huit ans croit tout perdu, tout désespéré, quand on lui dit en pareil cas qu'il n'y a plus que Dieu qui lui reste: c'est une idée grave et sérieuse qui effarouche sa petite confiance. A cet âge on ne se fie guère qu'à ce qu'on voit, on ne connaît guère que les choses de la terre. [p. 145]

This commentary establishes some distance from "cet âge" but nothing subsequent to this in the text ever asserts any change in vision from that which it expresses: as far as can be ascertained, Marianne II has nothing to add to it.[115] It is clearly the latter who says, "il faut que la terre soit un séjour bien étranger pour la vertu, car elle ne fait qu'y souffrir" (p. 18) — although that is not a violation of Christian views, with their emphasis on deferred compensation. And although Marianne's career is launched under the sign of virtue, which she maintains out of self-respect, nothing ever indicates that, as a specifically Christian attribute, it is endowed with any particular moral force. Virtue has a positive social value, to the degree that the curé's sister is accurate in her judicious affirmation, "les gens vertueux sont rares, mais ceux qui estiment la vertu ne le sont pas" (p. 19). The moral of the story is never clear; but on the other hand, this is not a work where, as in *Manon Lescaut,* it is both

---

from except as relates to Marianne's exterior struggle (specifically, her run-in with the proud young "princess").

[115] There is a similar observation by Tervire: "Confinée dans ma chambre, toujours noyée dans les pleurs, méconnaissable à force d'être changée, j'implorais le ciel, et j'attendais qu'il eût pitié de moi, sans oser l'espérer" (p. 480). Yet her prayer is heard, or at least she attributes the eventual turnaround to God in his mercy (p. 481). However, this is a religious talking, and we assume (from her goodness) that she has not embraced her vocation insincerely.

unclear and thematically pivotal. Everything here does not ride on the problem of God; indeed, it is rather the opposite which is true: nothing whatever depends on it.

What we have is a number of examples, then, of the text teasing if not eroding certain of its own discursive premises. This is partly a function of irony and partly an insidious action proper to the play of fiction, as though it were intrinsically self-undermining and unable to maintain straightforwardly its own argument.[116] There is a covert suggestion that no formalized discourse can avoid structural self-contradiction; that it must undo itself, call itself into question, like the sermon Marianne comments upon:

> Le service commença; il y eut un sermon qui fut fort beau; je ne dis pas bon: ce fut avec la vanité de prêcher élégamment qu'on nous prêcha la vanité des choses de ce monde, et c'est là le vice de nombre de prédicateurs; c'est bien moins pour notre instruction qu'en faveur de leur orgueil qu'ils prêchent; de sorte que c'est presque toujours le péché qui prêche la vertu dans nos chaires. [p. 204]

The institution undermines the integrity of the discourse. And there is a corresponding uncertainty of the autonomy and "truth" of plot. Marianne's great loss of Valville is a defeat which soon gives way to the relative triumph of her moral superiority in direct confrontation with him. Similarly, Tervire's story appears to be suspended — rather satisfactorily, from the standpoint of dramatic tension, for an uncompleted work — after a resounding forensic victory: the humiliation of her rich sister-in-law. But the text harbors indications that it was a losing cause, thus sabotaging its own crescendo.[117] "Le beau dénoûment!" — to use Marianne's own

---

[116] Henri Coulet notes, with regard to Marianne's awkward remark that at the La Fare's she encounters "Mme Dutour, de qui j'ai dit étourdiment, ou par pure distraction, que je ne parlerais plus, et qui, en effet, ne paraîtra plus sur la scène" (p. 263), that the supposed error was not in fact committed at all: "Quand Marianne s'excuse d'une distraction qu'elle n'a pas commise — car si elle a fait en pleurant ses adieux à Mme Dutour, p. 159, elle n'a pas dit qu'elle ne parlerait plus d'elle — où est la vraie distraction, et à qui l'imputer?" (p. 411, n. 202). Perhaps the only appropriate answer is: to the text.

[117] Tervire says (p. 572) that her mother for eight years received nothing of the pension that had been due her for the nearly two years since her son's

ironic phrase (p. 86). Yet the title announces an eventual triumph, the crowning of the principal goal, in titling Marianne "la comtesse de ***"—a triumph to which we have no access. The discovery of her beginnings, which was to come at the end of the story, recedes from grasp, making the ever-anticipated confirmation impossible.

Or rather, in the end there is only the story, and one which ironically disguises its consummation.

---

marriage, and which was the object of her visit to her sister-in-law: therefore she failed for some six years more to collect: and for all we know, at the end of that time she may have died.

LA RELIGIEUSE

The first thing to be said about *La Religieuse* is perhaps that its preface (pp. 209-46), describing the hoax perpetrated on the Marquis de Croismare which gave rise to the novel, should be read as a preface. That is not self-evident, particularly because many editions either suppress it entirely or relegate it to the note section, and the title "Préface-annexe" which it was given not by its author(s) but by the editor Assézat in 1875 has caused it always to figure after the novel proper. The editors of a recent critical edition, however, have finally asserted the conclusion, with which I concur, that its label of *préface* should be taken to mean just that.[1] Its appurtenance to the novel does not depend, actually, upon its authenticity as a work of Diderot, but rather on the act of will by which he chose to incorporate it into his own text: presumably written essentially by Grimm, who circulated it in his *Correspondance littéraire* ten years before he did the text of the novel, it does contain letters attributed to Diderot, who also revised it more than once in function of its relationship to the novel it concerns. The interplay

---

Denis Diderot (1713-1784), *La Religieuse*. Edition: Garnier-Flammarion, 1968. Although page numbers will refer to this edition, quotations will frequently be modified on the basis of the critical text established by Jean Parrish and others in Vol. XI of the *Œuvres complètes* (Paris: Hermann, 1975). The publication history of this novel is particularly complicated: it is thought to have been written, in the main, about 1760, and was first circulated in Grimm's manuscript *Correspondance littéraire* in 1780; but it was revised thereafter, and published only in 1796 after the suppression of official censorship. The text used here represents not the original but the final state of revision, completed probably in 1783.

[1] See above the note on editions. Jean Varloot points out ("Avant-propos," p. xii) that Diderot's vocabulary also included the term "postface," which he could have used.

between the two texts is far too complex for us to delve into here, especially because of numerous inconsistencies between them. But the first line of the novel — "La réponse de M. le marquis de C***, s'il m'en fait une, me fournira les premières lignes de ce récit" — seems properly introduced only when the *Préface* has been read first. It raises, though, explicit questions regarding the anecdotal origins of the entire production which must not interfere with an appreciation of *La Religieuse* and even of the *Préface* itself as fiction (even the supposedly authentic letters of Croismare were in fact retouched by Diderot). I will in what follows therefore assume its reading, but pass for the moment directly to the main body of the novel.

Even then, however, the beginning can appear somewhat perplexing. The first paragraph refers to the Marquis de Croismare in the third person, and the rest of the text, except for the very last paragraph, in the second. This fact provides the most obvious clue as to how those two passages should be read: as notes by Suzanne Simonin to herself regarding the manner in which the uncompleted manuscript (not uncompleted in historical fact, but within the fiction: the *Préface* makes it clear that she dies before she can finish) is to be finally assembled. That is, they appear to have been added at least in part after a preliminary rereading by Suzanne of her own letter-memoirs, at a point before Croismare's first reply to her; she assumes he will in writing to her have requested supplementary information: "vous avez voulu savoir si je méritais un peu la compassion que j'attends de vous" (p. 109). Thus the allusion to "l'abrégé qui les [= mémoires] termine" at the beginning is in no way absurd, although it points to another stage of incompletion: the *abrégé* remains fragmentary not because her intervening death cut short her redaction, but because she intends to let this sketchy conclusion stand temporarily, for possible completion at some unspecified future time, especially if Croismare so requests.

This paragraph serves too an important rhetorical function. The entire work is in the form of a plea for pity and help (unlike Des Grieux's story, for example, which is a plea only for pity and absolution): that is, something designed for, and to be judged by, its effect. But the function of a remark like "je peins une partie de mes malheurs, sans talent et sans art, avec la naïveté d'un enfant de mon âge et la franchise de mon caractère" is of an entirely different order: it seeks to condition the reading of the subsequent plea in a way that addresses it not to an impartial mind but to an already favorably biased one; ostensibly, she refers to her own naïveté and frankness only because she is sincere. It is thus all but impossible for the fictive or the actual reader, unless armed with cynicism, to approach the text as anything but a reliable version of the events represented, as least insofar as Suzanne herself can perceive them correctly.[2]

There is, then, a reader or *narrataire* inscribed in the text itself: the potential savior who is being invoked and beseeched throughout. He is the virtual, but absent, arbitor of its final value, in that, in the fiction's imaginary extension, he will determine by his willingness or refusal to succor her whether she is to be believed. But he is also her judge in a purely rhetorical sense, which does function directly in the text; he is called upon by Suzanne to judge on a continuing, and not just final, basis: "je pris un parti dont vous jugerez, Monsieur, comme il vous plaira" (p. 48); "qu'en pensez-vous?" (p. 63); "des actions que vous appellerez ou imprudence, ou fermeté, selon le coup d'œil sous lequel vous les considérerez" (p. 73). In such passages the narrator herself affects a certain impartiality concerning the practical interpretation to be drawn from her story; but under such modesty lies a subtle connotation that only a person firm in her own righteousness would appeal so confidently to impartial judgement (like Rousseau in his *Confessions*), as is more directly suggested by another version: "J'en appelle à votre jugement, j'en appelle au jugement de Dieu" (p. 69).[3] She even impersonates the reader, forcing him by fictional proxy into a dialogue with her[4] resembling passages in *Jacques le fataliste*. Be-

---

[2] This is not meant to deny that a doubt about her ingenuousness in so speaking can be raised: it will be dealt with later.

[3] She confuses this issue of who is judging later in referring to "la plupart de ceux qui liront ces mémoires" (p. 116) — one of the contradictions in the text which will be discussed further on. When she writes, "Brûlez donc ces lettres" (p. 85), the very existence of the book stands as an implicit violation of that injunction, just as Suzanne's promise to Sainte-Christine, "Personne n'en saura jamais rien" (p. 84) is a kind of reverse performative language, the oath being violated by its very inscription in the text. But as I have said earlier, all confessional writing implies to some degree a breach of discretion.

[4] "—Eh bien! que fîtes vous? —Vous ne devinez pas?... ... Cela est fort mal, direz-vous... [etc.]" (p. 197).

sides being an implied participant in this sense, Croismare is a character who figures tangentially in the story itself — "Vous fûtes de ce nombre" (p. 106)[5] — so the narrative serves not only to recount but also to recall, and to reappropriate Croismare into Suzanne's biography.

The fact that she is sacrificed via a religious commitment to the better fortune of her siblings gives her something in common with Des Grieux, but there the resemblance ends. The freedoms afforded a girl are much more limited, and the nunnery is the standard solution. And being bourgeoise (her father is a lawyer and her two brothers-in-law a notary and a silk merchant), Suzanne is nowhere treated with the deference accorded a Des Grieux. She is, besides, a sort of big-city provincial (pp. 63-64), more protected and less able to fend for herself than he. Indeed the convent appears initially as a kind of liberation from the hothouse atmosphere of the family, but only so long as it is envisaged as a waystation to some new life. At the first suggestion she remain there permanently, her joy turns to bitterness and incipient revolt: "Je me récriai sur cette étrange proposition." Suzanne has misread the signs: the constitution of her sisters' dowries, which she has taken as the promise of her own to follow, are precisely the opposite in reality: the proof that she will have none at all. (This gives an ironic value to the two "dowries" she obtains during the story, ones which are useless in the outside world and are obtained, indeed, only on condition she renounce forever her claim to a real one.) Simultaneously introduced is the theme of religion's collusion with the social power-structure: "La supérieure était prévenue.... Ô Monsieur, combien ces supérieures de couvent sont artificieuses!" (pp. 41-42); artifice combines with Suzanne's "sans art" to manipulate her, ultimately, into a partially consenting victim. Indeed the complicity of religious with social values goes deeper than she then can know: even the inner voice, even the voice of God are in the service of the status quo.[6]

---

[5] He has subsequently withdrawn his participation: "J'excusais ... tous ces gens du monde qui avaient montré tant de vivacité dans le cours de mon procès et pour qui je n'existais plus, et vous-même, Monsieur le marquis" (p. 135).

[6] "On n'invoque presque jamais la voix du Ciel que quand on ne sait à quoi se résoudre, et il est rare qu'alors elle ne nous conseille pas d'obéir" (p. 60); cf. Sainte-Christine's remarks on p. 97.

Yet she is not entirely artless: the "project" she realizes to terminate her first noviciate in scandal requires dissimulation on her part.

The purpose, of course, is to remove Suzanne from the economy — literally to take her out of circulation [7]; it is a sort of infanticide whereby things are made more opulent for fewer: "C'est la sentine où l'on jette le rebut de la société" (p. 122). Her sisters, in contrast therefore to her forced renunciation, are quintessential consumers: "elles prennent, elles emportent.... Elles soupirent après le peu que je laisse" (p. 72), confesses their dying mother, whose savings they try to steal even before her eyes are closed. In Dom Morel's words, the convent is a sepulcre where the young are buried alive (p. 195). The main interest of Suzanne is not her virtue or her docility but her anguished insistence on life in the face of the civil death to which she is being pushed: "je suis une malheureuse qu'on déteste et qu'on veut enterrer ici toute vive" (p. 42). Suicide is even, at least at times, a more attractive alternative to her, but she cannot avail herself of it — a fact she indeed cannot explain, but which is bound up in the total affirmation of the life principle for which she stands.

Nothing is more instructive of the social (and mental) forces at work than the corrosive logic by which Suzanne is designated for and coerced into the convent. It condemns the individual to effective responsibility for not only the civil but the spiritual consequences of her own birth. To be "illegitimate" as Suzanne is does not mean merely that one was conceived in particular (adulterous) circumstances, it determines an essence: one *is* illegitimate — that is, one's existence is fundamentally unsanctioned.[8] Bastards can never perfectly be "legitimized," they are a kind of unwanted baggage, the incarnated punishment for the sin that begot them: "Ma fille, car vous l'êtes malgré moi ..." (p. 59), says Mme Simonin. Suzanne is really — originally, in the theological sense — an orphan ("Je

---

[7] An implicit figure for this indeed involves money: "on permet à un enfant de disposer de sa liberté à un âge où il ne lui est pas permis de disposer d'un écu" (p. 104).

[8] Compare the case of the Virgin Mary in Church doctrine: in order to be essentially sinless, it does not suffice that she not sin; she must be immaculately *conceived* to avoid *original* sin. The essence is again implied in the conception, but the logic of course works in reverse for Suzanne.

n'avais point de père; le scrupule m'avait ôté ma mère" [p. 56])
who, to use Sartre's metaphor (concerned precisely with a modern,
existential sense of legitimacy), has no ticket on the train. She
moreover accepts that fatality insofar as the difference of treatment
between herself and her sisters goes: "Je ne suis plus surprise des
distinctions qu'on a mises entre mes sœurs et moi; j'en reconnais
la justice, j'y souscris, mais je suis toujours votre enfant" (p. 57).
Alas, yes: for that remnant of a claim is in fact mostly negative
in its consequences.[9] Mme Simonin's suggestion that she wishes
her daughter were dead is less dreadful than the burden she tries to
place on her living. For, in the tradition of the Old Testament,
the crime is visited upon the (illegitimate) progeniture: the declaration, "vos sœurs ont obtenu des lois un nom que vous tenez du
crime" (p. 59), makes of Suzanne a sort of thief who has *stolen* her
name; at the same time, she is deprived of her rightful one, that
is, knowledge of her real father. Symbolically (and civilly), she must
die so that her mother may live; or if she refuses this atonement,
her mother will die (of anguish), yet Suzanne will still be deprived
of life. She is trapped in an absurd circle: either, says her mother,
you disinherit yourself, or I shall have to tell your "father" — so
that *he* can disinherit you.

In addition to her mother's sin, Suzanne incarnates the memory
of her father's vice: "vous me rappelez une trahison, une ingratitude" (p. 58). Indeed, it is impossible to tell whether the roots
of Mme Simonin's reactions lie in remorse or in emotional sufferings; Suzanne might have been the *cher gage* of a love which
aborted. Thus the child is responsible for both her mother and her
father, for all the circumstances surrounding her conception and
birth. "Priez pour moi," says her mother's final letter; "votre naissance est la seule faute importante que j'aie commise; aidez-moi à
l'expier, et que Dieu me pardonne de vous avoir mise au monde"
(p. 71). In other words: you, the fruit of sin, must adopt it and
make it yours; as I gave you birth, you must sponsor my salvation.[10]

---

[9] The nosebleed scene (p. 52) symbolizes Mme Simonin's disgust with
Suzanne's blood, which has spontaneously burst upon her.

[10] Applying Mme de Moni's formula, it is Mme Simonin who really should
enter a convent: "la bonne religieuse est celle qui apporte dans le cloître
quelque grande faute à expier" (p. 100): once again, in this perspective,
Suzanne is the substitute who must expiate not her own, but another's, great

"Songez, mon enfant, que le sort de votre mère dans l'autre monde dépend beaucoup de la conduite que vous tiendrez dans celui-ci; Dieu, qui voit tout m'appliquera dans sa justice tout le bien et tout le mal que vous ferez" (p. 71).

In pragmatic terms, however, the threat Suzanne represents is really social: by her refusal she can only be, says her director, "une source de divisions domestiques" (p. 56), an injunction her mother twice repeats: "vous ne porterez point le trouble dans la maison" (p. 56); "surtout ne troublez point la famille" (p. 71). The implication of all this insistence is that a disruption of domestic tranquillity, whatever violence it has cost, is itself sinful. And the lesson incorporated into her later lawsuit makes clear why this is so; what is at stake in her revolt is in fact the social order — that is to say, the power structure and its vested institutions: "On sent secrètement que si l'on souffrait que les portes de ces prisons s'abattissent en faveur d'une malheureuse, la foule s'y porterait et chercherait à les forcer" (p. 119); it is significant that the lines following these concern the role of government in relation to the monastery.

Despite psychological coercion from the outside, Suzanne's life in both Sainte-Marie and Longchamp up to the time of Mme de Moni's death is placed rather under the sign of seduction — to which Suzanne, her hesitations notwithstanding, is vulnerable. In the name, ironically, of protection from "l'esprit séducteur" (p. 94), the young girl is showered with "tant de caresses, tant de protestations d'amitié, tant de faussetés douces" (p. 42) that she accepts a first noviciate. The flattery which attends the taking of the veil exploits a vestimentary nicety to insinuate a subtle transfer from the physical to the spiritual: "Mais voyez donc, ma sœur; comme elle est belle! Comme ce voile relève la blancheur de son teint! Comme ce bandeau lui sied, comme il lui arrondit le visage, comme il étend ses joues! Comme cet habit fait valoir sa taille et ses bras!" (p. 43).[11] By a kind of enthymeme, the sisters create the

---

sin. She turns the tables in declaring that her aversion for such a vocation is itself original: "je l'apportai en naissant" (p. 87).

[11] Although there is no obvious allusion to lesbianism, this passage foreshadows the eroticism of the Sainte-Eutrope episode, particularly in its progressive evocation of parts of the body (*teint, visage, joues, taille, bras*) which suggests the *blason*: see below, pp. 101-2. Suzanne, who later denies any

impression that physical appropriateness implies suitability for the state which the veil, by metonymy, signifies; and "sœur Suzanne est une très belle religieuse" adds perhaps to that the poetic inducements of the implied alliteration *belle/bonne*. Following this, the seductions of the noviciate are confided to a specialist:

> Une mère des novices est la sœur la plus indulgente qu'on a pu trouver. Son étude est de vous dérober toutes les épines de l'état; c'est un cours de séduction la plus subtile et la mieux apprêtée.... Je ne pense pas qu'il y ait aucune âme jeune et sans expérience à l'épreuve de cet art funeste. [p. 44]

At Longchamp, nonetheless, the tone is different, given the less contrived seductions of Mme de Moni's mysticism: "peu à peu on était entraîné, on s'unissait à elle, l'âme tressaillait et l'on partageait ses transports. Son dessein n'était pas de séduire, mais certainement c'est ce qu'elle faisait. On sortait de chez elle avec un cœur ardent, la joie et l'extase étaient peintes sur le visage, on versait des larmes si douces!" (p. 65). As is frequent in mystical discourse, the terminology closely approaches that of eroticism, which is all the more significant in the light of that which surfaces later in the novel at Sainte-Eutrope. In both instances, Suzanne, although fearful, is also susceptible: "Mon âme s'allume facilement, s'exalte, se touche.... Il est sûr que j'éprouvais une facilité extrême à partager son extase" (p. 89). The parallel manner in which the two mothers superior concerned (Mme de Moni and Mme ***) attach themselves passionately to her suggests too that she is both seduced and seducer. The suspicions of the vicar Hébert about her relations with Manouri (p. 137) and her voluntary or involuntary provocation of Don Morel at the end tend toward the same conclusion, and even Suzanne begins to suspect finally that she has been throughout her memoir in the process of seducing Croismare (p. 208).

The relationship between Suzanne and Mme de Moni still calls for further observation because of its complexity, underscored above

---

fascination with her own body (p. 165), is at least this once tempted to rehearse her attributes: "il faut que j'en convienne, quand je fus seule dans ma cellule je me ressouvins de leurs flatteries, je ne pus m'empêcher de les vérifier à mon petit miroir, et il me sembla qu'elles n'étaient pas tout à fait déplacées" (p. 43).

all in the curious way Suzanne shorts her spiritual circuit: "il me semble quand vous venez que Dieu se retire et que son esprit se taise" (p. 65). Whether this is interpreted in a purely spiritual manner or as an aspect of erotic interplay — and Suzanne herself is uncertain what terms can be used to account for it — something interrupts what had seemed to be a perfect harmony of inclinations. For there is also a sense in which Mme de Moni taps into Suzanne for replenishment,[12] which Suzanne later recalls in these terms: "Je conservais très longtemps l'impression que j'avais prise, et il fallait apparemment que je lui en restituasse quelque chose, car si l'on discernait dans les autres qu'elles avaient conversé avec elle, on discernait en elle qu'elle avait conversé avec moi" (p. 89). Despite suggestions that she is clairvoyant,[13] it cannot be determined whether Mme de Moni is attuned to something transcendent or ultimately similar in motivation to the mother superior of Sainte-Eutrope.[14] The cult which Suzanne devotes to the portrait of Mme de Moni, which she treats as a relic or amulet (p. 90), suggests a secret tie between them. Yet it is Suzanne who essentially kills her by cutting her life-line, just as it is Suzanne who drives the later superior mad by her very presence. Even indirectly, Suzanne for her part cannot tune in on the voice of God. Mme de Moni hopes for even a dream that could be interpreted as some sort of sign, but there is nothing (p. 67). Heaven is never a positive force for Suzanne; the best it can do is advise obedience, and console.

Only man has called Suzanne into the convent, and only man is offended by her recalcitrance. Although isolated as family, friends and even "sisters" withdraw human contact, her recourse takes the forms inspired by her background: like her father, Suzanne becomes

---

[12] "Tâchez de ne pas m'émouvoir; laissez les sentiments s'accumuler dans mon âme; quand elle en sera pleine, je vous quitterai" (p. 68).

[13] "Elle avait les yeux petits, mais ils semblaient ou regarder en elle-même, ou traverser les objets voisins et démêler au-delà, à une grande distance, toujours dans le passé ou dans l'avenir" (p. 68).

[14] One passage describes her in an erratic succession of disparate states characteristic of Mme *** of Sainte-Eutrope: "elle avait les yeux fermés avec effort, quelquefois elle les ouvrait, les portait en haut et les ramenait sur moi; elle s'agitait, son âme se remplissait de tumulte, se composait et se ragitait ensuite" (p. 68). Cf. Janet Todd's remarks about the "erotic feelings" between them in *Women's Friendship in Literature* (New York: Columbia University Press, 1980), pp. 114-15. See also on this subject the article by Walter E. Rex mentioned in n. 17 below.

a lawyer, not only in the training she imposes upon herself, but also by adopting an advocacy function on behalf of others, and at times turning the outside hierarchy into a court of appeals.[15] Although she admits to enormous tactical errors,[16] she carries out this "project" as willfully as she had the one at Sainte-Marie, and, as long as she can maintain it on her own terrain, is only too invincible; the provocation, in an institution where submission is the first principle, is consummate.

This bears mentioning primarily because the question of *vraisemblance* in the plot of *La Religieuse* has often been wrongly put. It is not really a matter of whether so many awful things could realistically have piled up against one person in a few short years, for she, after all, behaves in such a way as to attract the sort of reprisals she does.[17] The reader's attention is of course focused on her righteousness and innocence, and therefore the injustice of her systematic victimization. But in a convent one takes a vow of obedience without legalistic quibbles. It is an important aspect of her character that she does provoke her superiors, adopting behavior which cannot fail to irritate them, as a function of her personal revolt; she is, as she admits, a *mauvaise religieuse* (p. 87) in the strong sense of the term. Besides, she is herself hard for them to

---

[15] "Je lus les Constitutions, je les relus, je les savais par cœur. Si l'on m'ordonnait quelque chose ou qui n'y fût pas exprimé clairement, ou qui n'y fût pas, ou qui m'y parût contraire, je m'y refusais fermement; je prenais le livre et je disais: Voilà les engagements que j'ai pris et je n'en ai point pris d'autres.... Les grands vicaires de M. l'archevêque étaient sans cesse appelés; je comparaissais, je me défendais, je défendais mes compagnes, et il n'est pas arrivé une seule fois qu'on m'ait condamnée, tant j'avais d'attention à mettre la raison de mon côté" (p. 74).

[16] She speaks for instance of her "trois étourderies" (p. 78), and later of "des choses indiscrètes et ridicules que j'avais faites et dites" (p. 97).

[17] Vivienne Mylne is one of the rare critics to have taken note of this: "Suzanne herself is on more than one occasion the agent who brings out to their fullest extent the potential evils of conventual life" (*The Eighteenth-Century French Novel*, Manchester University Press, 1965, p. 204). This interpretation is pursued forcefully in a most insightful article by Walter E. Rex, who describes Suzanne's conduct as intentional: "faced with a new Mother Superior and unwilling to accept the change, Suzanne decides on a plan of behavior that will deliberately turn the new Superior, and everyone in her obedience, against her irrevocably" ("Secrets from Suzanne: The Tangled Motives of *La Religieuse*," in *The Eighteenth Century: Theory and Interpretation*, 24 [1983], 185-98, p. 192).

size up because of her unpredictability; she does not remain uniform in action as she does in the tone of her memoirs, but is instead sometimes docile and sometimes refractory. The accumulation of horrors is further accounted for by the fact that at every juncture after Sainte-Marie her reputation precedes her, predisposing others, whatever their degree of sympathy, to expect strange if not hostile behavior. It would thus be erroneous to insist only on Suzanne's sweet innocence: she is not *merely* a victim of inexorable persecution.

Nor does she escape the convent's influence. Just as she recognizes at the end that it has in spite of her moulded her habits to the degree that she catches herself making the sign of the cross whenever she hears a bell, so too has her language been affected by the Biblical lexicon which characterizes conventual language. For instance, she says that after her vows, "je restai au milieu du troupeau auquel on venait de m'associer" (p. 43), using unselfconsciously a "shepherd" metaphor like those of psalms and parables. From the standpoint of the real author, it may appear tinged with irony, but there is no reason to lend such irony to Suzanne.[18] And although Suzanne is much too modest ever to compare herself explicitly to Christ (when she is accused of doing so, it is unjust [pp. 83-84]), she comes very close to detailing the parallel between his wounds and hers: "Je lui dis en lui montrant ma tête meurtrie en plusieurs endroits, mes pieds ensanglantés, mes bras livides et sans chair, mon vêtement sale et déchiré: Vous voyez!" (p. 116).[19] Even ordinary metaphors, especially those of darkness and light, tend to take on Biblical (and sometimes ironic) overtones here.[20] They are complementary to the clair-obscur visual cast of the convent, its silence and its secrets, its many

---

[18] This is not to say that she is not at times capable of an ironic effect, witness the caricatural tone of a diminutive "troupeau" metaphor: "on [sortit de l'office] avec la vitesse et le babil d'une troupe d'oiseaux qui s'échapperaient d'une volière" (p. 148). The resonance of such a remark is hardly Biblical.

[19] Her "Vous voyez!" is also to be compared with St. John's "Ecce homo." Other parallels are the transfiguration of Suzanne described on p. 89, and the fact that she is resurrected from her dungeon on the third day (p. 83).

[20] E.g., "le concours de nos ténèbres fut nombreux" (p. 86); note too the obvious situational irony of the aria which comes immediately to Suzanne's mind upon entering Longchamp: "Tristes apprêts, pâles flambeaux, jour plus affreux que les ténèbres" (p. 63).

dramas,[21] where the positive Biblical sense of light hardly holds full sway: "il y a des lumières funestes," says Dom Morel (p. 194).[22] The convent is dark and constricted, and these qualities simultaneously stand for its psychological (or spiritual) character: it suppresses both *lumière* and *lumières*.

One can observe the same subtle confusion of the literal and figural with respect to numerous other metaphors. The sacrifice, a Biblical/pathetic image — "je soupirais après l'instant de me sacrifier" (p. 44) — seems only half figurative, like the numerous prison metaphors which not only reinforce the (literal) claustrophobia of the cloister, but reiterate aspects of Suzanne's own experience there: "un patient qui sort du cachot" (p. 124) is, *in situ,* a metaphor, but closely follows the occasion where she has herself emerged from a dungeon. After being symbolically pronounced dead by the sisters of Longchamp (p. 99), in a way which the repetition of the expression *en paix* explicitly links to her earlier form of burial in the dungeon (*in pace*), Suzanne eventually receives authentic last rites and re-dies (p. 130) — only once again doesn't really. "Je vis clairement qu'on était résolu à disposer de moi sans moi" (p. 48) is a rhetorically effective figure which soon is realized to the letter: "On disposa de moi pendant toute cette matinée qui a été nulle dans ma vie" (p. 69). She also compares this nothingness, this void, to a long alienation or illness (p. 70), commencing thus by semi-metaphor two of the "literal" themes of the novel. Although she takes care not to let any written evidence be discovered, she still cannot prevent her own words from turning against her, because metaphoric speech crystallizes into concrete act in ways ironically unrelated to its original intention; her desire to be free of the symbolic function of her vestments, which she expresses by exclaiming, "Ôtez-les-moi, j'en suis indigne"

---

[21] See "L'art du romancier," ch. 9 in Georges May, *Diderot et "La Religieuse,"* New Haven and Paris: Yale Univ. Press and Presses Universitaires de France, 1954.

[22] The thematic value of such a statement must not be overlooked either, since it poses the Adamic problem of the knowledge of evil: in principle God forbids access to such knowledge, yet like the Tree of Knowledge it is accessible, and the individual must will its denial; yet Suzanne who has not sought it must still contend with it. It also poses the question of knowledge as positive enlightenment: cf. the pertinent remarks on this subject in William F. Edmiston, "Sacrifice and Innocence in *La Religieuse,*" in *Diderot Studies* 19 (Geneva: Droz, 1978), 67-84.

(p. 97), seems to translate soon thereafter into her being stripped of them for other reasons. Guilt by inference is illustrated by the way something as simple as an alliteration seems to implicate her: "— Et de quoi puis-je être *coupable*? — De tout. Il n'y a rien dont vous ne soyez *capable*" (p. 81). This uncontrollable slippage of signifiers typifies a generalized abrogation of normal criteria for identifying reality and living truth.[23]

The cloister is the antithesis of *le monde,* the world, the exterior standard for truth; it is non-world, "*im*monde," and its weapon against the invader, like molten lead poured down from the parapets, is *immondices*: "Si je passais sous des fenêtres, j'étais obligée de fuir, ou de m'exposer à recevoir les immondices des cellules" (p. 101). Harboring the refuse of civil life, the convent responds with refuse[24] to any breach of its autonomy. It not only flays the (civil) body but tries to trap it in its own excremental function:

> Je vivais donc entre quatre murailles nues, ... sans aucun des vaisseaux les plus nécessaires, forcée de sortir la nuit pour satisfaire aux besoins de la nature. [p. 102]

> Je trouvais la porte des commodités fermée, et j'étais obligée de descendre plusieurs étages et de courir au fond du jardin, quand la porte en était ouverte. Quand elle ne l'était pas... Ah! Monsieur, les méchantes créatures que des femmes recluses ...! [107]

> C'est qu'on m'a privée d'eau, de pot à l'eau et de tous les vaisseaux nécessaires aux besoins de la nature [p. 114]

The nature of which Suzanne speaks here is not in revolt but merely insisting on its *needs*. Such vengeance on the body corresponds more generally to a defiance of nature in the form of its conventual denial:

> Toutes ces cérémonies lugubres qu'on observe à la prise d'habit et à la profession quand on consacre un homme ou

---

[23] "Il ne se passe pas une histoire fâcheuse dans le monde qu'on ne vous en parle; on arrange les vraies; on en fait de fausses.... Elles mentent toute leur vie" (pp. 44-45).

[24] "On me jetait les mets les plus grossiers, encore les gâtait-on avec de la cendre et toutes sortes d'ordures" (p. 101).

> une femme à la vie monastique et au malheur, suspendent-elles les fonctions animales? ... [Dans les couvents] *la nature, révoltée* d'une contrainte pour laquelle elle n'est point faite, brise les obstacles qu'on lui oppose, devient *furieuse,* jette *l'économie animale* dans un *désordre* auquel il n'y a plus de remède. [p. 120]

On this level, nature *is* in revolt, at once literal and symbolic: the social body of the convent must consume and recycle its own poisons, having refused the means for their normal psychological/metabolic discharge; and the track this evil takes is *furie* — in other words, folly in one of its avatars, all of which share common properties: possession, madness, perversion, damnation.

Unlike nature, which is the work of God and must be respected, madness can be blamed on the devil. Here we rejoin an ancient tradition, and in particular a Biblical one: demon possession in the Bible is undistinguishable from either insanity or epilepsy. The incursion of the world into Suzanne's thought and projects is equivalent to an invasion of Satan, and Sainte-Christine, successor to Mme de Moni as mother superior of Longchamp, reacts by declaring, "Mon enfant, vous êtes possédée du démon," protecting herself with rosary and cross (p. 95). In consequence, Suzanne is identified with Satan in what appears by the terms of her analysis to be itself a form of mass hysteria: "[les] *têtes faibles* ... me voyaient dans leur imagination *troublée* avec une figure hideuse, faisaient le signe de la croix à ma rencontre et s'enfuyaient en criant: Satan, éloignez-vous de moi" (p. 103). The concepts in play in the convent cannot well distinguish madness from possession — both unnatural — and can offer no remedy but exorcism: "quoique je ne fisse rien qui marquât un esprit dérangé, à plus forte raison un esprit obsédé de l'esprit infernal, elles délibérèrent entre elles s'il ne fallait pas m'exorciser, et il fut conclu ... que le démon résidait en moi" (p. 104).[25] Much later, Mme *** at Sainte-Eutrope is herself likened

---

[25] Cf. "il fallait que ce prêtre [Hébert] me vît obsédée, possédée ou folle" (p. 111); "S'il était de mon intérêt de paraître devant mon juge innocente et sage, il n'importait pas moins à ma supérieure qu'on me vît méchante, obsédée du démon, coupable et folle" (p. 106). One is nonetheless hard pressed to explain why she might be thought to be *feigning* possession: "Il venait avec la curiosité de voir une fille possédée ou qui le contrefaisait" (p. 107).

to Satan in person (pp. 180-81), and it is Suzanne in turn who is told to utter the scriptural "Mon Dieu, conservez-moi, éloignez de moi ce démon" (p. 183). Ill, mad[26] or possessed, Mme *** finally cries for protection by the crucifix or holy water, again reminiscent of the rites of exorcism (p. 201).[27]

Suzanne herself shows no interest in possession as a diagnostic term, but is much concerned with the problem of madness because it typifies what happens to *others* in a monastic system. Although in principle it also represents a potential threat to herself, all madness is viewed as if from the outside. Yet this involves such a refusal to subject her own behavior to scrutiny on this score that one is practically obligated to speak of it as a matter of repression. One finds merely symptoms or attenuated suggestions of disturbance, such as her "Mon esprit se troubla" (p. 50) just before the refusal of her first vows. The state of being "stupide ... imbécile" as the second vows approach is already a form of alienation, and she herself links her robot-like behavior to little convulsive movements (pp. 67-68). Other observers refer to her "esprit aliéné" (p. 76), and we are supposed to take this as a sign of *their* abnormalcy. But the same Suzanne who as novice was so struck by the sight of the mad nun she saw running through the corridor (p. 45) never asks how some other novice could have judged any differently the scenes she herself offers later:

> Combien de fois, dans le tumulte de mes idées, me suis-je levée brusquement et resolue à finir mes peines! Qu'est-ce qui m'a retenue? Pourquoi préférais-je alors de pleurer, de crier à haute voix, de fouler mon voile aux pieds, de m'arracher les cheveux et de me déchirer le visage avec les ongles? [p. 76]

> J'invoquais le Ciel, j'étais à terre et l'on me traînait; quand j'arrivai au bas des escaliers j'avais les pieds ensanglantés et les jambes meurtries; j'étais dans un état à toucher des âmes de bronze. [p. 83]

---

[26] She speaks of "des songes fâcheux qui me tourmentent" (p. 166), and Suzanne refers uncertainly to her *mal* (p. 189).

[27] The consummate irony on this subject is that Suzanne is, after this superior's death, accused of sorcery (p. 202).

> Cependant je tâchais de rajuster mon voile, mes mains tremblaient, et plus je m'efforçais à l'arranger, plus je le dérangeais; impatientée, je le saisis avec violence, je l'arrachai, je le jetai par terre, et je restai vis-à-vis de ma supérieure le front ceint d'un bandeau et la tête échevelée. [p. 95]

In such pathetic moments, Suzanne's objective symptoms approach those she herself has recognized as signs of madness in others. She even finds herself, filled with an obsessive fear, reacting hysterically in the face of an optical illusion (the odd illumination in the church on the head and fingers of Mme ***) she takes to be Satanic: "je me mis à courir dans le chœur *comme une insensée* en criant: Loin de moi, Satan!" (p. 184).

Folie is everywhere in *La Religieuse,* its metaphors pervading the discourse of Suzanne and others as well: "la fureur des religieuses" (p. 98); "la folle créature" (p. 143); "[sœur Agathe] fit les mêmes folies" (p. 150).[28] Besides the mad nun of Sainte-Marie, there are two others of whom it is said they went mad, one of them being Sainte-Ursule (pp. 121, 129). And in special relation to Sainte-Thérèse, who apparently is on the verge of insanity, the endless characterizations coming from Mme *** are cruelly insistent: "tu es folle avec tes idées" (p. 147); "elle a la tête perdue" (p. 151); "Sainte-Thérèse est folle" (p. 170); "peu s'en est fallu qu'il [= Lemoine] n'ait rendu folle cette pauvre Sainte-Thérèse" (p. 185). The world/cloister dichotomy finally comes down to these two symbols: "Vaut-il mieux vivre dans l'abjection que dans la folie?" (p. 154). The successive steps of degeneration in Mme *** as recorded by Suzanne are melancholy, piety, and delirium (p. 189) — which says something about the function of piety in all this. A pious evocation of "la folie de la croix" (p. 109) cannot fail, in such a context, to suggest a bitter irony at some level of the text, not to mention the perfectly unsubtle rhetorical question, "Quel besoin a l'époux de tant de vierges folles?" (p. 119).

According to Dom Morel, Mme *** cannot rightly be described as suspended between madness and mortal sin, as he first had said (p. 193), because the latter — in the form of sexual aberration —

---

[28] There are also numerous related terms such as *idiote* (p. 146) and *imbécile* (p. 158).

is already a form of madness: "Elle n'était pas faite pour son état, et voilà ce qui en arrive tôt ou tard. Quand on s'oppose au penchant général de la nature, cette contrainte la détourne à des *affections déréglées* qui sont d'autant plus violentes qu'elles sont mal fondées; c'est une espéce de *folie*" (p. 195). This madness thus results from a double perversion of nature, because the asocialization of the convent is also a forced asexuation; "elle n'était pas faite pour son état" comes down very simply to the affirmation that she was a sexual being. The theme of folly thus unites, at the deepest and most persistent level of the text, those of possession, damnation, and lesbianism: not just because the mother superior of Sainte-Eutrope is both lesbian *and* mad, but because the causes are themselves interrelated and simultaneously manifested. In her hallucinations (pp. 199-200) she sees the gulf of hell and the devil come to get her; full of desire, damned, possessed and mad, she rejoins the vision of the mad nun: "on la trouva pieds nus, en chemise, échevelée, hurlant, écumant [29] et courant autour de sa cellule" (p. 200).

Mme *** is first introduced with a volley of asymmetries and alternations in a pattern typical of what Leo Spitzer in a famous study called Diderot's "nervous" style:[30] there is, as Suzanne puts it, "quelque chose qui cloche." Her physical manner and her thought are alike disjointed: her eyes are akimbo, she stutters, she squirms and digresses randomly: "elle vous parle, et elle se perd, ... elle est tantôt familière ... tantôt impérieuse ... alternativement compatissante et dure" (p. 139). This is just the first suggestion of a process of unravelling: "sa figure *décomposée* marque tout le *décousu* de son esprit" (pp. 139-40); "elle joua des choses folles,

---

[29] This detail subtly recalls her sensuality, since Suzanne noticed it too during one of her orgasmic scenes: "ses lèvres se fermèrent d'abord, elles étaient humectées comme d'une mousse légère, puis sa bouche s'entrouvrit, et elle me parut mourir en poussant un grand soupir" (p. 155).

[30] "The Style of Diderot," in *Linguistics and Literary History*, Princeton, 1967. *La Religieuse* contains many anaphoras, often in combination with other mechanisms of repetition or parallelism. The effectiveness of Spitzer's enticing analysis depends a good deal, though, upon the choice of metaphors used by the critic in his own description; it may be that his discovery of sexual pulsations in Diderot's style corresponds in objective terms to no more than a predilection for parallelism, anaphora, and broken oratorical patterns (what Spitzer calls "the rhythm of orgasm itself").

bizarres, *décousues* comme ses idées" (p. 146).[31] The disorder within is also being sown without; Suzanne has entered a topsy-turvy world where order and disorder coexist ("l'ordre et le désordre se succédaient" [p. 140]), or where, as she later implies, order depends on disorder: "tout reviendrait à l'ordre; elles auraient dû dire au désordre accoutumé" (p. 190). In this context, the most simple accepted patterns of wisdom are thrown into doubt: the Sainte-Eutrope episode begins with a hopeful allusion to the proverb "un bonheur ne vient point sans un autre" (p. 138), but this changes to "une peine ne vient jamais seule" (p. 177): the two statements are logically speaking not mutually exclusive, but there is a major difference in the perspective emphasized. Saved from one convent by another, Suzanne has no great cause to admire the ways of Providence; nor does she.

There is even a sense in which the narrative partakes of the ambiant confusion. Unlike the first half of the novel, where periods of long months and years follow in rather well-defined sequence, the second, while chronologically more dense, loses us in a hazy interplay of vague memories with individual instances which are essentially nonlinear. This is not a flaw, it is merely a figure. For instance, one of the seduction scenes with the mother superior emerges imperceptibly from a description of general behavior in the imperfect tense ("Je voyais croître de jour en jour ..." [p. 154]) into what basically appears to be a singulative dialogue and action (beginning "J'allais l'en remercier chez elle ..."), except that all verbs remain in the imperfect: until, that is, the paroxysm approaches, when a preterite verb suddenly fixes the specificity of the occasion: "enfin il vint un moment ... où elle devint pâle comme la mort" (p. 155).[32] From here on the passage is riveted in the singulative *passé simple* until the transition "Le lendemain ..." (p. 158), which itself denotes a successive chronology rather than an iterative one. Coherent sequences are often lost in this manner, at least in part by virtue of the phenomenon that even specific recollections become by nature

---

[31] This description of rapid alternations returns towards the end: cf. pp. 201-2.

[32] Genette calls this the *pseudo-itératif*, the supposed *itératif* (repetition signaled by the imperfect) slipping towards the *singulatif;* there are notable examples which he cites in Proust ("Discours du récit," in *Figures III*, Paris: Seuil, 1972, pp. 151-53).

emblematic, standing for the repetitive and diffuse: "La scène que je viens de peindre fut suivie d'un grand nombre d'autres semblables que je néglige" (p. 165).

For not just memory as a record of objective events, but the consciousness of what experience has been acquired — and its meaning — is in question, the more so as the text advances. The most obvious subject matter on which this problematics operates is precisely that of (homo)sexual behavior. Much has been made, for instance, of the impossible innocence of Suzanne-narrator who, after all she has been through, can naïvely exclaim of her incomprehension in the face of Mme ***'s advances. Even before Sainte-Eutrope she has been exposed to some degree to sexual ideas, and wavers in acknowledging how much she has understood of them. Not only, indeed, has she, Suzanne, been accused of "des actions que je n'ose nommer et des désirs bizarres" (p. 103); she, Suzanne, has been the accuser: "Je m'étais échappée en propos indiscrets sur *l'intimité suspecte* de quelques-unes des favorites; la supérieure avait des tête-à-tête longs et fréquents avec un jeune ecclésiastique, et j'en avais démêlé la raison et le prétexte" (pp. 74-75). There is an ongoing process within her as both character and narrator, involving something she does not want to learn and, failing that, wants not to know. In part, perhaps, because she has narrowly avoided its enticing dominion.

The lexicon of the Sainte-Eutrope section of the novel (from pp. 139-203) reflects the frequency of passages relating to the body. Such language was not absent — far from it — from the earlier episodes, but it was characterized by an insistent sameness reflecting, for the most part, a topology of suffering. Now, however, it proliferates not only in frequency but in variety, deploying an extensive repertory of erotic foci. Some of the more repetitive terms are: *corps, tête, cheveux, visage, front, yeux, joue, bouche, lèvre, cou, épaule, bras, main, doigt, gorge/poitrine, genou, pied.* To this one can add certain predictable, obsessive actions linked by noun/verb roots: *embrasser, caresse(r), baiser.* None of these designations is exclusively erotic in itself, although one does note the absence of equally obvious anatomical features to which an erotic value is not commonly attributed, or which one might think of as less accessible to kisses than others: the nose, for instance, or the elbows and toes. And some of the parts, which would not usually figure in a description of convent life, appear often precisely because there they are normally covered by linen (*linge de cou* is often mentioned) which invites lifting: hair, neck, shoulders, and breasts in particular. *Genou* would seem more ordinary in this referential context, but its frequency here is not explained alone by the amount of time spent on one's knees — which in any event was not great at Sainte-Eutrope. For Suzanne, the education in lesbian ways takes place via an education in exterior anatomy; we might recall here the colorful metaphor with which she described her initiation to the personnel in her new convent: "on vous tâte partout" (p. 143).

It is always someone else who initiates these scenes, Suzanne herself being passive. But while emphasizing what she is merely reporting on at close range, she nonetheless gives sufficient cause for not overlooking the extent to which she is herself a participant. In the first place, she in some ways, willfully or not, entices and incites the mother superior, illustrating in her way the Heisenberg principle that one cannot innocently observe with no implication of effect on the observed. But further, Suzanne enters into the experience; her own quasi-orgasm is expressed in the same terms as that of Mme ***: "Elle était comme morte, et moi comme si j'allais mourir" (p. 156).[33] In another instance — one of "un grand nombre d'autres semblables" (p. 165): "Je ne me sentais aucune force, mes genoux se dérobaient sous moi ... et je lui dis: Chère mère, je ne sais ce que j'ai, je me trouve mal..." (p. 161). Now if Suzanne has felt this way a "great number" of times, even though from all appearances she lacks the sensuous passion of Sister Sainte-Thérèse or Mme ***, she is hardly less lesbian than, say, Proust's Odette de Crécy. If she "naïvely" conceives this drive as arising from a malady, it is precisely in function of its *contagion* which immediately implicates her: "le résultat de mes réflexions, c'est que c'était peut-être une maladie à laquelle elle [Mme ***] était sujette; puis il m'en vint une autre, c'est que peut-être cette maladie se gagnait, que Saint-Thérèse l'avait prise, *et que je la prendrais aussi*" (p. 158). The syntax here might be seen as revers-

---

[33] *Mourir* used in this sexual sense is a term borrowed in fact from gallant language: "mourir de plaisir," etc. Like other metaphors, it tends to literalize (ironically) in *La Religieuse:* Mme *** later says to Suzanne: "vous me ferez mourir" (p. 188).

ing the actual sequence of her thought, in which a (quasi)awareness of her own involvement is what provokes the medical explanation in terms of which Suzanne can indicate, but without quite naming it, the fact of her own situation: "Je ne sais ce qui se passait en moi, mais j'étais saisie de frayeur, d'un tremblement et d'une défaillance qui me vérifiaient le soupçon que j'avais eu que son mal était contagieux" (p. 160). But such is the deflective efficacy of Suzanne's rhetoric that in two centuries of commentary almost no one seems to have noticed that "son mal était contagieux" means "j'en étais atteinte"![34] Furthermore, she passes throughout the convent for Mme ***'s acknowledged lover: "on disait que je l'avais *fixée*" (p. 165); and her impatience during the night Mme *** spends with Sainte-Thérèse (p. 170) more than slightly suggests that the latter's jealousy for Suzanne is reciprocated. If, as a final irony, Suzanne finds herself, after her escape, sheltered in a "lieu suspect" (p. 204), this is not merely *another coincidence* added to what has preceded, but a *consequence* of the somewhat tainted reputation she has acquired in the convent: her young Benedictine can only have led her there because he has made certain deductions with regard to the severity of her moral scruples.

Mme ***'s fateful "je suis damnée" caps a theme tied to all the others in this constellation, that of damnation. Nor is the idea of being damned really just the secondary meaning of the term in this context: it is rather because it denotes damnation that it also connotes lesbianism. Its ambiguity is itself what melts the themes together. Thus the way Suzanne characterizes the fundamental irony of the convent establishes this double theme early on:

> ... un désespoir de quarante, de cinquante années et peut-être un malheur éternel; car il est sûr, monsieur, que sur cent religieuses qui meurent avant cinquante ans, il y en a cent tout juste de *damnées*, sans compter celles qui deviennent folles, stupides ou furieuses en attendant. [p. 45]

---

[34] Jacques Rustin has referred to the innocence of Suzanne as the result of "refoulement d'une tendance saphique de l'héroïne" ("*La Religieuse* de Diderot: mémoires ou journal intime?" in V. del Litto et al., *Le journal intime et ses formes littéraires*, Genève: Droz, 1978). Janet Todd (op. cit., p. 125) and William F. Edmiston (op. cit., p. 79) are the only critics I know to have picked up the clue regarding contagion.

Faire son salut is the ostensible purpose of the monastery, but it is turned into *faire sa damnation:* [35] and the *damnées* of this passage is just as much an allusion to the mortal sin of lesbianism as is the concluding "je suis damnée," especially since it is compared to the *other* pitfalls of monastic life with its consequent premature/eternal death. Even expressions like "je me déteste et je me damne" (p. 94) and the vindictive "mourez désespérée, et soyez damnée" (p. 104) are not free from such overtones, just as Sainte-Thérèse's "Je suis perdue!" (p. 149) contains suggestions of "je suis damnée." [36] Damned in advance, the superior cannot be saved even by repentence, and goes down to hell like Dom Juan, virtually dragging Saint-Thérèse along with her.

Suzanne herself is not *damnée,* of course: the whole rhetorical structure of the novel prevents such an application on either level of the terms. Logically and theologically, that would be the consequence of her story, but Suzanne's entire discourse avoids such categorization of herself, just as it avoids metaphysical conclusions of any sort, [37] leaving such matters open when they are raised at all. [38] Nor is there much question of any salvation, except social: Lemoine is the only one, Suzanne herself not excepted, who expresses any concern for her Christian salvation (p. 181). She never asserts to Croismare either that she will indeed damn herself within the cloister, or save herself without: she assumes that both can be equally well performed in either place, and that what is at stake, in her own case at least, is not particularly the fate of her soul.

---

[35] Cf. Dom Morel: "nous nous exposons à être perdus dans l'autre vie.... Au sein des pénitences, nous nous damnons presque aussi sûrement que les gens du monde au milieu des plaisirs" (p. 192). Again there is certain irony in Mme ***'s remark that in the world Suzanne "aurait damné autant d'hommes qu'elle aurait vus, et elle se serait damnée avec eux" (p. 152).

[36] Compare Mme ***'s remark: "La pauvre fille! elle est perdue à jamais" (p. 200), and even Suzanne's (in quite another context): "je serai perdue" (p. 206).

[37] "Je ne voulais entendre parler jansénisme et molinisme ni en bien ni en mal. Quand on me demandait si j'étais soumise à la Constitution, je répondais que je l'étais à l'Église; si j'acceptais la Bulle ... que j'acceptais l'Évangile" (p. 74).

[38] For example, after the illness following her vows: "Mais il reste à savoir si ces actions sont de l'homme, et s'il y est, quoiqu'il paraisse y être" (p. 70) (the meaning of the sentence, moreover, is itself obscure).

On the other hand, there is no reasonable motive for Suzanne's telling all this in such detail to Croismare if she did not have a strong inner need to put (nearly) all her cards on the table and pronounce herself innocent. This is not to suggest in the slightest that Suzanne can be presumed to have felt *good* about what has gone on: only, perhaps, that her naïve passiveness is a sort of rhetorical (and psychological, if you wish) stance of a piece with the other purposes governing her memoir. Effect upon the reader is, as I remarked earlier, a critical gauge as projected by the text itself, and Suzanne pauses frequently for various apostrophes to the Marquis — testing, as it were, the immediate effect of what she has just related, and in the wider view probing the cumulative effect as well. Unlike most other memoir-novels, this one is situated in such a way, by the function of the preface, that it does not serve only to justify the past but to determine future action, on which in turn will depend in large part the whole value of the narration. A rhetoric of persuasion is part of its basic stuff and not a secondary layer of extranarrative apparatus; its effects are calculated.

This is consistent with what Suzanne has reported concerning her presence of mind on other forensic occasions, and her consciousness as a dramatic artist. In the case of self-representation, the referent has a rather different status than in third-person narrative: the signified and the referent are in promiscuous collaboration on various levels. Hers is an oft-told tale, practiced at various stages in both oral and written versions.[39] Like the actress she is, Suzanne both plays herself and another: "Je *me représentais* mon rôle au pied des autels, une jeune fille protestant à haute voix contre une action à laquelle elle paraît avoir consenti; le scandale des assistants, le désespoir des religieuses, la fureur de mes parents" (p. 49). Such projection of a future self serves as a rehearsal, preparing her for the tragedy she is not just acting in but acting out. Rhetorically, such a passage allows her to represent the basic scene twice to Croismare, doubly emphasizing its dramatic value: it is a sort of anticipatory recapitulation (in Genette's terms, a prolepsis). Its

---

[39] She identifies her recapitulations to Mme de Moni (p. 64), to Manouri (pp. 90-91), to others unnamed (p. 98), to Mme *** (p. 159), to Dom Morel (p. 191), in addition the written memoir to Manouri.

abrupt end is in the same theatrical register, as if a stage curtain fell: "À ces mots une des sœurs laissa tomber le voile de la grille" (pp. 51-52). It occurs to her to compare the Lenten music at Longchamp to a stage spectacle when it is (literally) applauded, which she finds scandalous, but she does not fail to exact her share in the ovation: "*je* fus applaudie" (pp. 86-89). Similarly theatrical, although for a more limited audience of religious, is her Easter vigil: "je fus un *spectacle* bien touchant.... La *scène* du reposoir fit bruit dans la maison." Another spectacle, that of her court hearing, can be recounted only as she imagines it (p. 122) because she cannot attend.

That the same criteria apply to her appreciation of visual scenes and of discourse is shown by her use of the same qualifier in two instances. Her acts of faith performed before the grand vicar are described as "pathétiques" (p. 113), therefore effective ("j'arrachai des sanglots de quelques religieuses, ... les deux jeunes ecclésiastiques en versèrent des larmes"); and on the other hand she judges Manouri's brief lacking in *pathétique* (p. 119), just as she imagines her case inadequately pled by him at the hearing. One of the brief notes she leaves at the end is also revealing of this dramatic/literary vision: "C'est ici que je *peindrai* ma *scène* dans le fiacre. Quelle scène!" (p. 203). Such an unelaborated exclamation elicits an imaginative projection on the part of the reader, and thus produces a dramatic effect without representation. Thus all the "scenes" in *La Religieuse* also relate to the "tableaux," whose metaphorical basis is not theatre but painting;[40] in the contemporary theory of the *drame* the two are linked in a common idiom — Greuze, for example, on the one side, and Sedaine, Diderot, Beaumarchais on the other.

The artifice of Suzanne's innocence, which we have mentioned, can be rationalized to a degree on similar dramatic grounds — not to mention, on a technical level, the convention by which the narrator of memoirs at least partially reproduces the directness of his or her original point of view as actor in the diegesis. But Suzanne's case strains even these alibis. Her surprise at the mother superior's

---

[40] See: especially p. 171 "Vous qui vous connaissez en peinture, je vous assure, Monsieur le marquis que c'était un assez agréable tableau à voir..."

exquisite sensitivity to music (p. 152) is acceptable in these terms, as would be her disclaimer, "je n'y entendais rien" (p. 144); but what immediately follows — "... ni elle non plus, et à présent même que j'y réfléchis, qu'aurions-nous pu y entendre?" — explodes its plausibility. There is a suggestion that more complete understanding would have armed her for a lucid, effective defense which partial ignorance cannot marshal.[41] But the fact remains that Suzanne's lack of comprehension defies common sense. The standard explanation offered for this is that the author has, intentionally or otherwise, artificially maintained her innocence in a day-to-day perspective, just as he has kept her age, for the same purpose, impossibly low.[42] In this view, Suzanne, whom Lemoine compares to "une fleur délicate qu'on ne garde fraîche et sans tâche jusqu'à l'âge où vous êtes que par une protection spéciale de la Providence" (p. 180), is, precisely, unusually protected by her creator — Diderot, in this instance.

There is, however, an interior key to her discourse that should not be overlooked, provided, paradoxically, by the very Dom Morel who is keeping her in the dark: "Ma sœur, me répondit-il en prenant un air grave, tenez-vous-en à ses conseils [= those of Lemoine], et tâchez d'en ignorer la raison tant que vous vivrez" (p. 194).[43] All she has to do is to carry out these instructions as willfully as he suggests — "*tâchez* d'ignorer" — to produce a recital which not only reflects past ignorance but still *tries* with an on-

---

[41] She says, about one of her interviews with Dom Morel: "J'avais la plus forte curiosité d'en savoir davantage. Il aurait bien pu m'éclairer sur des questions que je m'étais faites et auxquelles je n'avais jamais pu me répondre, mais je n'osais l'interroger" (p. 193). The passage is not without ambiguity; in part, it emphasizes her active sexual curiosity, but the *il aurait bien pu* suggests that Morel has shirked his obligation, and the only explanation Suzanne obtains is the less than useful mythic one that Satan is at work.

[42] She tells Mme *** she is not yet nineteen (p. 156). According to my attempts to work out a coherent chronology for the story, it actually covers, at a minimum, about nine years, beginning when she is sixteen and a half, and Suzanne cannot have gone to Sainte-Eutrope before about age twenty-four ("A Note on Chronology in *La Religieuse*," *Romance Notes*, 12, No. 1, 149-56).

[43] Cf. what another priest says to the heroine of *La Vie de Marianne*: "Tâchez même de croire que vous avez mal vu, mal entendu; ce sera une disposition d'esprit, une innocence de pensée qui sera agréable à Dieu" (p. 144).

going effort ("tant que vous vivrez") not to understand. Trying not to know is the way she keeps her theological innocence, thereby avoiding damnation.[44] Thus she maintains a spectacular kind of virginity up to the moment when, although implausibly, the veil is objectively rent.[45]

There are thus, among the celebrated incongruences of *La Religieuse*,[46] some for which the text itself offers a reading principle. It is possible to overlook them for many reasons, including the fact that they are dissimulated in the text not only by the laws of Suzanne's own discourse but also by technical problems inducing misreading. The best example of the latter category is a modern sense of punctuation, which leads one to overlook the fact that Mme Simonin "ends" her strangely incongruous farewell letter (pp. 71-72), half-way through ("Adieu encore une fois."). Because this is followed by no new indentation or quotation marks, readers invariably fail to notice that she has said *adieu*. But if one trusts the words themselves, the unimaginably maladroit remark about the letters' supposedly having been sent yesterday ("je lui avais remis ce petit paquet avec cette lettre qu'il a écrite sous ma dictée") is rationally comprehensible: to the original letter, Mme Simonin has had time later to adjoin, again through the mediation of her *dépositaire*, a second note which will also accompany the package, and which describes what has happened — notably the attempted theft by her sisters of the money destined for Suzanne — since the first was dictated the day before. This solution to the ambiguity is not

---

[44] Such is also the reading of William F. Edmiston: "The problem is that she confuses innocence (lack of guilt) with ignorance (lack of knowledge about guilt).... An innocence based on ignorance is thus her only defense, and Suzanne goes to extreme lengths to preserve its semblance.... She is only acting as she has been taught by her confessor: in order to be free from guilt, she believes she must not know of its existence" (op. cit., pp. 80, 82).

[45] "Le voile qui jusqu'alors m'avait dérobé le péril que j'avais couru se déchirait" (p. 198) is an exceptionally rich diegetic metaphor. *Le voile* can equally well be the veil of the religious or the veil of the convent church/temple. As a Biblical allusion (the veil of the temple rent upon Christ's death), the metaphor evokes a cataclysmic change in the relationship between heaven and earth; secondly, it denotes the sudden understanding which enters her "veiled" mind; and finally, it is hard not to see in it a metaphor for another metaphor, rent virginity.

[46] They have been frequently detailed, for example by Jérôme Catrysse in *Diderot et la mystification* (Paris: Nizet, 1970), pp. 224-31.

all that evident in terms of typographical clarity, but it is there and can be found.

That is certainly not true in every case, however, Suzanne's assertion that Sainte-Ursule is still alive and threatened (p. 85), whereas she dies later in the novel, is unaccountable for by the addendum, "Voilà ce que je vous disais alors; mais hélas elle n'est plus, et je reste seule," because the *alors* cannot be situated referentially. There is no explanation for it within the text itself as a closed system (as opposed to a paleographical explanation which examines the different states of the manuscript) except as a function of a self-subverting text. But this apparent violation of the law of noncontradiction is not in itself a valid reason for dismissing the hypothesis: a text can, after all, be self-subverting. To some extent Suzanne the narrator knowingly subverts it herself, as in this example: "... je ne continue que parce que je me flatte secrètement que vous ne lirez pas ces endroits.... Voilà encore un de ces endroits que j'écris parce que je me flatte que vous ne le lirez pas; cependant cela n'est pas vrai, mais il faut que je me le persuade" (p. 197). Her rationalization is revealing, in more than one way. It tends, for one thing, to bring out the extent to which, while projecting the dramatic fiction of her own interlocutor ("il me semble que vous êtes présent, que je vous vois et que vous m'écoutez"), she is really talking to herself — a subtle form of autoeroticism. (Note in this regard a reply of Mme *** which makes of speech a metaphor for sex: "Quand on parle, c'est toujours à quelqu'un, cela vaut mieux sans doute que de s'entretenir seule, quoique ce ne soit pas tout à fait sans plaisir" [p. 163].)[47] But its main interest here is its self-refutation, doubly inscribed: first, in the contradiction of writing what she ostensibly does not want read, and then in denying the pretext just proffered to explain that contradiction. "Cela n'est pas vrai" does not erase what precedes: logically it should, but if performed the erasure would not figure at all in the actual, present text.[48] It stands, instead, as a sign of sabotage by Suzanne of her own writing.[49]

---

[47] There are similar metaphors in Crébillon: cf. my *Le Masque et la parole* (Paris: José Corti, 1973), pp. 162-63, and Bernadette Fort, *Le Langage de l'ambiguïté dans l'œuvre de Crébillon fils* (Paris: Klincksieck, 1978), pp. 101-2.

[48] The stages of revision which an *author* has put his manuscript through in the process of its elaboration has of course nothing to do with the revisions

It is at this point that the function of the preface must be taken into account, for it participates in this movement at the same time that it provides the framework fiction for Suzanne's memoirs (most importantly, in terms of the plot, it includes her death). In many details, it contradicts quite plainly what Suzanne says, and in ways which can hardly contribute plausibly to a rounding-out of the complexity of her character. To take a simple example, it gives different professions and locations for her two brothers-in-law: are we to conclude from this that Suzanne is lying about them? Such a problem is of course false because the preface "fictionalizes" everything concerning Suzanne, locating everything she has said outside its own reality-framework. Those contradictions, then, hardly matter. But once that has been said, the same effects must be recognized in the internal inconsistencies of her own text: the whole is self-undermining, in much the way that *Jacques le fataliste* is. And just as it contains its own statement that it cannot entirely be trusted, it incorporates its own principle of incompleteness and revision in its beginning and ending. If a work published in several parts may contain allusions to its own earlier parts' existence in book form, and even to critical reactions to them (as in *Don Quixote*), then the Suzanne who rereads her own draft can leave commentary on it and notes for its continuation or revision, even before (logically speaking) the preface reduces even this to fiction. What the preface affirms unambiguously, and even if its doing so represents a sort of impossible challenge to the reader, is that the whole must be read as a fiction, not beholden to "truth" nor, in consequence, to the principle of total consistency which prevails as the benchmark of truth's domain.[50]

---

practiced by the character when she is represented in the text as a writer; there is no equivalent for the palimpsest or *repentir* on the fictive level, unless the fictive author leaves traces of her own rewriting process within the text — as Suzanne in fact does.

[49] Georges May's argument, according to which the strength of the illusion for the reader is dependent in some way upon the implausibilities of the text, implies that *artifice* requires *error:* he identifies mistakes with untruth, and groups the ensemble under the umbrella term "tricheries" (p. 218).

[50] This problematizing function of the preface calls for some nuancing of Susan Suleiman's formulation, in an otherwise valuable exposition, that "la rhétorique du roman à thèse est une rhétorique *simple* — c'est-à-dire, sans retour ironique sur elle-même" ("La Structure d'apprentissage," in *Poétique,* 37 [1979], p. 28).

Perfect comprehension, however, is not to be had even on the exclusive level of Suzanne's perspective: she cannot guarantee the meaning of what she puts forward, which is one of the reasons the Marquis is invoked as judge. There are several senses in which this is true. For one thing, it is a function of the difficulty of analytic interpretation. Despite the ostensible straightforwardness of her overall argument, our "subtle movements" (p. 77) — what she refers to in another place as "la structure intérieure de l'homme" (p. 120) — resist identification and introduce an insistent *peut-être*. Suzanne is not certain what she herself was expressing when she uttered a "chère mère" during her lethargy, and must attenuate her explanation that she meant Mme de Moni by an *apparemment* (p. 131). The status of facts is insecure, since they are manipulable in discourse: "l'on fit de cette imprudence tout ce qu'on voulut" (p. 75); "pour l'aventure de la jeune religieuse, on en fit tout ce qu'on voulut" (p. 105). All of a society has a tongue in common, but there are segments of it where force is exerted through the power to give local definition to the terms. Explanations themselves are tendencious: "Il me paraissait assez singulier que la même chose vînt de Dieu ou du diable, selon qu'il leur plaisait de l'envisager.... Le même mal vient ou de Dieu qui nous éprouve ou du diable qui nous tente" (p. 49). In the second formulation of this example, the human mediator of truth has disappeared — thereby suggesting more broadly the uncertainty of signs, which is disconcerting not just because of the theological ramifications but because, on a purely semantic plane, of the utterly antipodal nature of the two signifieds in uncertain conflict: between diametric opposites, the ambiguity is total.

Moreover, not everything Suzanne has to tell, as she herself recognizes, is interpretable only in her favor. Her isolation at Longchamp is due to her failure — but not her lack of attempting — to rally others to the same defiant conduct. "J'eus bientôt l'air et peut-être un peu le jeu d'une *factieuse*" (p. 74): the term is strong, despite her double attenuation (*peut-être, un peu*) preparing it. Her suit, indeed, cannot be based upon the whole truth, which would contain elements "qui m'auraient rendue odieuse sans me servir" (p. 63). It is because Suzanne knows full well that her case is not unambiguous that she is not very hopeful about its outcome; and it is for the same reason that she pleads so hard to Croismare, and recognizes the necessity of a judgment (that is, an interpretation) in addressing herself to him. The thesis is clear, but not its demonstration or even the evidence of its demonstrability.

This is one of the reasons why the theme of knowledge, and in particular self-knowledge, latent through most of the text, can emerge into the openly problematic realm so effectively at the conclusion.[51] Knowledge, as we have seen, takes on in the convent perverse and antithetical connotations.[52] As the end of the novel approaches, this motif becomes more intense, not only with regard to things outside the self, but within — "Je ne me connaissais pas, je me connais" (p. 196) — and dovetails to a degree with the problem of good faith. Finally, and it is significant that this comes only as she rereads her own writing, Suzanne must raise questions both about the moral truth of her narrative and about the more disturbing matter of her motives — both "je m'étais montrée ... beaucoup plus *aimable* que je ne le suis" and a possible consequence: "Cependant si le marquis, à qui l'on accorde le tact le plus délicat, venait à se persuader que ce n'est pas à sa bienfaisance mais à son vice que je m'adresse, que penserait-il de moi?" There is a fine delicacy in this passage which allows it both to raise the terribly compromising suggestion of a seduction, and to nuance and attenuate it to the maximum: first, in phrasing it in the form of a query, thus permitting the doubt to subsist over the whole; then in lending the perception to the Marquis (that is, she has tried to read her own text as the Marquis might); thirdly, in suggesting that even then, only the extreme sensitivity ("le tact le plus délicat") with which the prospective reader is endowed would detect it; fourthly, in further distancing these factors through the circumlocution "venait à se persuader que"; fifthly, through the euphemism "à son vice que je m'adresse," which must itself be interpreted (although without difficulty); and finally, by what is not said: in

---

[51] Cf. May, pp. 215 et passim.
[52] This is expressed, for example, in the parallelism and anaphora of the formula: "on m'a fait lire le nombreux fatras de ce que les religieux ont débité de leur état qu'ils connaissent bien et qu'ils détestent, contre le monde qu'ils aiment, qu'ils déchirent et qu'ils ne connaissent pas" (p. 44).

avoiding speculation about his response — and hers to his — if he does interpret her memoirs as she suggests he well might.

She retreats, as she has a couple of times previously, into truisms regarding femininity, but again with an ambiguous distanciation. In the first step — "En vérité il aurait bien tort de m'imputer personnellement un instinct propre à tout mon sexe" — she admits the general law and sets herself above it. Step two — "Je suis une femme, peut-être un peu coquette, que sais-je?" — she hints that she may fall under the general rule after all, but treats this as undecidable. And then, in her softly winsome but devious final word — "mais c'est naturellement et sans artifice" — she integrates the *coquette* of the previous utterance into the realm of nature and renders it innocent. But if seduction is natural, so much so that it can be done unconsciously by a weak and innocent creature, why should it be evil? She does not say that it is: only that she is afraid of what the Marquis will think.

What he will think has, in one respect, already been determined for the reader by the preface: he has responded favorably. On the other hand, in terms of the preface, Croismare never read until after her death the long letter Suzanne had written to detail her experience. Therefore her story proper still ends on a concentric series of open questions: ones the text asks about itself, just as the preface, taken separately, ends with an explicitly formulated question ("Question aux gens de lettres"). The thesis — and no one has ever doubted that this is a *roman à thèse* — is itself engulfed in the power to doubt . . . [53] which is simultaneous with the power and freedom to live. That too, however, has been nipped in the bud by that convoluted end that was in the beginning: Suzanne's death.

---

[53] See Carol Sherman's analysis of the uncertainty of meaning in "Changing Spaces," in Jack Undank and Herbert Joseph (eds.), *Diderot: Digression and Dispersion* (Lexington: French Forum Publishers, 1984), 219-30: "for if there are several ways of saying and if she can hesitate among them, what assurance has the reader of the (monolithic) truth of what was just presented? . . . Sense is thus never conferred, not even by the ending" (pp. 228-29). Cf. also her "The Deferral of Textual Authority in *La Religieuse*," in *Postscript*, 2 (1985), 57-65.

JULIE, OU LA NOUVELLE HÉLOÏSE

This grand and perplexing novel turns upon itself, in mid-course, to seek a resolution that is at once a denial and a sublimation of its passion-imbued first half. According to its second, dialogical preface,[1] this shift corresponds to a moral strategy, a didactic gamble: after rising to sensuous bait, the reader will be in a position to be moved by the superior truths of hard-won virtue. The book will seduce, then cleanse, in a manner parallel to the development of its plot — or it won't. There is nothing unclear about all this in terms of the text's overall, overt stance. But in truth such a schematic reading is possible only superficially, and a more thorough understanding of this work is to be had in recognizing its textual complexity throughout rather than just its linearity whereby a pathetic interest comes to be supplanted by an heroic one. The rhetoric is, in one sense, constant throughout, faithful to the same obsessions and dilemmas, and at the same time diachronically differentiated, inasmuch as the "truth" of the love story is reversed and the wrong values originally posited set aright. A complete reading therefore involves being aware and taking account of the pendant function of the two halves in plot and purport, while being willing to ap-

---

Jean-Jacques Rousseau (1713-1778), *Julie, ou la nouvelle Héloïse: lettres de deux amants habitants d'une petite ville au pied des Alpes, recueillies et publiées par Jean-Jacques Rousseau*, 1761. Édition: Classiques Garnier, ed. René Pomeau, 1960.

[1] The "Préface de Julie ou entretien sur les romans," although it did not appear in the first edition, can without abuse be considered as part of the total text inasmuch as Rousseau apparently intended it to accompany the novel; in the edition cited it is appended in pp. 737-57.

proach the whole as a uniform surface which can be scanned in any order.

That *Julie* is ultimately ambiguous is not a new idea. Traditionally, however, its ambiguity is approached as a case study the ultimate cause of which lies elsewhere, namely in the persistent contradictions of its author. This discussion will attempt instead to make it evident that the themes can be worked out within the novel's own, self-contained dimensions; that, in other words, the logical disparities and the like are functions of the text as such, a text which consistently undermines its own pretensions as consistent discourse. This pattern will emerge gradually as various aspects of the work are discussed. What we find ultimately is not merely the movement from one preoccupation to another, but a general tension underlying the whole; there is at once a certain terminological harmony running the length of the novel, and, within that, contradictory impulses which infuse it from start to finish. It is possible here as in few letter novels to treat the discourse at least in certain respects as situated all on one plane no matter what the source of particular utterances, rather than always relating it to the context of characters acting forever on and against each other (as one must do, for example, in *Les Liaisons dangereuses*). Certainly there is interaction, just as there is character differentiation; yet the centripetal forces override these because, by their common opposition to society at large, the several characters largely think, and express themselves, alike.[2]

One way to summarize the sense of the work is to see in it the aleatory itinerary of a search for value — perdurable value. Chastity has value; love has value; filial duty, honor, compassion, domestic tranquility, patriotism and piety all have value: but can they all be satisfied equally well, and which of them guarantee the surest recompense? The need for transcendent value, at least as

---

[2] "N" says, in the second preface, "J'observe que dans une société très intime les styles se rapprochent ainsi que les caractères et que les amis, confondant leurs âmes, confondent aussi leurs manières de penser, de sentir et de dire" (p. 755). Similarly, the identity of the addressee loses importance when the characters themselves stress so much their lack of disguise and secrecy, their openness to each other.

personified by Julie herself, is absolute; [3] its realizations, relative: and herein lies the tragedy of the quest.

It will be easier to grasp some of the symmetries and the overall movement in this architectonic text if we describe its composition somewhat in numerical terms. There are 163 letters,[4] varying enormously in length and density as we move from the book's first half to its last:

Part	No. of letters	Pages	Ave. no. of pages	Approximate Lapse of time covered [5]
I	65	159	2.5	3 years
II	28	121	4.3	1 1/2 years
III	26	91	3.5	3 years
				(Interval: 4 years)
IV	17	127	7.5	6 months to a year or so
V	14	117	8.4	"
VI	13	109	8.4	"

Of course these figures give only general indications, since some letters, for instance, are only a line or two while others go on for thirty pages; still, they indicate the rapid succession of letters in the first three parts (119 letters, average 3.1 pages) and the much slower, elegiac tempo of the last three (44 letters, average 8 pages). This uneven balance and inverse proportion between letter length and diegetic time clearly correspond nonetheless to a general thematic equilibrium, which Claire characterizes as "douze ans de pleurs et six ans de gloire" (p. 486).[6]

---

[3] "Ce n'est pas assez, croyez-moi, que la vertu soit la base de votre conduite, si vous n'établissez cette base même sur un fondement *inébranlable*" (Julie, p. 355).

[4] For convenience, I count only the letters numbered in the text; there are numerous unnumbered "billets," "fragments," etc. which would affect the statistics somewhat, but these distinctions are somewhat arbitrary.

[5] I rely here principally on the chronologies given in the Pléiade edition (Paris: Gallimard, 1961, Vol. II in *Œuvres complètes*), pp. 1825-29, and by François Van Laere in *Une Lecture du temps dans "La Nouvelle Héloïse"* (Neuchâtel: La Baconnière, 1968). I can find in them only small details to quibble over, but the text does not finally permit a more specific chronology to be fixed; it is, as it stands, quite coherent despite its frequent lack of temporal precision.

[6] That is, twelve anguished years in all, six of which are glorious. Cf. Julie: "Après avoir perdu *la moitié* de ma vie à nourrir une passion malheureuse, je consacrais *l'autre* à la justifier" (pp. 600-601).

The expression "lettres de deux amants" in the subtitle really accounts for only a little less than half of the letters, but if we include Claire we come to three quarters (121) of the total exchanged just between this troika, as follows:

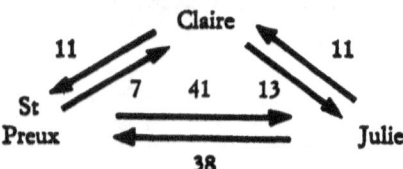

(By counting Edouard Bomston, we would reach 140 letters, or 86 %.) This heavy loading of the correspondence among the principals is even clearer if we make a table including all ten characters involved in some way in the exchange (next page). Even Wolmar's part is, in this regard, quite small. Saint-Preux both writes and receives more than anyone else. But he is also the organizational principal in a subtler way, since all the letter headings indicating points of exchange assume his place as central referent (a simple "à Julie" or "de Claire" without further qualifiers always means "Saint-Preux à Julie" and "Claire à Saint-Preux").[7] There is, of course, a shift in axes over time. In part I Saint-Preux writes only to Julie, and 50 out of 65 letters pass between them, whereas there will be an interval of seven years (p. 662) between parts III and VI during which she never writes to him at all. The focal attention is during that time concentrated on her, as she is observed and described, but she herself writes only ten letters in the entire last half of the novel and Saint-Preux fifteen. Claire's role is more uniform, and except for one letter to her fiancé at the end of part I, she writes exclusively to Julie and Saint-Preux. It should be noted that Mme d'Étange and M. d'Orbe exist only in the novel's first half and Wolmar appears only in the last; still it is interesting that there are no letters from Wolmar to Julie.

---

[7] This device both privileges his perspective and suppresses his name. It could be shown too how socially slanted the novel's dominant perspective is: though a commoner, Saint-Preux hardly views society from the under side and falls in easily with an ostensibly neutral *on* (e.g., "une famille qui voit qu'*on* a daigné s'occuper d'elle" [p. 541]) which is that of the rich master.

TABLE OF CORRESPONDENCE AXES [8]

SENDER \ ADDRESSEE	Saint-Preux	Julie	Claire	Edouard	Wolmar	Fanchon	d'Orbe	d'Étange	Mme d'Étange	Henriette	TOTAL	%
Saint-Preux	X	40+1	5+2	3+10	0+2	—	—	1+0	1+0	—	65	39.8
Julie	35+3	X	6+5	2+0	0+1	1+0	—	—	—	—	53	32.5
Claire	7+4	7+6	X	—	—	—	1+0	—	—	—	25	15.3
Edouard	4+2	2+0	1+0	X	0+1	—	—	—	—	—	10	6.1
Wolmar	0+3	—	0+1	0+1	X	—	—	—	—	—	5	3.0
Fanchon	0+1	1+0	—	—	—	X	—	—	—	—	2	1.2
d'Orbe	—	1+0	—	—	—	—	X	—	—	—	1	0.6
d'Étange	1+0	—	—	—	—	—	—	X	—	—	1	0.6
Mme d'Étange	—	—	—	—	—	—	—	—	X	—	0	0
Henriette	—	—	0+1	—	—	—	—	—	—	X	1	0.6
RECEIVED: T	60.	58	21	16	4	1	1	1	1	0	163	
%	36.8	35.0	12.9	9.8	2.5	0.6	0.6	0.6	0.6	0		

[8] I have separated in this table, in order to reveal the asymmetries, figures for the two halves of the novel; it must be noted, however, that it is not formally divided in any way into two but only into six *parties*.

The letter as a material object does not play a particularly large role, but enough of one (especially in the first half) to recall to mind occasionally the fictive medium. The letters are not dated, but they frequently answer to each other or allude to the interval required for postal exchange, and Julie informs Saint-Preux to whom he can address letters intended for her. Pen and paper are not frequently alluded to except in two circumstances where their presence seems fortuitous (in the icy wilds at Meillerie, p. 65, and in Julie's dressing room, p. 122) and when Saint-Preux copies all Julie's letters into a book. Julie once refers to her trembling hand (p. 38), which presumably means, in epistolary equivalence, her quivering writing; and once, by evoking "l'état de ce papier" (p. 356), connotes the trace of tears on the stationery. Secret letters, of course, usually exist in fiction in order to be found, and the discovery of Julie's cache by her mother is an important if not indeed crucial point in the plot. Moreover, these particular letters provide one of the rare extended secrets in the story since, although Julie thinks she has witnessed their destruction, they later appear (it is not clear precisely how transmitted) in Wolmar's hands to prove he has known all along about Julie's past. Wolmar is a curator of letters, having saved these from the fire as well as the one Saint-Preux concluded with "brûlez ma lettre et oubliez ce qu'elle contient" (p. 612): when one reads this in a book, the very presence of the utterance is proof that the wish was not respected, and thus constitutes a further meaning beyond what it "says." Similarly, Wolmar was free, by Julie's own charge, to suppress her last letter to Saint-Preux (p. 708); consequently, part of its significance lies in its very appearance. (To this one might add, on another level, the implied indiscretion inherent in the publication of any private paper.)

Although emphasis on the missives themselves is moderate, there is a problematics of writing, and an intriguing sort of equivalence between writing and action. When Julie writes, "recevez dans votre sein des larmes dont vous êtes l'auteur" (p. 295), the transmission of the tears is purely epistolary, and the metaphor of Saint-Preux as their "author" is a reliteralization inasmuch as their cause is his just-discovered letters. The period of correspondence coincides with one of sexual involvement, the one standing for the other; the latter's termination is signaled by repeated allusions — by

Saint-Preux, Julie, and Claire — to an end to writing.[9] Similarly, Julie's writing is a sign of her purity which is implicitly suspect for an instant when another man (Bomston) becomes a recipient.[10] And when after years of silence she once more writes, Saint-Preux will ask whether the same writing can mean something different (p. 662). Saint-Preux refers to his letter on his infidelity as one which "il ne fallait jamais écrire" (p. 272)[11] — the equivalent of the thing which shouldn't have been done. Wolman seems to intuit that Saint-Preux's living under the same roof with Julie is not a danger so long as he has no *written* communication with her; she, in turn, offers to submit all her writing to her husband's inspection and control (p. 412); and Claire, to protect her, proposes that during Wolmar's absence she keep, in lieu of letters, a journal for him (p. 488). Julie's first letter had been to confess her love, and when she ultimately declares, "j'achève de vivre comme j'ai commencé" (p. 731) one can nearly equate *vivre* with writing, especially since in this last paragraph of her last letter she abruptly reverts to the long banished *tu* form and affirms once more that she loves him still.

Quite aside from the many letters whose suppression the editor indicates here and there, there are numerous mentions of additional writings, distinct from the letters, which although held in abeyance purport to exist. Concerning Saint-Preux's visit to Le Valais: "Je ne vous ferai point ici un détail de mon voyage et de mes remarques; j'en ai fait *une relation* que je compte vous porter" (p. 50). But if Julie has seen it, this is not further certified. Then there is his copy of Julie's letters, with space left over to "write" in: "[Le livre] est assez gros; mais je songe à l'avenir, et j'espère ne pas mourir assez jeune pour me borner à ce volume" (p. 205). Besides his descriptions of the Parisian arts, there is one form, lyric drama, of

---

[9] Pp. 291, 296, 318, 354.

[10] "... une lettre ... écrite d'une main qui n'en écrivit jamais à d'autre homme qu'à moi" (p. 139). Arnolphe in *L'École des femmes* likewise equates Agnès's writing with her sexual favors. The reader already knows here what Julie's heroic letter (I.59) contains, but the footnote calls attention to the erotic implications of Saint-Preux's remark with a surprising qualification regarding the father: "Il en faut, je pense, excepter son père."

[11] As if fearing that words can get out of control and concatenize events, Julie exclaims, "Mon ami, jamais je n'écrirai ce mot-là" in alluding to the possible day where Saint-Preux might say "je ne t'aime plus" (p. 85): such a blasphemy cannot be "quoted" without fear of realizing its performative effect.

which he says, "j'en ai fait une *petite dissertation* à part que vous trouverez ci-jointe" (p. 267) — but which, for *us*, is not appended. He speaks of a copy for Julie of his circumnavigation narrative (p. 406). And she, whether or not she followed up on Claire's idea for a journal (p. 488), has written an illustrated book consisting mostly of Bible stories for her children (p. 568). Based upon her and Wolmar's theories, Saint-Preux has written and submitted for their approval (p. 599) a system of education which Julie herself has read and in turn commented upon (p. 730); she also has read the relation of Saint-Preux's voyages, as well as the account of Bomston's adventures (p. 677) which thus "exists" qua allusion — "quelque chose à deviner" (note p. 612).[12]

They are therefore authors in ways going far beyond just their letters, and their thoughts in all domains draw very heavily on literary sources. Of these, and however opposed they may be to the sophisticated ways of the cultural capitals, these provincials embrace a quite remarkable range. There are, most noticeably, the numerous quotations from Italian love poetry, principally in the most lyrical part one. These presumably emerge from the readings Claire, Julie and Saint-Preux have done together, for they quote freely from Petrarch, Metastasio and Tasso without mention of their names. But their range of allusion is much broader than that; besides general evocation of Greek or Roman antiquity and occasionally of classical myth, there are frequent references to Greek and Roman writers, philosophical or literary,[13] particularly Plutarch; to other Italians,[14] to four English writers (Pope, Locke, Berkeley, Hyde); rarely, a Biblical allusion; and a whole bevy of French writers running from Montaigne to Montesquieu and Voltaire[15] — not to mention Sinbad,

---

[12] "Les Amours de Milord Edouard Bomston" (pp. 759-71) was included as an appendix in some subsequent editions of the novel.

[13] Euripides, Plato (4 times), Homer, Alcibiades, Aristophanes, Menander, Pythagorus, Pliny, Cato, Terence, Plautus, Suetonius, Tacitus.

[14] Lamberti and Marini: although the first discussion of Marini is based on a mistaken attribution (pp. 214-15), there is a quotation further on from his *Adone* (p. 270).

[15] I count seventeen, not all of whom are identified by name. One could add *L'Astrée* and Mme Riccoboni, but Julie and Claire do not read novels, of course ("Jamais fille chaste n'a lu de romans"): the allusion to *L'Astrée* is a mere mention of the name of Céladon by Claire (p. 649), and Madame Riccoboni's novels are cited only in a footnote (p. 539).

Saint Theresa, and the *Roman de la Rose*. The occurrences of Plutarch (nine) and Muralt for his *Lettres sur les Anglais et les Français* (five) relate rather evidently to particular moral and social themes of the novel; in the case of Plutarch, one has only to think of Saint-Preux's injunction, "proposons-nous de grands exemples à imiter" (p. 32): great models are more valuable than grand principles.[16]

Now one of the most suggestive models proposed by the text is Heloise, itself literary (and epistolary) since it derives from the presumed letters of Abelard and Heloise of which many contemporary translations and adaptations had appeared. Her name in the book's title seems to announce an heroic, tragic love ultimately transposed into a spiritual essence. On the other hand, the rest of the title seems to work in just the opposite direction, for the thought of such a romantic drama transpiring in "une petite ville au pied des Alpes" is antithetical in any context and thus constitutes a juxtaposition, ostensibly, of the grandiose and the quaint. The famous episode of Abelard and Heloise was eminently Parisian in all its aspects. *Julie* sets out from the start to shock expectations, and this Swiss Heloise is going to make sense precisely because only in her country will one find a worthy modern heroism, "des hommes antiques dans les temps modernes" (p. 33). For the whole parallel is set up in terms of similarity tied to a critical difference, and based upon a certain reading of the model. The protagonists here have themselves read that story, and it is Saint-Preux who, early on, brings it up with reference to theirs:

> Quand les lettres d'Héloïse et d'Abélard tombèrent entre vos mains, vous savez ce que je vous dis ce cette lecture et de la conduite du théologien. J'ai toujours plaint Héloïse; elle avait un cœur fait pour aimer: mais Abélard ne m'a jamais paru qu'un misérable digne de son sort, et connaissant aussi peu l'amour que la vertu. Après l'avoir jugé, faudra-t-il que je l'imite? Malheur à quiconque prêche une morale qu'il ne veut pas pratiquer. [p. 60]

---

[16] Cf. Julie: "Souviens-toi des ... transports qui nous élevaient au-dessus de nous-mêmes, au *récit* de ces vies héroïques qui rendent le vice inexcusable et font l'honneur de l'humanité" (p. 199).

The complexities of this comparison highlight the overall ambiguity of this text's ostensible relationship to romance tradition. Its hero maintains he will not become a "vil corrupteur" like Abelard,[17] yet this passage appears only a few pages before the parallel is drawn tighter by their imitation of Abelard's and Héloïse's fornication. Nothing in the novel remotely parallels in literal terms the most famous consequence of Abelard's guilt, namely his castration. Symbolically, of course, one can say that Saint-Preux is emasculated and thereby loses Julie just as definitively. Conversely, the fact that they cannot marry should logically bring into play another literary myth implicitly involved because of the theme of adultery which hangs over the novel's last half: Tristan and Isolde. (The mention of Abelard and Heloise in the *Roman de la Rose* occurs precisely in the context of rejecting the idea of marriage.) In this sense, the fact that Saint-Preux and Julie do not marry seems to coincide with the courtly romance tradition celebrating a glorious but death-bound, adulterous love; the return of Saint-Preux to Clarens sets the stage for such a development. But the reversal of this expectation is keyed to a return of the Héloïse parallel. Claire writes: "Cousine, tu fus amante comme Héloïse, te voilà dévote comme elle; plaise à Dieu que ce soit avec plus de succès!" (p. 483). Transcendence again becomes the model; but at the same time, Claire's appended clause foreshadows the failure of the transition from carnal to purely spiritual love.

The ambiguity of the fictional connection does not attach clearly to either side of the editor/character distinction. *Julie*'s preface seems at first to announce a novel: "Il faut des spectacles dans les grandes villes, et des romans aux peuples corrompus. J'ai vu les mœurs de mon temps, et j'ai publié ces lettres" (p. 3). The equation *romans : peuples corrompus :: ces lettres : les mœurs de mon temps* appears quite clear, yet immediately the text's fictional status is explicitly raised ("la correspondance entière est-elle une fiction?") only to bring forth a sarcasm ("Gens du monde, que vous importe? C'est sûrement une fiction pour vous"). The literal enigma is dissolved into metaphor, and "fiction" changes meanings. The second preface takes this process much further, even insisting on the crucial

---

[17] The Editor says nonetheless that Saint-Preux has "imité la conduite d'Abélard" (p. 673).

nature of the dilemma, but still without offering a resolution. As Paul de Man has so elegantly shown in his analysis of that preface, it both forces the issue of the text's referentiality, positing it as pivotal to the manner appropriate for its reading, and imposes a reading unassisted by such a distinction.[18] Saint-Preux, who has read *Le Roman de la Rose* and *Don Quixote,* among other works, himself intones that "les romans sont peut-être la dernière instruction qu'il reste à donner à un peuple assez corrompu pour que tout autre lui soit inutile," and he proposes novels "qui ne montrassent pas tout d'un coup la vertu dans le ciel hors de la portée des hommes, mais qui la leur fissent aimer en la peignant d'abord moins austère et puis du sein du vice les y sussent conduire insensiblement" (p. 255). That description can hardly be read as other than a blueprint for *Julie* itself, and indeed it corresponds to the strategy "R" describes for it in the second preface.

The text lays claim to a heroism the concept of which belongs largely to romance, yet (partially) denies this appurtenance. The second preface, moreover, instructs us to read it not as a novel but as a collection of letters [19] — again suggesting the Abelard-Heloise parallel. This is an *as if* injunction, not claiming factuality but stressing the distinction to be made between the present letters and what the term *novel* usually evokes. At the same time, the characters model their descriptions and even their roles on novelistic premises:

> L'amour véritable est un feu dévorant qui porte son ardeur dans les autres sentiments, et les anime d'une vigueur nouvelle. C'est pour cela qu'on a dit que l'amour faisait *des héros.* Heureux celui que le sort eût placé pour le devenir, *et qui aurait Julie pour amante!* [p. 34]

And this, in the same letter proscribing love stories from their program of study (Julie replies: "vouloir attendrir sa maîtresse à l'aide des romans est avoir bien peu de ressource en soi-même"). But Saint-Preux did not glean an idea like "l'amour véritable" from

---

[18] "Rarely has a preface been less able to shed light on the meaning of the text it introduces, to the point of thematizing this impotence into the knowledge of an ignorance" (*Allegories of Reading,* New Haven and London: Yale University Press, 1979, p. 205).

[19] "Vous jugez ce que vous avez lu comme un roman. Ce n'en est point un; vous l'avez dit vous-même. C'est un recueil de lettres..." (p. 739).

Plato nor even from Petrarch. Where but in the romances did these two learn expressions like "miracle de l'amour" (p. 257) or "deux amants infortunés" which they both repeat (pp. 67, 136), or the general rules they quote so spontaneously:

> [Ton cœur] n'est pas ... de ceux qui peuvent aimer deux fois. [p. 81]
> Nous ne saurions longtemps vivre après avoir cessé d'aimer. [p. 83]
> L'amour sera la grande affaire de notre vie. [p. 83]
> L'inconstance et l'amour sont incompatibles. [p. 663]

Quoting Edouard's remark that "l'amour passera," Saint-Preux qualifies it as "blasphemy" (p. 140). They have invented nothing new about love; this aspect of their story is perfectly conventional except for their attempt to conflate this discourse with one of virtue.[20] The elopement proposed by Saint-Preux too is as novelistic as the scenes where words are overheard by an eavesdropper.[21]

Of course they frequently take their distance from such shopworn rhetoric, even by irony, as when Julie parodies chivalric fealty while enticing Saint-Preux toward a lonely chalet:

> C'est là, mon féal, qu'à genoux devant votre dame et maîtresse, vos deux mains dans les siennes, et en présence de son chancelier, vous lui jurerez foi et loyauté à toute épreuve; ... de ne point commettre acte de félonie, et de déclarer au moins la guerre avant de secouer le joug. Ce faisant, aurez l'accolade, et serez reconnu vassal unique et loyal chevalier. [p. 86]

Julie also plays other roles, among them that of a disconsolate Magdalene: "Ma faute est irréparable, mes pleurs ne tariront point.

---

[20] For a discussion of this repertory of traditional amorous rhetoric in the novel, see Jean-Louis Lecercle, *Rousseau et l'art du roman* (Paris: Armand Colin, 1969), pp. 165-76.

[21] There are three instances of the latter: Claire overhearing the heated discussion between Bomston and d'Étange about Saint-Preux; Saint-Preux listening to Bomston in his room (talking to himself! [p. 194]); and finally the scene after the dream where Saint-Preux hears Julie and Claire over the Elysée wall. *Les Amours de Milord Edouard,* more like a novel from the standpoint of plot, is relegated to an appendix; it also breaks with the letter format.

Ô toi qui les fais couler, crains d'attenter à de si justes douleurs; tout mon espoir est de les rendre éternelles" (p. 76). And to my knowledge no one has ever thought to detect a tinge of humor when Saint-Preux for his part intones: "je ferai dire un jour à ceux qui nous auront connus: 'Ô quels hommes nous serions tous, si le monde était plein de Julies et de cœurs qui les sussent aimer!'" (p. 205). *Novels* to them suggest, in contrast, what is cold and artificial, or immature;[22] they stand not so much for what is untrue as opposed to historical, but rather for what is phony. But consider an allusion like this, from the Parisian letters: "Les mots mêmes d'amour et d'amant sont bannis de l'intime société des deux sexes, et relégués avec ceux de *chaîne* et de *flamme* dans les romans qu'on ne lit plus" (p. 248, italics in the text). Although Saint-Preux neither espouses nor eschews terminology such as *chaîne* and *flamme*, what he says reveals the degree to which, from this vantage point, *Julie* represents a rehabilitation of the romantic in the face of a society which has trivialized or otherwise devalued it. There is a large wager riding on a necessary quantum leap underlying the value structure of the work, one which seems in ways to carry us back into a world of fantasy: as the Editor so well puts it, in rationalizing the verisimilitude of these characters: "Le problème entier dépend d'un point unique; trouvez seulement Julie, et tout le reste est trouvé" (p. 719).

Also in their ostensibly artless way, they often engage in emphatic diction whose most consistent patterns are probably the hyperbole and the epithet. Adjectives foremost, and particular groups of them, gravitate to nouns with epithetic regularity, in phrases like *tristesse mortelle, une mortelle impatience, ce baiser mortel, ma constance immortelle, abstinence éternelle et volontaire, liqueur funeste, sainte amitié, transport sacré, sainte ardeur.*[23] Julie shows

---

[22] Saint-Preux remarks that in reading novels he has often laughed at the "froides plaintes des amants" (p. 44); he classes "faiseurs de romans et de comédies" together as distorted painters of the world (p. 255). Later Wolmar compares extreme passion to puerile reactions, and a footnote applies this explanation to taste for theatre and novels (p. 726).

[23] An erotic undertone in such expressions is not belied by lines like "Douce pudeur, suprême volupté de l'amour" (p. 275), which can scarcely on the level of diction be distinguished from chaster passages evoking "ravissements célestes" (p. 348) or "un transport sacré ... un si doux saisissement" (p. 403).

on one occasion that she knows such terms must be largely discounted [24] — another one of the ways she sporadically undercuts what she does not otherwise cease to valorize. Lecercle remarks that the adjective thus often assumes the function of rhythmic modulator, bearing no informational value. [25] A phrase like "le plus fidèle amant du monde" (p. 502) has no referent, implies no comparison with other lovers; it is a purely rhetorical construction (indeed, cliché) based upon the principle of the superlative justified by a language of love. It might well be right out of *L'Astrée* or any number of other novels. "Le principe de cette rhétorique," remarks Lecercle, "consiste à donner à tous les mouvements de l'âme le maximum d'expressivité. Le style de Saint-Preux est tout en exclamations et en interrogations. Les mots les plus intensifs sont toujours choisis" (op. cit., p. 147). A case in point: "Julie, laisse-moi respirer; tu fais bouillonner mon sang, tu me fais tressaillir, tu me fais palpiter; ta lettre brûle comme ton cœur du saint amour de la vertu et tu portes au fond du mien son ardeur céleste" (p. 203). Indeed they repeatedly let themselves fall into the most flagrant platitudes of rhetorical pomposity; and this is precisely, and paradoxically, supposed to be an aspect of their extreme simplicity. The second preface asserts that "la passion, pleine d'elle-même, s'exprime avec plus d'abondance que de force; elle ne songe même pas à persuader" (p. 741): since persuasion was one of the traditional purposes of rhetoric, this tends to undo in the reader any wariness of rhetorical intentions on the characters' part. So too with the concession about the "style emphatique et plat" in the first preface, a trait justified only by the fact that the authors are provincials, "de jeunes gens, presque des enfants."

From the very first page of the novel, however, we are plunged into a field of highly tendencious language. "Il faut vous fuir, mademoiselle, je le sens bien": what could be less literal than this first line, whose purpose is hardly to announce a departure? (Idem the *adieu*'s and *il faut partir*'s on pp. 11-12.) We read a good deal about

---

[24] "D'ailleurs, il y a quelquefois plus d'adresse que de courage à tirer aventage pour le moment présent d'un avenir incertain, et à se payer d'avance d'une abstinence éternelle à laquelle on renonce quand on veut" (p. 177). One finds other sarcasms, such as the beginning of her letter 11 in part I (p. 23).

[25] Op. cit., p. 195.

danger (*danger* and *dangereux* are quite frequent throughout, not to mention *péril* and so forth), about love as poison causing pain, suffering, illness, and in consequence provoking pity. All that stands in its way is *cruel* and *barbare*: even Claire is *barbare* when she separates them (pp. 154, 292, 311), and Julie once, surprisingly enough, although in jest, speaks of "la plus cruelle des mères" (p. 119) who has deprived them of an opportunity to sneak away together. Quite aside from the suasive intention which may motivate such terms, they are not innocent merely by virtue of being mechanistic and banal. It may seem contrived when Saint-Preux begs pity for "le feu qui me consume" (p. 9), but Julie will later affirm its fatal effect: "Je le vis, dans des agitations convulsives, prêt à s'évanouir à mes pieds. Peut-être l'amour seul m'aurait épargnée; ô ma cousine! c'est la pitié qui me perdit" (p. 70). For no one ever denies here that conventional seduction *works,* and its mechanism is no different from elsewhere; what is different is the original integrity of the intention: "Il prit le langage honnête et insinuant avec lequel mille fourbes séduisent tous les jours autant de filles bien nées; mais seul parmi tant d'autres il était honnête homme et pensait ce qu'il disait" (p. 712).

Terms relating to family ties, "sacred" if anything is in *Julie,* are epithetically qualified with particular regularity. The word *mère,* above all, these characters seem utterly incapable of using without some sort of superlative qualifier: "cette incomparable mère" (pp. 239, 295), "la plus respectable des mères" (p. 291), "la meilleure des mères" (pp. 294, 295, 326), "ma triste mère" (p. 295), "une tendre mère" (pp. 297, 301, 380), "la plus tendre des mères" (p. 307), "cette mère tendre et chérie" (p. 298), "cette mère infortunée" (p. 298). There is little difference between the three main protagonists on this score. For this phenomenon there seem to be two complementary explanations. First, the mother has to be quintessentially good for the shape of the plot, as a counterbalance to the father, seldom so qualified.[26] It is largely, in this respect, a

---

[26] More often characterized by his bilious side — "un père emporté" (pp. 158, 288), "un père irrité" (pp. 189, 293) — he can nonetheless become "mon vénéré père" (p. 333), even "le meilleur des pères" (pp. 45, 496) and "ce père si tendre" (p. 708). But in general the flattering side of fatherhood favors d'Orbe ("le meilleur des pères," p. 420) and Wolmar.

matter of definition: that is, the mother is posited as ultimately good,[27] rather than this being a trait of deducible characterization. The plot itself does not furnish us with much evidence to justify this quintessence, except for the fact that Mme d'Étange does keep her daughter's secret from her husband; but when we consider that anything less would — she herself is persuaded — result in Julie's death, then it is not such an unambiguous proof of compassionate generosity. (She also turns out to have pleaded for the marriage of the two lovers.) Secondly, there operates here a sort of categorical imperative of the signifier: *mère* pulls in its wake, like a magnet, a set of semically related epithets; in its essence, *mère* really connotes them all, and the reinforcement is tautological. This is just one example among many, characteristic of the way sentimentally charged words can operate in the text.

A mythical apparatus works thus to transform everything into an archetype. Amorous enthusiasm alone might suffice to account for something like "Jamais sentiments humains n'approchèrent de ceux que m'inspira votre adorable fille" (p. 291) or "Vous êtes celle qui méritez les hommages de tout l'univers" (p. 345); but it is not alone the object of love which is so transmogrified. Virtually every significant aspect of the plot is raised to a superlative dimension: "modèle unique des vrais amants" (p. 175), "une amitié qui n'eut jamais d'égale" (p. 171), "tendres et inséparables amies, femmes uniques sur la terre" (p. 377), "unique et parfait modèle d'amitié, qu'on citera seule entre toutes les femmes" (p. 196; cf. p. 377), "Jamais homme n'entreprit ce que vous avez entrepris" (p. 598), "Il n'y aura jamais qu'une Julie au monde" (p. 516). Above all, of course, this process applies to Julie, whom we can watch the text transforming into a myth like the first Héloïse. Saint-Preux's propensity for the future citation contributes to this process: "C'est maintenant pour sa gloire que je dois vivre. Ah! que ne puis-je étonner le monde de mes vertus, afin qu'on pût dire un jour en les admirant: 'Pouvait-il moins faire? Il fut aimé de Julie!' " (p. 196). This verbal mechanism can take us very far in its implications, as we shall have occasion to see later, even to the point of reversing the

---

[27] So is motherhood: "le doux nom de mère" (p. 554), "l'honneur d'être mère" (p. 324).

apparently normal relation of things. An epigram such as "rien de ce qui touche à Julie n'est indifférent pour la vertu" (p. 518) would seem to have "Julie" and "vertu" in the wrong syntagmatic slots: simple hyperbolic slippage? Which, of virtue or Julie, is now more of an abstraction? Allegory ultimately threatens referentiality, even fictive.

The transparency of character which Jean Starobinski has so effectively analyzed[28] in *Julie* does not mean that everything uttered is perfectly literal. This remark may seem paradoxical, but it is quite clearly authorized, and even explicitly, in the text. Quite aside from questions of outright deceit — Julie once accuses Saint-Preux of dissimulation (p. 23) — Julie challenges his use of metaphor, not to mention *jargon du bel esprit*, stressing the equivalence in her eyes of pure sentiment and its pure expression: "je ne veux pas pour cela que l'amour soit toujours triste; mais je veux que sa gaieté soit simple, sans ornement, sans art, nue comme lui; qu'elle brille de ses propres grâces, et non de la parure du bel esprit" (p. 215). Saint-Preux in turn not only rejects this contention but argues, in effect, that the possibility of figureless discourse is an illusion: "Pour peu qu'on ait de chaleur dans l'esprit, on a besoin de métaphores et d'expressions figurées pour se faire entendre. Vos lettres mêmes en sont pleines sans que vous y songiez, et je soutiens qu'il n'y a qu'un géomètre et un sot qui puissent parler sans figures" (p. 217). Indeed she metaphorizes as spontaneously as he; the very letter scolding him, for instance, concludes with a comparison of Claire, before her marriage, to "une eau pure et calme [qui] commence à se troubler aux approches de l'orage." Ultimately, her reproach does not relate to metaphor in principle but to relative degrees of style, to affectation and contrived analogies; but the fact remains that the text is replete with figural expression which are no one's monopoly, even if Saint-Preux is more likely than others to use obvious oratorical devices such as apostrophe and anaphora.[29] After all, the idea of ornamentation associated with figures

---

[28] *Jean-Jacques Rousseau: la transparence et l'obstacle* (Paris: Plon, 1957, reed. Gallimard, 1971), ch. 5.
[29] Examples of apostrophes can be found on pp. 116, 121, and 314: but note that the latter is in a letter of Julie's; the most evident anaphora of Saint-Preux are on pp. 33-34 and 115; cf. Wolmar's on p. 718.

is not entirely foreign to their studied, lucid style. Julie herself *is* an ornament (p. 47) and "*orne* son âme de connaissances utiles; elle ajoute à son goût exquis les agréments des beaux arts" (p. 65). Saint-Preux equally, says Bomston, has "l'esprit *orné*" (p. 143).

Besides — simply put — not everything is said straightforwardly. Obliqueness serves a variety of purposes. On the one hand, there is the game of coding allusions in a somewhat playful manner: their little exchange over the "chalet" is obvious enough in its purpose and not without similarity to Mme de Ferval's *papiers* in *Le Paysan parvenu* or to Swann's and Odette's *cattleya*. But there is, too, a much more serious side. Indeed there is so much indirection in their discourse that it is not unusual for a reader new to *Julie* to finish part one quite unaware that Julie's and Saint-Preux's immaculate love has in fact been quite thoroughly consummated. Expression is hedged in ways that are important to the characters, and not just out of fear the letters will be intercepted: the code serves a function intrinsic to their own actions. The one time when Julie must really upbraid Saint-Preux for his indecency, he replies in consternation with a letter which, since it cannot dare broach an outright denial, displaces the whole discussion into abstractions and conditionals. Rather than assert, as he cannot, that he did not do what he is accused of, he in so many words asks rhetorically: how *could* I have done that? Himself deploring "les discours déshonnêtes," he says: "Julie, ange du ciel! dis moi comment je *pourrais* apporter devant toi l'effronterie qu'on ne peut avoir que devant celles qui l'aiment. Ah! non, il n'est pas possible. Un seul de tes regards *eût contenu* ma bouche et purifié mon cœur. L'amour *eût couvert* mes désirs emportés des charmes de ta modestie..." (p. 115). Then, avoiding the event in question, he cites as "proof" the delicacy with which he has made love to her: "Dis si, dans toutes les fureurs d'une passion sans mesure, je cessai jamais d'en respecter le charmant objet. Si je reçus le prix que ma flamme avait mérité, dis si j'abusai de mon bonheur pour outrager ta douce honte. Si d'une main timide l'amour ardent et craintif attenta quelquefois à tes charmes, dis si jamais une témérité brutale osa les profaner." All these "Dis si..." clauses call for an emphatic "Non!" in response from her, and the whole process serves to absolve Saint-Preux (as the conclusion of the letter makes clear) from any responsibility for what has, he will finally concede, happened.

Nor is Julie herself above dissimulation. Of course her pregnancy "project" is benign in that its secrecy serves Saint-Preux's interests; but another of her ellipses — this time a formal one in grammatical terms — is more ominous: "Nous serons séparés à jamais, et, pour comble d'horreur, je vais passer dans les... Hélas! j'ai pu vivre dans les tiens! Ô devoir! à quoi sers-tu?" (p. 307). At stake here is more than the word *bras* and the image of a *devoir* Julie shrinks from facing. For at this point she has hidden from Saint-Preux *for two years and more* (140 pages in the text) her knowledge that her hand in marriage has been formally promised to Wolmar. By now, the difficulty of revealing that fact is compounded with the discomfort of avowing her long dissimulation. The eclipse of a long illness which immediately follows spares her, finally, this necessity.

Much more evident overall than talk of deceit and miscomprehension is the confident tone of clear perceptions, of knowledge that has been mastered through intuition if not intellect. Frequently it takes on the sententious and highly literary form of the maxim, a general idea allied with a convention of terse formulation.[30] All the major characters produce such utterances. Taken from their immediate context, a reader would be hard-pressed to identify the specific authors of even such a small sample as the following: [31]

    a) Le vulgaire ne connaît point de violentes douleurs, et les grandes passions ne germent guère chez les hommes faibles. [p. 185]

    b) Si le plus méchant des hommes pouvait être un autre que lui-même, il voudrait être un homme de bien. [p. 200]

    c) Toutes les grandes passions se forment dans la solitude. [p. 79]

    d) Il n'est point de route plus sûre pour aller au bonheur que celle de la vertu. [p. 294]

    e) Remonte au principe, et toutes les règles s'expliqueront. [p. 484]

---

[30] Maxims bring to mind, of course, what the Editor calls La Rochefoucauld's "triste livre" (p. 352): a counterpoint rather than a model, because of its negativism.

[31] Julie (a-c), Claire (d-f), Saint-Preux (g-h), Edouard Bomston (i-j), Wolmar (k), the Editor (l).

f) L'amour veut faire tout son progrès lui-même; il n'aime point que l'amitié lui épargne la moitié du chemin. [p. 629]

g) Quiconque aime à se cacher a tôt ou tard raison de se cacher. [p. 406]

h) On a peu de désirs quand on souffre. [p. 665]

i) L'âme ne peut guère s'occuper fortement et longtemps d'un objet sans contracter des dispositions qui s'y rapportent. [pp. 168-69]

j) [Les] douleurs de l'âme ... pour vives qu'elles soient, portent toujours leur remède avec elles. [p. 369]

k) Le mariage est un état trop austère et trop grave pour supporter toutes les petites ouvertures de cœur qu'admet la tendre amitié. [p. 412]

l) Tout ce qui donne prise à l'imagination excite les idées et nourrit l'esprit. [p. 466]

Maxims proliferate as a function of the search for the widest possible statement of human truth, and all the characters use them because they all assert their own control, in one way or another, of knowledge of man. When someone says, "Discutons la proposition générale" (p. 357), it means that the rest of the discussion is going to take place on this level.

There is an obsession not only with maxims but with *maximes*, meaning not only sayings but guiding principles; a "maxime" is a truth if it is a good one — but most are bad. *Maximes* appears sixty-three times in the text in this way,[32] often qualified by a pejorative epithet such as *basses, viles, fières, empoisonnées,* or *honteuses. Sophisme* is usually a good synonym (eight occurrences); *règle, précepte* and *principe,* on the contrary, are more neutral or even positive. The insistent castigation of "maximes" constantly recalls the identity of the enemy: not merely the world in general with its nefarious wisdom, but that wisdom precisely in the form of enticing but satanic verbiage: "je hais les sophismes" (p. 42), says Julie, and Claire, "je hais les mauvaises maximes encore plus que les mauvaises actions" (p. 72). "Ô Julie!" writes Saint-Preux

---

[32] Exact totals obtained from the *T.L.F.* database; cf. note 96 below.

sarcastically from Paris, "nos cœurs grossiers n'ont jamais rien su de toutes ces belles maximes" (p. 226). Everything is predicated thus upon the sharing of privileged values.[33]

Such language does not simply provide mutual assurance of clarity of vision; it also serves to draw attention, insidiously, to terrible uncertainties which must be confronted through language. There is a need for formulaic knowledge to assuage anxieties, and its most extreme forms therefore may not correspond at all to areas of greatest security. Wolmar, precisely he who lacks transcendental faith, even attempts to condense everything into one metamaxim to rival the Golden Rule: "Un seul précepte de morale peut tenir lieu de tous les autres, c'est celui-ci: ne fais ni ne dis jamais rien que tu ne veuilles que tout le monde voie et entende" (p. 406). Here transparency and universal truth merge. There is a constant dialectic between truths derived from apparent outward consensus and those found in the inner recesses, but even this distinction will not always account for disparities of position. Saint-Preux returns from his voyage, according to Julie, less given than before to generalities of the first kind: "Je trouve ... qu'il est moins prompt à juger les hommes depuis qu'il en a beaucoup observé, moins pressé d'établir des propositions universelles depuis qu'il a tant vue d'exceptions, et qu'en général l'amour de la vérité l'a guéri de l'esprit de système" (p. 409); but this does not prevent his invoking "un usage constant de tous les peuples du monde" (p. 432) a little farther on. Despite much show of assurance, these characters grope for their truths, with especial anguish in the last half of the book where distinctions of words and facts become equally problematic. "Tout ce que je sais très certainement, c'est que si mes sentiments pour elle n'ont pas changé d'espèce, ils ont au moins changé de forme" (p. 407): the *certainement* tends to obscure an awareness that really Saint-Preux is begging the question, contending with something most unclear to him. He sorts it out neatly later by the clear division: "vous ne verrez jamais en moi que *l'ami* de votre personne et *l'amant* de vos vertus" (p. 663);[34] but the immediate

---

[33] Cf. second preface: "les écrits faits pour les solitaires ... doivent combattre et détruire les maximes des grandes sociétés, ils doivent les montrer fausses et méprisables, c'est-à-dire telles qu'elles sont (p. 748).

[34] She had already spiritualized the libido in her invitation: "soyez l'amant de mon âme" (p. 343).

context shows that this designates merely a formal version of a somewhat less regenerate state.

In some ways the most equivocal discourse of all is that of the Editor. His name, given on the title page, is explicitly "Jean-Jacques Rousseau," and he shares at least one authorship with the biographical Rousseau (the *Lettre à d'Alembert* [p. 439]), but he can still be discussed as an entity in terms of his role *in this text*.[35] Many of his notes concern routine forms of "annotation": explanation that certain letters have been suppressed, or abbreviated, or lost (and once he cites an extract from an omitted one); he glosses events and vocabulary. His apparent doubts about the purported diegetic facts,[36] lending to his role an aura of disinterested arbiter, lead him at times to cast doubt on the claims of the whole to credibility: "Ces lettres sont si pleines de semblables absurdités, que je n'en parlerai plus; il suffit d'en avoir averti" (p. 161). The sense of such intervention is, however, anything but univocal, as we shall see. As a disabused man of fifty (p. 207), on the other hand, he is not beyond ironizing on his own role (e.g., p. 81).

Far too from always maintaining a neutral posture with regard to sentiments expressed in the letters ("Je me garderai de prononcer sur cette lettre" [p. 256], he several times explicitly states his own opinion, and approves or disapproves that of a character; or sometimes his remarks appear a simple extension of those in the text (Bomston's p. 144, Saint-Preux's p. 227). Ostensible disapproval often takes the form of mild condescension, signaled by apostrophe: "Bonne Julie" (p. 198); "mon cher philosophe" (p. 244, cf. p. 669). But even a sarcasm in such circumstances can be carressing, as when he says, "les deux amants séparés ne font que déraisonner et battre la campagne; leurs pauvres têtes n'y sont plus" (p. 165), or "Le galimatias de cette lettre me plaît" (p. 511). For the flaw as perceived on one level is precisely a virtue viewed differently, and these editorial glosses, through irony, turn deviously on these two poles. He points out an "error" in Saint-Preux's reasoning, for instance, in order to say that he is after all correct: "Saint-Preux fait de la

---

[35] He has also had some sort of public quarrel with the Académie de Musique (p. 260).
[36] See examples pp. 145, 161, 375, 489, 498, 651.

conscience morale un sentiment, et non pas un jugement; ce qui est contre les définitions des philosophes. Je crois pourtant qu'en ceci leur prétendu confrère a raison" (p. 671: the sarcasm of *philosophe* is evident here too). And in condemning Saint-Preux's role in the Étange household, he nonetheless adds: "On sent pourtant qu'il aime sincèrement la vertu," and in the end he declares only the mother guilty (p. 59).

His real affection for the characters is thus expressed not directly but indirectly, sometimes by turning his commentary against the very things they oppose. Never unambiguously, however. France for example is played off against Switzerland through ironies usually damaging to her (e.g. p. 393), yet which suggest too a disparagement of the corrupting influences undermining the privileged Switzerland as well. Similarly, a lack of social graces tends to reflect less to the character's detriment than to that of society. "Douce Julie, à combien de titres vous allez vous faire siffler! Eh quoi! vous n'avez pas même le ton du jour!" (p. 277) constitutes approval of Julie and a backhand swipe at society (which is directly addressed in the following note, p. 278). But there is often no way to summarize just what these interventions "mean." He takes off from a serious distinction between the actual Julie and the one in Saint-Preux's imagination to make this remark about love:

> Vous êtes bien folles, vous autres femmes, de vouloir donner de la consistance à un sentiment aussi frivole et aussi passager que l'amour. Tout change dans la nature, tout est dans un flux continuel et vous voulez inspirer des feux constants! ... Mais changer sans cesse, et vouloir toujours qu'on vous aime, c'est vouloir qu'à chaque instant on cesse de vous aimer; ce n'est pas chercher des cœurs constants, c'est en chercher d'aussi changeants que vous. [p. 493]

Now this seems to satirize simultaneously the myth of love (or at least a certain practice utilizing the myth), the moral flippancy of society, libertine and/or materialist discourse, the caprices of fashion — and even the depreciation of love (what the women referred to are offending perhaps more than anything else is love itself). The Editor's stance is complex and defies simple categorization.

Numerous asides to the reader reveal that only an active intuition on his part can decide such questions. "C'est un pair d'Angleterre qui parle ainsi! et tout ceci ne serait pas une fiction!

Lecteur, qu'en dites-vous?" (p. 176) seems once more to beg the question of fictionality, as will the final note (p. 733) which adopts an "author's" perspective toward the characters.[37] But "fiction" itself is ambiguous, since it may connote simply whatever contrasts with conventional "maximes":[38] it then functions as an ironic swipe at a certain kind of reader, like the "c'est sûrement une fiction pour vous" of the preface. One of the many remarks in the footnotes on the supposed flaws of the letters ends with a curt cutoff which serves as a kind of *avis au lecteur:* "Au reste, sans prétendre justifier l'excessive longueur de plusieurs des lettres dont ce recueil est composé, je remarquerai que les lettres des solitaires sont longues et rares, celles des gens du monde fréquentes et courtes. Il ne faut qu'observer cette différence pour en sentir à l'instant la raison" (p. 543). *Sentir à l'instant* becomes a qualifying act of reading — the *only* one adequate to the text. There is a point beyond which logic will not go, or does not need to go. Based on such a sentimental tautology, which we will discuss later, a note like the following is a sarcastic way of baiting any reader not among what Stendhal would call the "happy few": "Pourquoi l'éditeur laisse-t-il les continuelles répétitions dont cette lettre est pleine, ainsi que beaucoup d'autres? Par une raison fort simple: c'est qu'il ne se soucie point du tout que ces lettres plaisent à ceux qui feront cette question" (p. 619). Certain kinds of resistance disqualify the questioner rather than eliciting a reasoned response. Thus the Editor's role, far from rectifying the complexities of the letters, compounds and overlays them with irony, leading perambulatorily to the only — however

---

[37] A similarly tantalizing posture is assumed in a note on p. 207, which, moreover, begins with a curious diegetic interference by the Editor: "Sans prévenir le jugement du lecteur *et celui de Julie* sur ces relations..." This kind of "authorial" game is more characteristic of the comic novel. Cf. too a perfectly ambiguous note on p. 584 regarding letters omitted: "Le lecteur dira qu'on se tire fort commodément d'affaire avec de pareilles omissions, et je suis tout à fait de son avis," which can be taken to mean either that one is perfectly well off without them, or that the author has gotten by with a cheap trick in refusing to present them.

[38] One of the hallmarks of these privileged characters is of course that they do *not* conform to exterior norms, cannot be analyzed through the spectacles of a La Bruyère or a La Rochefoucauld; cf. Wolmar: "Je sais bien que ma conduite a l'air bizarre, et choque toutes les maximes communes; mais les maximes deviennent moins générales à mesure qu'on lit mieux dans les cœurs; et le mari de Julie ne doit pas se conduire comme un autre homme" (p. 479).

flawed — truth the letters can themselves ultimately posit, that of sentiment. To say, "Quoi, Julie! aussi des contradictions!" in part six is to concede that an ideal is itself unfaithful: "Au reste, j'avoue que cette lettre me paraît le chant du cygne" (p. 682).

Love in particular, but also other intense human commitments, are seen as an investment of the self outwardly. Saint-Preux: "moi qui ne suis plus rien que par vous" (p. 57); "Je ne suis plus à moi, je l'avoue; mon âme aliénée est toute en toi" (p. 75). And Julie: "Sois tout mon être, à présent que je ne suis plus rien" (p. 77); "viens te réunir à toi-même" (p. 121). It can be seen that this implies a self-spending evacuation and alienation; the word *égarement* has a dozen similar uses in the text. The possibility of self-recuperation is problematic: Julie writes to Claire, "c'est à toi de me rendre à moi-même" (p. 17), and, by an opposite movement, to Saint-Preux: "Sépare-moi pour jamais de moi-même, donne-moi la mort s'il faut que je meure" (p. 152). Saint-Preux manifests even more radically than Julie the insubstantiality of the self when this literal alter-ego is withdrawn, or merely threatens to be. "Hélas! je commençais d'exister, et je suis tombé dans l'anéantissement" (p. 165); "je ne suis plus rien, un instant m'a tout ôté" (p. 167); "je ne suis plus rien à mes propres yeux" (p. 298). And, like Julie, "abandonné de moi-même" (p. 193), he invokes Claire, "daignez me rappeler à moi-même" (p. 196).

This language sounds similar to that used by Saint-Preux to describe the Parisians, whose influence even causes him to "oublier quelques instants ce que je suis et à qui" (p. 233). But there is a difference. The antidote to this influence is easily found in the thought of Julie: "Avec quel charme je rentre en moi-même.... Je sens respirer mon âme oppressée, je crois avoir recouvré mon existence et ma vie" (p. 233); whereas the alienated Parisian has no such recourse. For his existence is defined not by the investment of the self but in its dispersal, his only commitment being to society: "nul homme n'ose être lui-même" (p. 227); "les hommes y deviennent autres que ce qu'ils sont, et ... la société leur donne pour ainsi dire un être différent du leur" (p. 251). The Parisian is a void from start to finish, but at the same time less vulnerable to the radical disvestiture of the self that lies in wait for Julie and Sain-Preux.

As for Claire, she both emulates her cousin and intuits her very being. "Je me pare de toutes tes perfections, et c'est en toi que je place mon amour-propre le mieux entendu" (p. 182): nothing could be farther from La Rochefoucauld's *amour-propre* than one focused outside the self. Rather than feeling estranged, Claire though has defined her existence from the start through Julie: "Si tu n'avais pas été Julie, ... je ne sais ce que j'aurais été moi-même" (p. 628). There is in a sense no *moi-même* for Claire, who compensates for it with a more marked personality than Julie, one which lends her identity.[39] In a formal and highly literal sense, Claire gives herself up in marriage; as Julie says, "elle a aliéné sa liberté" because the husband is authorized to provide all the definitions: "s'il la blâme, elle est blâmable; et, fût-elle innocente, elle a tort sitôt qu'elle est soupçonnée" (p. 235). There is no way to *be* "innocent" or anything else in this situation. But in another way, doubtless facilitated by d'Orbe's early disparition, Claire retains a certain identity and thus through the transition between the two halves of the novel can provide an anchor: "je n'ai point changé pour vous," she says to Saint-Preux (p. 399).

Much of the problematics of the second half has to do with whether the same self is indeed still involved; the "je te verrais survivre à toi-même!" (p. 315) of Saint-Preux poses the question of continuity of the self such as it was posited in the first panel of the dyptique. The replacement of one Julie with another is not really accomplished by the formalities of the marriage contract but through the concomitant reinvestiture of the self by exterior agency. When she describes how God "me rend à moi-même" (p. 335) and asserts that Wolmar "m'en devient plus cher pour m'avoir rendue à moi-même" (p. 344), she postulates the recovery of a self no longer exclusively defined by Saint-Preux — perhaps not entirely a pre-Saint-Preux self (such is part of the dilemma), but at least an identifiable entity. She will never more admit to alienation until the day when it concerns only a separation from God to be bridged: "Mon âme aliénée est-elle en état de s'élever à lui?" (p. 703). Saint-

---

[39] A symptomatic passage suggesting the superficiality of her dominant personality trait is the following: "Tu sais bien que si je ris quand je pleure et n'en suis pas moins affligée, je ris aussi quand je gronde et n'en suis pas moins en colère" (p. 416). What essence then does the laughter have?

Preux for his part seeks a similar recovery; Meillerie will be, he hopes, "la crise qui me rendra tout à fait à moi" (p. 505); but the dream of the veil reveals still that, as Edouard puts it brutally, "vous n'êtes rien" (p. 604).

The most threatening form of alienation for them is posed by money: to receive it suggests being bought; the mercenary is the "vile" image of the alienated self.[40] One of the first and most tense disagreements between the lovers comes over money provided by Julie which Saint-Preux instinctively sees as dishonoring (pp. 39-41); and well he might, for d'Étange — himself, it is well worth noting, a mercenary[41] — unable to bear "owing" something to an inferior, will try to fix Saint-Preux in his place by putting a price on his services (p. 49). I think it has been much too little noted that Julie's last letter before the fatal fault bears this cry of rage: "Enfin mon père m'a donc *vendue*! Il fait de sa fille une *marchandise*, une esclave! Il s'acquitte *à mes dépens*! Il *paye* sa vie de la mienne!" (pp. 68-69). This violation of the self (in Julie's eyes) precipitates the fall; for although she says she has succumbed out of pity, one could equally well say she *gives herself* away to spite the father who sold her.[42]

Exchanges (and indeed d'Étange's promise of her hand to Wolmar was in the form of a gallant quid pro quo) are always threatening in this way when they are mediated. The genius of Wolmar's domestic economy is that it has no need for an abstract medium of exchange; Wolmar is "rich" only in productive resources, not in money, of which he has little, and this recalls the virtues of the Valais economy which Saint-Preux described in part one.[43] Love,

---

[40] "Je pense ... qu'il n'est pas permis de *s'aliéner* à des princes auxquels on ne doit rien, moins encore de *se vendre*, et de faire du plus noble métier du monde celui d'un *vil mercenaire*" (p. 82).

[41] As a nobleman, he is an officer of course, but inasmuch as he works for the French army he remains one of "les militaires de profession qui vendent leur sang à prix d'argent" (p. 133), and falls, as Saint-Preux is well aware, under the anathema quoted in the previous note.

[42] The assimilation of her situation to that of a prostitute is suggested indirectly by her remarks later about the possibility that Saint-Preux might succumb to the temptations of a servant: "Ah! périsse l'homme indigne qui marchande un cœur et rend l'amour mercenaire! ... Comment ne serait pas toujours à vendre celle qui se laisse acheter une fois?" (p. 656).

[43] "En effet, à quoi dépenser de l'argent dans un pays où les maîtres ne reçoivent point le prix de leurs frais, ni les domestiques celui de leurs soins,

however, delights in money metaphors because the tables are turned: the "debts" contracted in a loving enchange are free from constraint and unmediated. In this context they evoke a pure generosity and joyful consummation: "ce soir même peut acquitter mes promesses, et payer d'une seule fois toutes les dettes de l'amour" (p. 120).[44]

If the self is harder to relocate for Saint-Preux than for Julie, it is because it was epistemologically less well endowed to begin with. Claire qualifies him "un petit bourgeois sans fortune,"[45] and his lack of adequate social standing is indicated by many other symbols, most overtly the baron's disdain for him and his whole class of "jeunes gens sans état et sans nom" (p. 148). For him, Saint-Preux is not socially "capable" of repairing a girl's honor (because he could not be accepted in marriage, which is the reparation an equal would offer) and is not even worthy of matching his sword (pp. 147-48). Despite his ire, d'Étange underscores his daughter's station precisely by repeatedly calling her *chère fille* (pp. 150-51): there is no one to call Saint-Preux *cher fils*. On the d'Étange social stratum, Saint-Preux can only be a supernumerary: "que peut-on croire qu'il fait ici?" (p. 126) asks Claire. *Sans nom* is d'Étange's way of putting all that in a nutshell. To have a "name" is to be invested with a being, a socially valid definition; the only names he has for Saint-Preux are ciphers like *quidam* — "noms injurieux à un homme d'honneur" (p. 143). Nor could the text itself symbolize this more forcefully than by representing Saint-Preux as a man without a name — "cet amant anonyme," quips the Editor (p. 161).[46] Saint-Preux is a name invented by Claire during the smallpox episode, and which she decides he will keep (pp. 311, 399).[47] All

---

et où l'on ne trouve aucun mendiant? Cependant l'argent est fort rare dans le Haut-Valais; mais c'est pour cela que les habitants sont à leur aise" (p. 54).

[44] Cf.: "Avec quel plaisir tu dois voir augmenter sans cesse les dettes que l'amour s'oblige à payer!" (p. 99).

[45] His is also ambiguously styled "honnête," but this adjective is applied equally to Claude Anet and Fanchon, who clearly have no social rank (p. 98). For a thorough and illuminating discussion of the proper understanding of Saint-Preux's social status, see J. S. Spink, "The Social Background of Saint-Preux and d'Étange," in *French Studies*, 30, No. 2 (1976), pp. 153-69.

[46] See too Tony Tanner's discussion of this point in *Adultery in the Novel* (Baltimore and London: Johns Hopkins, 1979), p. 138.

[47] There is every reason to think that both the sanctimonious and the chivalric implications of this double name are willful, particularly since the pseudonym Julie herself confers on one occasion, M. du Bosquet (p. 236), has

we know of his "real" name is that its initials are S. G. (p. 306); he is never named in these pages anything but Saint-Preux.[48]

"Sans famille et presque sans patrie" (p. 47), Saint-Preux also has no home to revert to, topographically and epistemologically, when he is thrust forth from Vevey. The whole world becomes undifferentiated: "Ne suis-je pas désormais partout en exil?" (p. 396). Part and parcel of Wolmar's attempt to "cure" him is to provide him in the second half of the story with a home, with a room which will be his — which will be *empty* if he is not there to occupy it (p. 404). For a long transition period, Julie, who had asked never to hear his name again spoken (p. 296), apparently respects the pseudonym, until she breaks her epistolary silence and once more writes his true — but still mysterious — name (p. 662).

It is thus not a purely "psychological" dimension which determines Julie's ascendancy over Saint-Preux. His passivity begins under the aegis of romantic obeisance, as he writes in his second letter, "daignez au moins disposer de mon sort; ... je ne saurai qu'obéir" (p. 9). This sort of language keeps up for a long while and in truth never ceases to operate, but it becomes imbued with a constraint that is not simply gallant. Julie's "laissez-vous conduire" (p. 29) signals the launching of her "projects" which require Saint-Preux's uncomprehending submission: "votre âme a deux corps à gouverner" (p. 48), he writes. Further on, there are allusions to a formal obligation which she invokes more than once,[49] and many references, by no means all in jest, to her "orders." And just as Julie sometimes gets tough in the tone of her early letters (I.9 and I.17 particularly), she can be pretty stern on the matter of who is entitled, between them, to take initiatives: "ne sens-tu pas," she even says once, "que tu ne peux rien à notre bonheur que de n'y point mettre obstacle?" (p. 111).

---

an obvious relation to their own private mythology. (The only invented names in the novel are apparently Saint-Preux and d'Étange, but the latter is close to a village name of Étagnières.)

[48] Only three times in letters (pp. 399, 614, 659), and twice in footnotes (pp. 311, 662). The letter headings naming him, such as "De Saint-Preux à Milord Edouard," are not part of the original edition but derive from the synoptic tables developed for the Duchesne edition of 1764. Cf. supra, n. 7.

[49] "J'use en cette occasion du droit que vous m'avez donné vous-même" (p. 135); cf. pp. 138 ("mon vœu d'obéissance"), 330. On this subject cf. again Tanner, p. 117.

All the ideas, indeed, are hers. Saint-Preux responds with passion, but it is Julie who offers and stages the kiss in the bower, and subsequently — at a moment, it is true, of exceptional aggressive courage on her part ("une hardiesse que je n'eus jamais") — the nocturnal rendez-vous which she bills as "le prix de ton obéissance et de tes sacrifices" (pp. 120-21). "Il fera tout ce que tu lui commanderas" (p. 126), remarks Claire, who later notes his weakish quintessence in referring to him as "cette âme simple, qui ne cherche, pour ainsi dire, qu'à s'accrocher à ce qui t'environne" (p. 162). As he endows her kisses with phallic force ("trop pénétrants," "ils percent, ils brûlent jusqu'à la moelle" [p. 38]), she flinches at signs of effeminate plaintiveness in him (p. 189) and congratulates him on the return of "cette vigueur de sentiments qui convient au courage d'un homme!" (p. 197).[50] Some years later, she will recall somewhat uncharitably that she saw in him "je ne sais quelle contenance servile et basse dont tu t'es plus d'une fois moquée avec raison" (p. 409).

But if anything, this tendency is exacerbated in the second half, where Saint-Preux lives a totally tributary existence. At Clarens, as he puts it himself, he is taken possession of (p. 403); and it is now to Bomston that he is, to the extent that any career aspirations remain, "attached" (p. 419). He indeed considers himself, as does everyone else, "l'enfant de la maison" (p. 511). "Nous avons pris une si grande habitude de le gouverner," confesses Claire, "que nous sommes un peu responsables de lui" (p. 416): so the Saint-Preux who once was free to drink himself under the table now has his wine meted to him by the two sollicitous cousins (p. 596). To be sure, such language thus isolated gives him a tendenciously feeble outline, for he does manifest in counterpoint what Claire call "male" vigor of thought (p. 156). As he says, he takes with Julie the tone sometimes of father and sometimes of child, and she replies in kind: "Votre lettre est, comme votre vie, sublime et rampante, pleine de force et de puérilités. Mon cher philosophe, ne cesserez-vous jamais d'être enfant?" (pp. 674-75).

---

[50] This exchange precedes, although in some ways it relates to, the discussion of the loss of proper sexual identity in Parisian society, where women are bold and men effeminate.

How in truth could it be otherwise, without a father (inexistent to the text)? For Julie the father's role is critical. "Ma mère est faible et sans autorité" (p. 13): the least one can say is that the opposite goes for the father, who is most often characterized — and not for Julie alone — by his severity, pride, violence, and arrogance. Only during his absence is she vulnerable to Saint-Preux. But she is, of course, highly ambivalent toward him. There is an unquestionable element of erotic attraction in his contact: "quel charme c'est de sentir, dans ces purs et sacrés embrassements, le sein d'un père palpiter d'aise contre celui de sa fille" (p. 45).[51] On the other hand, there is a repulsion which asserts itself most clearly in Julie's argument against duelling, where her father's example enters into her disgust. Above all, she feels guilty, even without him, but unbearably in his presence: "le remords déchire et la honte écrase en sa présence" (p. 148). Guilt stalks her but not Saint-Preux, as she herself remarks: "la honte qui m'humilie est sans dédommagement.... Mais toi qui n'as nulle violence à craindre, que la honte n'avilit point..." (p. 189). She cannot quite perceive here the equivalence between violence (feared) and shame (experienced). The violence is real, and not merely because the beating she receives at her father's hands destroys the promised seed and thereby her "project." Its threat is heavier yet: for neither Julie herself, nor Claire, nor her mother — those who know d'Étange best — ever doubts that if he knew the truth about what had transpired between Julie and Saint-Preux, he would *kill* his daughter.[52] This murder, though unrealized, is constantly present in the text. Indeed it underlies Julie's plan at more than one stage, first of all because she imagines that they may very well be caught during their night of love and that this will solve all problems by prompt and mutual death (p. 121), and then because, by declaring her

---

[51] On this subject, and in particular for a commentary on the scenes of crisis and reconciliation with her father, see once more Tanner, p. 121 and *passim*.

[52] This is expressed indirectly several times, but directly also: "Si mon père les [lettres] voit, c'est fait de ma vie!" (p. 285); Claire evokes "une mère tremblante pour les jours de sa fille [qui] veut cacher ce dangereux secret" (p. 288), who feared to expose her daughter's life (p. 302); and d'Étange himself writes to Saint-Preux that Julie "ne serait plus si j'osais soupçonner qu'elle eût porté plus loin l'oubli d'elle-même" (p. 305).

pregnancy openly before a minister, "je savais que mon père me donnerait la mort ou mon amant" (p. 324).

Yet it is she who is accused of killing, and who, having internalized the value system, accuses herself of what is, significantly enough, called *parricide* (p. 295) — the only term available at the time for designating murder of a kinsman. "Ah! veux-tu donner la mort à toute la famille?" (p. 327), d'Étange asks her in one of his moments of sentimental extortion. (The consummate irony here is that, according to Claire, it is d'Étange who is the parricide, having by his many infidelities driven his wife to the grave [p. 302].) Needless to say, Julie is easily touched by any overture on her father's part, and if anything, his brutality, which he blames not on himself but on Saint-Preux,[53] eases the reconciliation with his daughter who, torn between guilt and revolt, "[serait] trop heureuse d'être battue tous les jours au même prix" (p. 151). His rivalry with Saint-Preux is, on different levels, both explicit and implicit. Virtue, according to Julie, will not at this stage help her choose between conflicting duties (p. 177). And it is true, as Saint-Preux says, that "la chaîne qui nous lie est la borne du pouvoir paternel" (p. 305): that is why it must yield, and indeed this apparently challenging remark comes in his letter of capitulation to the father's irresistible victory.

Order is the superego's legacy from the father, and to it Julie will consecrate her married life. Wolmar is himself a father, not merely because he is her father's companion in arms and a good deal older than she, but also because of his sense of authority symbolized by his ineradicable, controlling presence.[54] Julie must believe in his infallibility,[55] and the resistance will be overcome by his role as their common father: he is Saint-Preux's savior too, like God.[56]

---

[53] "Je le hais, surtout à présent, pour les excès qu'il m'a fait commettre, et ne lui pardonnerai jamais ma brutalité" (p. 151).

[54] That is, he is present whether present or absent. "Mais vivez dans le tête-à-tête," he says to her and Saint-Preux, "comme si j'étais présent, ou devant moi comme si je n'y étais pas" (p. 406). Indeed Wolmar is even more present when absent: cf. Saint-Preux's remark p. 495: "Je me sens plus contraint qu'en sa présence même."

[55] "Claire, il est impossible que Wolmar me trompe, *et qu'il se trompe*" (p. 615).

[56] Saint-Preux to Wolmar: "J'étais mort aux vertus ainsi qu'au bonheur; je vous dois cette vie morale à laquelle je me sens renaître. Ô mon bienfaiteur!

But the constraint has not disappeared from this role, it has only become benign and nonviolent; the description we have of Clarens as a community modeled on the family (p. 427) is one where duty implants itself within the will, so that the subjects "pensent vouloir tout ce qu'on les oblige de faire" (p. 436). Wolmar is not, positively speaking, a deist, but he is in this sense a deist's God: "On y reconnaît toujours la main du maître et l'on ne la sent jamais" (p. 351). He is the very personification of order.[57]

Once the violence which has displaced choice has had its effect, Julie totally subscribes to its formal consequences, not recognizing that things *should* be so[58] (although she does affirm that arbitrary authority has done *better* by her than she could have done by herself), but engaging herself totally as once and future wife, and if not wife, then widow.[59] In marrying, she opts for identifying virtue, heretofore ambiguous, with a social system which is guarantor of order and peace. It coincides in the broadest way with self-interest, because the family is the social base, and its bonds — in particular that of conjugal fidelity — congruent with the body politic.[60] The order that reigns at Clarens is tied to sexual as it is to other temperances.[61] At the same time, it achieves an esthetic ideal where the dichotomy of *utile/agréable* is transcended[62] and even its

---

Ô mon père! En me donnant à vous tout entier, je ne puis vous offrir, comme à Dieu même, que les dons que je tiens de vous" (p. 598).

[57] "Mon seul principe actif est le goût naturel de l'ordre" (p. 474).

[58] There is no final statement on this matter, though Bomston argues that neither love nor reason should absolutely govern the matter of marriage (p. 170): he posits a new social order founded upon choice (love) and merit (the new form of rank), and will seek to promote Saint-Preux via talent into the new aristocracy.

[59] Wolmar "laissera du moins une chaste veuve" (p. 353): this projection, already a defense mechanism against the eventuality of a Princesse de Clèves-type situation, tries to seal off all contingencies.

[60] "Je veux être fidèle, parce que c'est le premier devoir qui lie la famille et toute la société" (p. 336); "il intervient un engagement tacite de tout le genre humain de respecter ce lien sacré ... sans lequel rien ne peut subsister dans l'ordre légitime des choses humaines" (p. 339).

[61] "Dans une maison bien réglée les hommes et les femmes doivent avoir peu de commerce entre eux" (p. 432).

[62] "Partout on a substitué l'utile à l'agréable, et l'agréable y a presque toujours gagné" (p. 424).

magnificence is simply order so perfectly prescribed that anything superfluous would be an impoverishment.[63]

If order played no such role in the novel's first half, that was not because of any bias for disorder, but rather because it was assumed that the world's order was safely in the hands of nature, with which the characters themselves have an implicit alliance. They know that *their* nature is impelling them beyond social constraints, but this is subservient to their assurance that desire is, in effect, the voice of predestination.[64] For Bomston, that is not merely a romantic notion but a matter of dogma: "Ces deux belles âmes sortirent l'une pour l'autre des mains de la nature.... Pourquoi faut-il qu'un insensé préjugé vienne changer les directions éternelles et bouleverser l'harmonie des êtres pensants?" (p. 169). They love nature by intuition and by design, believing implicitly in its availability for observation[65] and seeking its arbitration; even the priority accorded mimetic (Italian) music is rationalized by its relation to nature. Paris is, of course, the very antithesis of nature: there the natural is systematically displaced, and first of all in the moral domain, where *pudeur* is relegated to the common folk and *impudence* takes its pedestal (p. 245). In the city lives "l'homme de l'homme au lieu de celui de la nature" (p. 540).

Needless to say, however, this line of reasoning (really never more than an adjunct of their other systems of thought) easily runs into impasses. The difference of sexual roles, male and female, is entirely ordained by nature: this is a theme of the novel and Julie has no problem with it in essence;[66] but did nature equally authorize paternal authority when it is tyranny, and if so why does it counter love, that other voice of nature? "Je serais à lui si l'ordre humain n'eût troublé les rapports de la nature" (p. 319), writes Julie early in her great letter of recapitulation. She has faced a sort

---

[63] "Ajoutez-y du galon, des tableaux, un lustre, de la dorure, à l'instant vous appauvrirez tout" (p. 533).

[64] "Pourquoi rendre incompatible ce que la nature a voulu réunir?" (p. 26); "le ciel et la nature nous avaient unis l'un à l'autre" (p. 346).

[65] "Le bon et l'honnête ne dépendent point du jugement des hommes, mais de la nature des choses" (p. 132).

[66] See pp. 102-3 in particular. "Ce qui nous sépare des hommes," writes Claire later, "c'est la nature elle-même" (p. 484).

of Corneillian situation where neither nature nor reason could be consulted with any confidence.[67] Saint-Preux at his point of greatest despair asks whether any action can really be decided by consulting God's or nature's laws: "Faut-il ne rien faire en ce monde de peur d'enfreindre ses lois, et, quoi que nous fassions, pouvons-nous jamais les enfreindre?" (p. 363). This notion is remarkably bold, for if one cannot, in fact, offend nature by violating its laws (to which, in offending, one would still be subject), then absolutely everything one can do is natural: and that is precisely what Sade will assert. Subsequent to such a defiance, the Saint-Preux who then calls Clarens "un état si conforme à la nature" (p. 540) seems toothlessly domesticated; and even aside from that, the engineered version of natural appearance which is Clarens' forte must itself come under critical scrutiny.

"Nature, ô douce nature! reprends tous tes droits; j'abjure les barbares vertus qui t'anéantissent. Les penchants que tu m'as donnés seront-ils plus trompeurs qu'une raison qui m'égara tant de fois?" (p. 314). This exclamation, which thus isolated appears to represent rather well the priority of nature over reason in *Julie,* is in fact a temporary conclusion coming at what will later be identified as Julie's moment of greatest aberration from true principles: this fact alone well illustrates how problematic are the fundamental logical relationships between different sources of value. For both nature and reason are, as well, sources of error. Reason is deceptive in several ways, the first being that, *pace* Descartes, its mechanics are unreliable. The proper corrective then lies in a perception more intimate than the clear and simple idea: "Je me suis souvent trouvée en faute sur mes raisonnements, jamais sur les mouvements secrets qui me les inspirent, et cela fait que j'ai plus de confiance à mon instinct qu'à ma raison" (p. 235).[68] Worse still, reason can corrupt truth and become a tool of seduction; Julie alerts Saint-Preux that "la mauvaise compagnie a commencé par abuser votre raison pour corrompre votre vertu" (p. 277). Indeed the most damning thing

---

[67] Claire writes: "Mais ici, quelque parti que tu prennes, la nature l'autorise et le condamne, la raison le blâme et l'approuve, le devoir se tait ou s'oppose à lui-même; les suites sont également à craindre de part et d'autre; tu ne peux ni rester indécise ni bien choisir" (p. 178).

[68] Cf. Saint-Preux: "[j'abhorre] ces honteuses maximes ... sans savoir les combattre; et ma conscience y répond mieux que ma raison" (p. 317).

about reason is the company it keeps: the philosophers — "dangereux raisonneurs" (p. 338), "tristes raisonneurs" with their "arguments subtils" (p. 199).[69] Their stance here betrays a degree of fear and insecurity before logical discussion, a tool which tends to get out of hand and turn against them. It is then subversive, almost irresistably so, as Saint-Preux shows in his Parisian letters:

> Si quelquefois j'essaie de secouer les préjugés et de voir les choses comme elles sont, à l'instant je suis écrasé d'un certain verbiage qui ressemble beaucoup à du raisonnement. On me prouve avec évidence qu'il n'y a que le demi-philosophe qui regarde à la réalité des choses; que le vrai sage ne les considère que par les apparences; qu'il doit prendre les préjugés pour principes, les bienséances pour lois, et que la plus sublime sagesse consiste à vivre comme les fous. [p. 233]

Here it is not the philosophers but the Parisians who abuse reason and in whose society "toute la morale est un pur verbiage" (p. 226). A clear criterion of discrimination is lacking: how is one to distinguish "un pur verbiage qui *ressemble beaucoup* à du raisonnement" from real reason? Because of this failure, all reasoning is suspect; whereas there is no such thing as a similarly false voice "qui ressemble beaucoup à la *conscience*."

Still, this is to overlook the fact that reason is very important indeed, not just to the likes of Edouard and Wolmar, but to Julie and Saint-Preux themselves. In their letters to each other they have frequent recourse to reason; "voilà le principe sur lequel il faut raisonner" (p. 127), says for example Julie. However great a role sentiment plays as the novel develops, it does not do so simply at the expense of reason,[70] which if anything becomes progressively

---

[69] These phrases are Julie's; Saint-Preux says likewise: "ah! ne me parlez plus de philosophie: je méprise ce trompeur étalage qui ne consiste qu'en vains discours" (p. 196).

[70] Christie Vance has written: "Julie and Saint-Preux see their passion alternatively as being natural (and divinely inspired) or base (and denatured).... When passion is viewed as sacred, predestined and blessed by nature, they refer to the world of *sentiment*. When, on the other hand, *raison* is evoked, passion is seen as corrupting" (*The Extravagant Shepherd: A Study of the Pastoral Vision in Rousseau's "La Nouvelle Héloïse"*, Studies on Voltaire and the Eighteenth Century, Vol. 105, 1973, p. 79). Despite the merits of her discussion, however, this opposition seems to me too schematic.

more important. For Julie, this is because it has strayed from its true origin and must return there; in the same letter that states, "mes prières n'étaient que des mots, mes raisonnements des sophismes" (p. 336), she identifies the way for moving from bad reasoning to good: "Mais où chercher la saine raison, sinon dans celui qui en est la source, et que penser de ceux qui consacrent à perdre les hommes ce flambeau divin qu'il leur donna pour les guider?" (p. 341). Divine light is then not the exclusive province of feeling as opposed to logic, but the text provides us with no complete synthesis of these oppositions. For Julie even goes so far as to give at one point a distinct priority to reason in terms that are remarkably decisive (if not, perhaps, definitive): "le cœur nous trompe en mille manières, et n'agit que par un principe toujours suspect; mais la raison n'a d'autre fin que ce qui est bien; ses règles sont sûres, claires, faciles dans la conduite de la vie" (p. 349). Julie thus moves toward intellectual control of her destiny. "Je ne comptais que sur ta vertu," Claire writes to her, "et je commence à compter aussi sur ta raison" (p. 415). The "raison qui m'égara tant de fois" in the passage cited earlier in fact refers *not* to false and corrupting reason, but to true and right reason — one which was momentarily overwhelmed by nature.

Although Saint-Preux is the book's "philosophe," his gift for reason is severely tempered by the leeway given his imagination. Its most charming functions are erotic:

> Je n'ai traîné dans mon exil que la moindre partie de moi-même: tout ce qu'il a de vivant en moi demeure auprès de vous sans cesse. Il erre impunément sur vos yeux, sur vos lèvres, sur votre sein, sur tous vos charmes; il pénètre partout comme une vapeur subtile, et je suis plus heureux en dépit de vous que je ne fus jamais de votre gré.... La vie active qui me rappelle à moi tout entier m'est insupportable. [pp. 42-43]

Similarly, one can compare what he says about the sensual satisfactions afforded by Julie's modest attire — "L'œil avide et téméraire s'insinue impunément sous les fleurs d'un bouquet, il erre sous la chenille et la gaze, et fait sentir à la main la résistance élastique qu'elle n'oserait éprouver" (p. 56) — with the more brazenly revealed but less exciting bodices of the Parisians: "Quoique je n'aie aperçu ces objets que de fort loin, l'inspection en est si libre qu'il reste peu de chose à deviner. Ces dames paraissent mal entendre en cela leurs intérêts; car, pour peu que le visage soit agréable, l'imagination du spectateur les servirait au surplus beaucoup mieux que ses yeux" (p. 243). For in the first instance the eye does not operate directly; what it sees is veiled and imagination supplies the rest. But when Saint-Preux dwells with the same intensity on less delightful subject matter, his thoughts run amok. If on the one hand what is dreamed outruns real pleasures, it is equally true, as he says of himself, that "l'imagination va toujours plus loin que le mal" (p. 499), and Julie warns him of "pièges de l'imagination" (p. 655). Excitement threatens the coherence of his discourse,[71] and, even in the letter where he mentions the need to bring it under control, he repeatedly alludes to extreme agitation: "je suffoquais"; "mon imagination troublée ne me présentait que des objets confus.... Enfin je puis dire n'avoir de ma vie éprouvé d'agitation plus cruelle"; "un transport sacré"; "presque oppressé d'aise"; "cet état violent" (p. 402-4). Now it is true that these pages describe a paroxystic moment by any criterion, that of Saint-Preux's return to Julie and Clarens; but the language is no stronger than that found in numerous other passages. One cannot imagine Julie using the same terms, for she has, as Claire describes it, a sort of internal feedback mechanism that moderates her behavior: "votre amour à tous deux, quoique égal en force, n'est pas semblable en effets; le vôtre est bouillant et vif, le sien est doux et tendre; vos sentiments s'exhalent au dehors avec véhémence, les siens retournent sur elle-même, et, pénétrant la substance de son âme, l'altèrent et la changent insensiblement" (p. 303). That opposition, minus Claire's analysis, had been évoked by Saint-Preux himself: "je veux jouir, et tu veux aimer; j'ai des transports, et toi de la passion; tous mes emportements ne valent pas ta délicieuse langueur" (p. 124). *Emportements* is indeed a word often applied to him by others too,[72] and Edouard Bomston's remarks about the indistinguishability of Julie and Saint-

---

[71] "Mes idées sont trop vives pour se succéder; elles se présentent toutes ensemble; elles se nuisent mutuellement. Je vais m'arrêter et reprendre haleine pour tâcher de mettre quelque ordre dans mon récit" (p. 400).

[72] "Un homme aussi emporté que vous," "vos emportements" (pp. 324-25); "tu a trop d'emportement" (p. 111).

Preux (p. 173) must be taken as relating to their moral character rather than to their temperaments in the strong, physiological sense.

Several times Saint-Preux describes in the early pages the ecstasies of love in terms of *délire*.[73] "Ce que tu me fais éprouver approche d'un vrai délire, et je crains d'en perdre enfin la raison" (p. 91): it is moot at what point simple hyperbole fades into the realities of hypersensitivity. At Meillerie he evokes "les violents transports qui m'agitent" (p. 64). The word *délire* returns for the first kiss and for the night of love as it does for the effects of wine. Several times *délire* along with related terms such as "fureur" and "insensé désespoir" (p. 193) accompany his removal to Paris. There, Julie's letters have the same effect: "En les relisant je perds la raison, ma tête s'égare dans un *délire* continuel, un feu dévorant me consume, mon sang s'allume et pétille, une *fureur* me fait tressaillir" (p. 220). Then the setback of the discovered letters brings on *rage* and the *délire* of suicide (pp. 292, 367). The return to Meillerie occasions "des accès de fureur et de rage ... la crise de ma *folie* et de mes maux" (pp. 504, 511), as the return to the room at Sion brings "une extase, un ravissement, un délire" (p. 602). As Edouard's actions also show in the latter instance, there is often concern at these moments over Saint-Preux's ability to control himself. He never really does lose control, though, and when pushed to the limit of bearable emotion tends rather to lapse into a sort of syncope.[74]

In order to realize that such allusions to states approaching folly are not innocently metaphorical in import, one need only think of the transition from the banter about Claire's craziness — she even says, when discussing the idea she should have married Saint-Preux: "que je sois folle ou non, je l'aurais infailliblement rendu fou" (p. 628) — to her close scrape with delirium at the end, not to mention the collective folly[75] and that with which Julie herself in

---

[73] *Égarement* also appears several times with this gist (e.g., pp. 38, 75, 91, 196, 273), as do other terms, for example: "les fougueuses saillies d'une imagination téméraire" (p. 37).

[74] During the smallpox scene: "En passant dans l'antichambre les forces lui manquèrent; il respirait avec peine, et fut contraint de s'asseoir" (p. 311); cf. the moments before his reunion with Julie as described on p. 402, and the general failing of the grand reunion on p. 585.

[75] "Tout le monde est dans le transport ... la tête avait tourné à mes propres gens" (p. 723).

fact felt threatened.[76] Claire's ravings and convulsions at Julie's death are described by Wolmar (pp. 722, 726-27) with great concern lest she slip irretrievably into alienation. This is why, in fact, he puts an end to Henriette's imitation of Julie, however therapeutic it may have been for the others involved.

Clinical differences aside, there is of course a distinction to be made on sound rhetorical grounds between such scenes and ones where Saint-Preux describes *his own* behavior. There is enough testimony from others to show that his *emportements* and *délires* are neither mere figments of his imagination nor improvised acts;[77] nonetheless they cannot but be structured by the way he wishes, consciously or otherwise, to represent them. Needless to say, some of the scenes quoted or alluded to here have erotic overtones; indeed Saint-Preux describes his explicit sexual ecstasies in very similar terms. I have no quarrel with analogies one might make between his descriptions of great excitement of whatever sort and orgasmic rhythms. Nevertheless, one is induced by the text into a simple literalistic trap if adequate heed is not taken of the rhetorical instance. A case in point is Tony Tanner's commentary of letter I.54, written in Julie's boudoir while Saint-Preux awaits her, passionately contemplating her underthings:

> Julie! ma charmante Julie! je te vois, je te sens partout, je te respire avec l'air que tu as respiré; tu pénètres toute ma substance: que ton séjour est brûlant et douloureux pour moi! Il est terrible à mon impatience. Ô viens, vole, ou je suis perdu.
> Quel bonheur d'avoir trouvé de l'encre et du papier! J'exprime ce que je sens pour en tempérer l'excès; je donne le change à mes transports en les décrivant. [p. 122]

As Tanner constructs it, what effectively transpires here is this:

> At this stage he is clearly on the point of involuntary orgasm or masturbation. Then — and we should not attribute this to the exigencies and constraints of the epistolary

---

[76] "Qui sait si, me voyant si près de l'abîme, la tête ne m'eût point tourné?" (p. 728).

[77] Julie: "Je le vis, dans des agitations *convulsives,* prêt à s'évanouir à mes pieds" (p. 70).

mode — he seeks relief in writing.... To a modern reader this moment is comic indeed; but in fact it has far-reaching reverberations. Saint-Preux is indeed forced away from the body of the loved other, and into writing, an inherently solitary activity.[78]

This is a reasonable reading of what is *represented* but it shunts aside a critical matter of *representation*. For in no literal sense can the pen and ink have been found at the point in the passage where Saint-Preux *says* "Quel bonheur d'avoir trouvé de l'encre et du papier!": he found them before he started writing the whole letter. There is a symbolic, *rhetorical* displacement from a masturbatory situation to a writing one, and one which is profoundly revealing of the function of writing for Saint-Preux. But that function is not purely and simply to tell what "happened": it involves his own role-playing and persuasive intentions, not to mention his unconscious, and, more abstractly, the problems of language and expression.

Certainly there is, willfully or not, plenty of voluptuousness in Saint-Preux's language. The kiss in the bower provokes a powerful paroxysm for both of them — his controlled by lyrical sublimation: "Le feu s'exhalait avec nos soupirs de nos lèvres brûlantes, et mon cœur se mourait sous le poids de la volupté..."; and hers, a physical syncope: "...quand tout à coup je te vis pâlir, fermer tes beaux yeux, t'appuyer sur ta cousine, et tomber en défaillance" (p. 38). This leads him to suggest something further, mixing metaphor and suggestion: "il faut enfin que j'expire à tes pieds... ou dans tes bras" (p. 39).[79] But much of the eroticism he expresses comes from exercises of the imagination: he savors a symbolic ecstacy ("je passais le torrent lentement, avec délices" [p. 57]) and savors at a distance, with the help of a phallic telescope, pleasures not yet experienced directly: "à travers les airs et les murs il [= je] ose pénétrer jusque dans ta chambre. Tes traits charmants le frappent encore; tes regards tendres raniment son cœur mourant; il entend le son de ta douce voix; il ose chercher encore en tes bras ce délire qu'il éprouva dans le bosquet. Vain fantôme d'une âme agitée qui

---

[78] *Adultery in the novel*, p. 122.
[79] It must be remembered that at the time the terms *mourir* and *expirer* were current in gallant contexts for orgasm; Saint-Preux may be far from such jargonistic "intention," but cannot control what the words imply.

s'égare dans ses désirs!" (p. 65). He is excited too by the physical intimacy of Julie with Claire [80] and, implicitly, by the sound of Italian music.[81] His metaphors of love are frequently, sensuously ambiguous: "ces plaisirs célestes" (p. 166), "cette suprême félicité" (p. 167). An expression of his platonic sympathy with Julie becomes agressively sexual: "les puissants élancements de deux cœurs l'un vers l'autre ont toujours une volupté secrète ignorée des âmes tranquilles" (p. 221).

In Julie's case it is rather something else that seems to transpire. Her first simulacrum of an orgasmic experience comes with what is, to her, surprising gentleness (it must be remembered that she thought "nul intervalle" separated the first step from the ultimate one) when she has first answered to Saint-Preux's expressions of love: "je n'eus pas parlé, que je me trouvai *soulagée*; vous n'eûtes pas répondu, que je me sentis tout à fait *calme*.... Que ne puis-je vous apprendre à jouir tranquillement...!" (p. 25). This is the perfect stage. The sexual experience itself on the other hand produces a rather acute, though terminologically veiled, withdrawal. In his first letter to her after their first tryst, Saint-Preux concedes, "mes emportements t'effrayent, mon délire te fait pitié, et tu ne sens pas que toute la force humaine ne peut suffire à des félicités sans bornes" (p. 75). The terror is in part prompted by crossing the divide that separates chastity from defilement; but Julie's terms imply also the effect of an animalistic frenzy which threatens to annul the essential distinction between ethereal lovers and the vulgar lot:

> Notre jouissance était paisible et durable, nous n'avons plus que des *transports*: ce bonheur *insensé* ressemble à des *accès de fureur* plus qu'à de tendres caresses. Un feu pur et sacré brûlait nos cœurs; livrés aux erreurs des sens, *nous ne sommes plus que des amants vulgaires*; trop heureux si l'amour jaloux daigne présider encore à des plaisirs que *le plus vil mortel* peut goûter sans lui! [p. 76]

---

[80] "Non, rien, rien sur la terre n'est capable d'exciter un si voluptueux attendrissement que vos mutuelles caresses; et le spectacle de deux amants eût offert à mes yeux une sensation moins délicieuse" (p. 90).

[81] There is an analogy between Julie and Italian music in that he says her voice will naturally attune to it; that there are sexual overtones is shown by his revulsion "de voir sortir de la bouche d'un vil *castrato* les plus tendres expressions de l'amour" (p. 109, italics in text).

Julie in consequence tortures herself with shame, fears she may not be suffering enough.[82] She insists on the role of *pudeur* in sex and in effect attempts verbally to asexuate it by concentrating it on a single object of desire,[83] finally denying that the sex drive as such, unmotivated by an exclusive sentimental fixation, is even natural: "Tous ces prétendus besoins n'ont point leur source dans la nature, mais dans la volontaire dépravation des sens" (p. 280).

The calm of innocent pleasure is to a certain extent recovered in the aftermath, which brings a more stable sensation surpassing that of satisfied desire: "Quel *calme* dans tous mes sens!" exclaims Saint-Preux after their unique night together, "Quelle volupté pure, *continue,* universelle! Le charme de la jouissance était dans l'âme; il n'en sortait plus, il durait toujours. Quelle différence des *fureurs* de l'amour à une *situation si paisible*" (p. 123).[84] But even before, there were suggestions of a longing for the non-violent manifestations, so to speak, of passion, as when Saint-Preux in Le Valais evokes in contrast "je ne sais quelle volupté tranquille qui n'a rien d'âcre et de sensuel" (p. 52), and the simpler joys: "combien vous surpassez ... tous les transports qu'une ardeur sans mesure offre aux désirs effrénés des amants!" (p. 90).

Volupté gets its revenge on Julie through the way it conditions her life at Clarens, but it does so precisely in a lucidly controlled way. To the sensual pleasures there allowed, Julie applies an essentially erotic gradation: eager to avoid the disgust that follows satiation, she cultivates the art of savoring "avec délices" — which

---

[82] "Ma honte n'est-elle pas écrite sur tous les objets?" (p. 69); "le pire de mes maux serait d'en être consolée" (p. 76). Claire remarks: "Cette âme tendre craint toujours de ne pas s'affliger assez, et c'est une sorte de plaisir pour elle d'ajouter au sentiment de ses peines tout ce qui peut les aigrir" (p. 301).

[83] "Je ne sais si je m'abuse, mais il me semble que le véritable amour est le plus chaste de tous les liens. C'est lui, c'est son feu divin qui sait épurer nos penchants naturels, en les concentrant dans un seul objet; c'est lui qui nous dérobe aux tentations, et qui fait qu'excepté cet objet unique un sexe n'est plus rien pour l'autre" (p. 113). Ultimately, in the very different context of Clarens, Saint-Preux seems to rally to this ideal: "Tout le reste de votre sexe ne m'est plus rien" (p. 665) — but this seems to represent a burned-out drive more than chaste focalization.

[84] A remarkable note on p. 124 (which Voltaire was to mock) draws attention to the absence of such a pleasurable plateau in any instance where love has not provided the preliminary bond.

means restraint.[85] Custom spoils enjoyment;[86] so, since Julie especially likes coffee, for instance, she drinks it infrequently: "elle en a quitté l'habitude pour en augmenter le goût.... C'est une petite sensualité qui la flatte plus, qui lui coûte moins, et par laquelle elle *aiguise et règle à la fois* sa gourmandise" (p. 537).[87] This economy of pleasure is related explicitly by Wolmar to its sensuous origin, as is, equally clearly, her very aspiration to purity: "Julie a l'âme et le corps également sensibles. La même délicatesse règne dans ses sentiments et dans ses organes. Elle était faite pour connaître et goûter tous les plaisirs, et longtemps elle n'aima si chèrement la vertu même que comme la plus douce des voluptés" (p. 526).[88] Although this depiction applies to a phase through which Julie presumably has passed, nothing determines precisely when it is supposed to have been outgrown.

There is in Julie and Saint-Preux alike an intense aspiration toward purity, the antithesis of the "vices de parade" required in Paris (p. 256). The early pages of the book are replete with evocations of the purity of Julie's soul, mind, taste, beauty, and love. To Saint-Preux's "Ma flamme et son objet conserveront ensemble une inaltérable pureté" (p. 15), Julie can echo, "je goûte le plaisir délicieux d'aimer purement" (p. 24). She must be less certain of that after the first kiss, when she extolls instead the "purs et sacrés embrassements" (p. 45) not of Saint-Preux but of her father.[89]

---

[85] Cf. Claire's observations on pp. 300-301 on the necessity of obstacles for passion, and "le dégoût de ce qu'on possède."

[86] "Je ne connaissais point cette charmante salle [le salon d'Apollon], dis-je à Mme de Wolmar; pourquoi n'y mangez-vous pas toujours? — Voyez, dit-elle, elle est si jolie! ne serait-ce pas dommage de la gâter?" (p. 529).

[87] Julie has already been called "sensuelle et gourmande" (p. 435) and her "penchant à la gourmandise" (p. 527) is later noted again.

[88] Paul de Man puts us on guard against the "language of religious awe" applied to virtue in this text: "Actually, there is nothing in the structure of Julie's relationship to virtue or to what she calls God that does not find its counterpart in her previous and now so rigorously demystified relationship towards Saint-Preux.... Neither is it surprising that virtue will later be identified, by Wolmar, as being a passion among others, with a structure similar to that of love" (op. cit., pp. 217-19).

[89] Her filial guilt is brought back into play when she confronts her father in a less chaste state, and when she sheds "impure tears" at her mother's death (p. 295).

Saint-Preux associates even the purity of the mountain air with moral purity [90] — both aspects of Starobinski's "transparency." Because nature is "pure," she helps to sustain the conviction (by later terms, the illusion) of purity even after societally formal chastity is gone: "N'as-tu pas suivi les plus pures lois de la nature? ... Ô mon épouse! Ô ma digne et *chaste* compagne!" (p. 74). [91]

The persistence of such language causes unsuspecting readers to be easily misled. There is indeed something bald and daring about maintaining it in the presence of sensual fulfillment, on which level it exacts no sacrifice. Once, when the lovers forego a promised tryst to perform a good deed for Fanchon, Saint-Preux delights in the chance to "réunir ainsi dans le même soin les charmes de l'amour et de la vertu" (p. 96); but such te1 s carry over also to sexual acts because, as he says with notable directness, "Le véritable amour ... sait tout accorder aux désirs sans rien ôter à la pudeur" (p. 113). No repentance is possible in a proper sense, for it would require a willingness to renounce sin. [92] "Nous serons coupables, mais nous aimerons toujours la vertu" (p. 317), writes Julie. The terminological compatibility of virtue with such a set of other terms conventionally held to be in opposition with it is what sustains for a long time the erroneous mode of thought and makes it difficult for them to perceive the paradox. Ultimately, the disparity between words and the facts as experienced leads to perplexity based just on this: "Non, j'ose le croire, un feu si pur n'a point produit de si noirs effets. L'amour nous inspira des sentiments trop nobles pour en tirer les forfaits des âmes dénaturées" (p. 298). This painful juxtaposition of pure intentions and evil effects betokens a crisis of terms and with it of categories and essences.

Very soon thereafter, Julie will denounce their mistaken notion of virtue. But the force of that illusion will nonetheless be explained

---

[90] "Tout me rappelait à vous dans ce séjour paisible; et les touchants attraits de la nature, et l'inaltérable pureté de d'air, et les mœurs simples des habitants, et leur sagesse égale et sûre, et l'aimable pudeur du sexe" (p. 57).

[91] Cf. "nos chastes amours" (p. 249), "le plus *pur,* le plus sacré lien qui jamais ait uni deux cœurs" (p. 291). There is one anomalous, contrary outburst of Saint-Preux's when he is sent away, of which it is extremely difficult to determine the tone: "cette odieuse vertu que vous me supposez et que je déteste" (p. 96).

[92] "Dieu! quel état cruel de ne pouvoir ni supporter son crime, ni s'en repentir" (p. 111).

by their attachment to virtue;[93] indeed, in this construction, they have been seduced *by* the appearance of virtue.[94] The turnabout at mid-point therefore brings a recovery of purity, even with regard to her relationship to Saint-Preux: "ce sentiment est aussi pur que le jour qui m'éclaire" (p. 354); "une amitié pure et sainte" sets the fallen angel on the ethereal path to beatification: "si le sentiment de sa faute la rendait alors plus touchante, celui de sa pureté la rend aujourd'hui plus céleste" (p. 403).[95] Symbolically, in the intimacy of the Salon d'Apollon the use of unadulterated wine is reintroduced (p. 529). The fire of purification emanates from Julie and eventually encompasses Saint-Preux: "Mon cœur s'épurait au feu de son zèle, et je partageais sa vertu" (p. 580); "les feux dont j'ai brûlé m'ont purifié" (p. 666).

There is a whole constellation of other lexical witnesses to these obsessions. A fear of becoming tainted, and consequently a revulsion for things unclean or base, is expressed for example in thirty-nine occurrences of the adjective *vil,* predominantly (31) in the novel's first half. Its starkest forms are the excoriating *vil séducteur* (pp. 12, 16) and *vil corrupteur* (pp. 60, 342), terms raised precisely with reference to whether or not Saint-Preux deserves them. It has both social and moral implications: Saint-Preux's condition — a romantic commonplace — is based on "ce contraste insupportable de *grandeur* au fond de mon âme et de *bassesse* dans ma fortune" (p. 64). The high and the low are thus usually combined in some paradoxical

---

[93] "La vertu est si nécessaire à nos cœurs que, quand on a une fois abandonné la véritable, on s'en fait ensuite une à sa mode" (p. 325).

[94] "L'amour se parait à nos yeux de tous les charmes de la vertu.... L'on se réveille épouvanté de se trouver couvert de crimes avec un cœur né pour la vertu" (pp. 331-32). Edouard Bomston contributes for his part to their purity by clearing Saint-Preux on the score of formal honor; to have been challenged, he asserts, "est toujours une sorte de tache, et l'amant de Julie en doit être exempt" (p. 141). It is a sign of Saint-Preux's moral austerity towards the end of the novel that Laura must meet the same criteria: "Ce n'est pas assez qu'elle soit vertueuse, elle doit être sans tache" (p. 640).

[95] There still lurks the possibility of illusion, to be sure; Claire notes that "la pure amitié [a] encore un peu l'air de l'amour" (p. 415). The uneasiness behind a language of firm conviction is substantiated by the appearance, in the second half of the text, of blushing, quite absent earlier ("nous pouvons parler de la vertu sans rougir" [p. 25]). *Rougir* appears both metaphorically (pp. 598, 613, 619, 634, 658, 676) and literally, applied to Saint-Preux (p. 405) and to Julie (pp. 434, 596).

admixture. Celestial Julie feels cheapened by the physical pleasure "que le plus vil mortel peut goûter" (p. 76); this knocks her from the pedestal she is determined to maintain, except of course when she aberrantly *elects* to become "vile et malheureuse" (p. 314). Nor should we dismiss in this context the relevance of a homonym which in *Julie* is in fact semantically allied: "mon aversion pour la *ville*" (p. 385), "les vices des *villes*" (p. 431); honest and virtuous servants cannot come from the *ville* (p. 427). It is precisely the city mentality that undermines and perverts the noble values of *Julie*: "Cette pudeur charmante qui distingue, honore et embellit ton sexe, leur a paru *vile* et roturière" (p. 245).

Related adjectives [96] are *bas* and *abject* and a number of verbs semantically similar, having to do with downward movement and disparagement: *avilir* and *s'avilir* (40 occurrences), *rabaisser, souiller, profaner, prostituer, ravaler, abrutir* and, passim, *précipiter, corrompre, gâter*, etc. A corresponding cluster of substantives: *avilissement* (4 occurrences), *souillure, abrutissement, bassesse, abîme, précipice*. Structurally echoing the falling movement of these images is a whole series of terms of undoing, built with negative prefixes: *dégrader, dénaturé, dépraver, déshonneur/déshonorer/déshonnête, déranger, désordonné, discorde, dépérissement* and, above all, *désordre*.

To be sure, there is also a lexical countermovement, for all does not run downhill in this novel. Saint-Preux puts the two tendencies into counterplay when he writes from Meillerie: "Telle est la situation cruelle où me *plongent* le sort qui m'accable et mes sentiments qui m'*élèvent*" (p. 63). [97] And unlike the previous register, this one will dominate in the second half, not only because of the general theme of redemption but also because of the specific role of a religion "qui, loin d'*abrutir* l'homme, l'*ennoblit* et l'*élève*" (p. 712). Saint-Preux's adoring posture valorizes Julie's "sentiments élevés" (p. 30), [98] which simultaneously also allude to her social standing

---

[96] I was able to check precisely some of these terms by consulting the ARTFL data base (compiled in France for the *Trésor de la Langue Française*) at the University of Chicago; only in these instances have I indicated a figure in parentheses.

[97] Christie Vance has remarked too on the vocabulary of rising and falling in *Julie*: see op. cit., pp. 168-69. The exhilaration of the mountains also has a great deal to do with the symbolic sense of elevation.

[98] More hyperbolically: "Ô pureté que je respecte en murmurant, que ne puis-je ou vous *rabaisser* ou m'*élever* jusqu'à vous!" (pp. 26-27).

— and to it (that is of course their dilemma) the loftiest of feelings cannot hoist him: "L'amour qui rapproche tout n'élève point la personne: il n'élève que les sentiments" (p. 291).[99] Gravity, so to speak, carries one downhill; to counter its force takes some kind of leverage. Saint-Preux recalls as a form of reciprocal bootstrap operation "cette grandeur intérieure où nos cœurs enflammés s'élevaient réciproquement" (p. 199),[100] but Julie remembers as well the importance of inspiring models, even if their effect sometimes resembles erotic provocation: "Souviens-toi des larmes délicieuses qui coulaient de nos yeux, des palpitations qui suffoquaient nos cœurs agités, des transports qui nous élevaient au-dessus de nous-mêmes, au récit de ces vies héroïques qui rendent le vice inexcusable et font l'honneur de l'humanité" (p. 199).

Julie herself, needless to say, turns to a higher source after her marriage and seeks uplifting through a divine model: "C'est à la contemplation de ce divin modèle que l'âme s'*épure* et s'*élève*, qu'elle apprend à mépriser ses inclinations *basses* et à *surmonter* ses *vils* penchants" (p. 338).[101] The new social role is also brought to bear: "Le rang d'épouse et de mère m'*élève* l'âme et me *soutient* contre les remords d'un autre état" (pp. 382-83). And when Julie seems to need shoring up, Claire invokes her whole new environment: "Regarde tout autour de toi, tu n'y verras rien qui ne doive élever et soutenir ton âme" (p. 485). At other times, less worried about her cousin, Claire allows herself to tease the lofty Julie: "Les objets éloignés et *bas* se confondent maintenant à ta vue; dans ta *sublime élévation*, tu regardes la terre et n'en vois plus les inégalités" (p. 627). And, of course, most important even in the early parts of the novel is the role of Julie as beacon for the wayfarers. Claire (referring to her in an abstract plural) writes, "on ne peut les connaître sans les vouloir imiter, et de leur sublime élévation elles attirent à elles tout ce qui les environne" (p. 180). The challenge for Saint-Preux, then, is to rise to Julie's level of exemplarity: "j'ai beau m'élever jusqu'à vous en votre présence, je retombe en

---

[99] Once it is no longer a question of a consenting father, Julie will propose to Claire to "élev[er] à toi le mérite outragé par la fortune" (p. 620).

[100] Cf. Bomston's comment that "vous vaudriez moins l'un et l'autre si vous ne vous étiez point aimés" (p. 140).

[101] She invites Claire too with the injunction: "Nous éleverons nos cœurs ensemble à celui qui purifia le mien par tes soins" (p. 386).

moi-même en vous quittant" (p. 666), and he tries to think in terms of her pseudo-theological language: "Tous les actes de l'entendement qui nous élèvent à Dieu nous portent au-dessus de nous-mêmes; en implorant son secours, nous apprenons à le trouver. Ce n'est pas lui qui nous change; c'est nous qui changeons en nous élevant à lui" (p. 673). Yet both allude still to a mutual sustenance that they provide each other.[102] Ultimately, Julie seeks to lift herself to "la source du sentiment et de l'être" (p. 683).[103]

The impossibility of knowing certainly what and whom to trust is frequently rendered in the text by the problem of confidence and trusteeship, and particularly by the term *dépôt,* a metaphor for responsibility which easily takes on a highly charged emotive or erotic value. Julie, who capitulates on all the essentials from the first moment she writes, delivers herself to and confides herself in the very source of danger, Saint-Preux. With an excited fascination, he refers to this delicate burden as "le plus sacré dépôt dont jamais mortel fut honoré" (p. 15), "le précieux dépôt dont tu m'as chargé" (p. 16) — only to give back quickly "ce dépôt trop dangereux" (p. 22) when he is no longer so sure he wants to protect it. When Julie refers to "un si dangereux dépôt" (p. 29) and later "un dépôt si cher" (p. 321) it is quite unambiguous that it means virginity. But other highly valued articles are referred to by the same term: honor, for Saint-Preux (p. 40); Fanchon, for Julie (p. 92); letters from Julie (pp. 46, 141); even Saint-Preux himself, for Edouard (p. 171). By turns, all are called *dépositaire* of someone's secrets, complaints, feelings. Comparing Julie wife and mother to the one who once, less pure, intervened for Fanchon, Wolmar reawakens the weighty meaning of the term when he leaves Saint-Preux and

---

[102] Saint-Preux: "jamais nos yeux ne se rencontrent, sans offrir à tous deux un objet d'honneur et de gloire qui nous élève conjointement" (p. 674); Julie: "C'est dans cette délicatesse qui survit toujours au véritable amour ... qu'il faut chercher la raison de cette élévation d'âme et de cette force intérieure que nous éprouvons l'un près de l'autre, et que je crois sentir comme vous" (p. 676).

[103] This is one of what Hugh Davidson describes as the dialectic aspects of Julie, "a pervasive movement upward, motivated by the imitation of models and in particular of one model whose aspirations are infinite" ("Dialectical order and movement in *La Nouvelle Héloïse,*" in Alfred J. Bingham and Virgil W. Topazio [eds.], *Enlightenment Studies in Honour of Lester G. Crocker,* Oxford: The Voltaire Foundation, 1979), p. 79.

Julie alone by design, saying: "Je remets ma femme et mon honneur en dépôt à celle qui, fille et séduite, préférait un acte de bienfaisance à un rendez-vous unique et sûr" (p. 481). *Dépôt* is hardly economic; there is never any collateral. It is a term which speaks both of the intimate trust prevailing between privileged individuals, and of the insecurity of a fragile but precious sense of value.

It is not as if trust were always well kept. Especially since, virginity being lost, they place such great store in its surrogate chastity, fidelity.[104] Once their relationship has been endowed rhetorically with legitimacy and virtue, it is the thought of marrying another which becomes adultery (pp. 74-75).[105] Just as Julie's betrothal to Wolmar in effect precipitates her capitulation to Saint-Preux, it is his infidelity in Paris which makes her marriage possible. She makes no reproach, but the purity has been compromised; suddenly in her reply reappears the *vous* banished between them for more than a year (from p. 186 to p. 276) — to reappear again in one brief spasm (III.15) after the smallpox episode before once more vanishing until the last paragraph of Julie's final letter. But it is he who cries "Infidèle!" treating her as a traitor and Wolmar as a sort of rapist.[106] Over this subject there is, for all their warmth of feeling, a symbolic cold war going on in part four: being allowed in the gyneceum, Saint-Preux enjoys a privilege explicitly refused to Wolmar, the favor of Julie's intimate company (p. 434); admitted also to the locked and exclusive Élysée, he wants not only a key but precisely Wolmar's own key (p. 469) — again an obvious sort of figurative adultery.[107] Wolmar in turn "profanes" the mythic bower,

---

[104] Julie, speaking of herself and Saint-Preux in the third person: "s'ils cessèrent d'être chastes, au moins ils étaient fidèles" (p. 331).

[105] "L'on force au crime une malheureuse victime en la forçant de manquer de part ou d'autre au devoir sacré de la fidélité" (p. 188).

[106] "C'est à moi seul de réclamer le bien que M. de Wolmar m'a *ravi*" (p. 346). Wolmar, who *has read Saint-Preux's letter,* recalls this later by saying to Claire, "Ce n'est pas de Julie de Wolmar qu'il est amoureux, c'est de Julie d'Étange; il ne me hait point comme le possesseur de la personne qu'il aime, mais comme le *ravisseur* de celle qu'il a aimée" (p. 492).

[107] "Given the very obvious phallic associations of keys, the fact that Julie immediately hands over her key to her ex-lover, who in turn would rather have been given the key of the husband, certainly suggests that there is something rather uneasy going on here, some kind of hidden and unexamined sexual malaise" (Tanner, pp. 160-61). To this degree the significance of Julie's key is overdetermined; for there is the simple practical consequence as well

in which the renewed Julie has never set foot (p. 468), by having them repeat the kiss before his eyes (p. 482).

The pervasive perversion of the city is epitomized by the way their fundamental truth, when turned into jargon and abstractions, existential:

> Un des sujets favoris de ces paisibles entretiens, c'est le sentiment; mot par lequel il ne faut pas entendre un épanchement affectueux dans le sein de l'amour ou de l'amitié, cela serait d'une fadeur à mourir; c'est le sentiment mis en grandes maximes générales, et quintessencié par tout ce que la métaphysique a de plus subtil. Je puis dire n'avoir de ma vie ouï tant parler du sentiment, ni si peu compris ce qu'on en disait. [p. 226]

Maybe this indeed represents where the young "philosophe" was himself headed before he learned philosophy's antidote, according to Claire, in Vevey: "En nous apprenant à penser, vous avez appris de nous à être sensible; ... si c'est la raison qui fait l'homme, c'est le sentiment qui le conduit" (p. 299). Reason cannot guarantee the viability of its own conclusions, and one way to tell good reasoning from sophisms is to test it against a more powerful intuition of what is right.[108] But sentiment is not only intuition in the philosophical sense for it combines several other functions: the inner voice of moral conviction; the capacity for feeling that Jane Austen called "sensibility"; and what we would tend to refer to as sentimentality. Sentiment in *Julie* evokes all these, singly or in combination, and stands in the aggregate for a life where emotion or feeling is the dominant and controlling faculty. "C'est dans mon trop sensible cœur qu'est la source de tous les maux et de mon corps et de mon âme," asserts Julie (p. 330). Sometimes abetting the appetites of the senses[109] and sometimes driving them back, sentiment is a

---

that if Julie gives Saint-Preux her key, she will never be in the Elysée without Wolmar.

[108] "J'entends beaucoup raisonner contre la liberté de l'homme, et je méprise tous ces sophismes, parce qu'un raisonneur a beau me prouver que je ne suis pas libre, le sentiment intérieur, plus fort que tous ses arguments, les dément sans cesse" (p. 671).

[109] Cf. Lecercle's discussion of "la volupté du sentiment" in op. cit., pp. 194-99.

quality of the soul which is ultimately metaphysical in origin: "Ô Julie! que c'est un fatal présent du ciel qu'une âme sensible! Celui qui l'a reçu ... cherchera la félicité suprême sans se souvenir qu'il est homme: son cœur et sa raison seront incessamment en guerre, et des *désirs sans bornes* lui prépareront d'éternelles privations" (p. 63). Sentiment is unlimited desire, the ultimate eroticism; with all its ecstasies, it is a curse in disguise, for its contentments will forever also be disillusions.

Membership in the novel's privileged circle can be determined by a formal criterion: the logical priority accorded to feeling; but even before that, it is communicated by some kind of telepathic, nonmaterial means. Saint-Preux relates, discussing Bomston: "Cependant nous sentîmes que nous nous convenions; il y a une certaine unisson d'âmes qui s'aperçoit au premier instant.... J'estimai qu'il en jugeait avec plus de sentiment que de science, et par les effets plus que par les règles, ce qui me confirma qu'il avait l'âme sensible" (p. 100). By these words, Saint-Preux certifies that Edouard is worthy of them. All of the inner circle belongs of course in that category, even, despite his restraint, Wolmar. Saint-Preux calls it a "bizarre inconséquence" that Wolmar should think like an unbeliever and live like a Christian (p. 578); but the paradox is only apparent because religion is only tangential to the remark: what is "Christian" about him is precisely his qualities of soul. The one thing, however, that he refuses to get excited about is the relationship of all that to God. Wolmar is cool by temperament but hardly an unfeeling monster. Consider his role in the scene of Claire's supposedly definitive return to Clarens, the most climactic of the novel in terms of personality manifestations. Julie, then Claire, fall into a faint, after which Saint-Preux becomes so distraught as to be quite useless (Henriette and Fanchon come to their aid); Wolmar alone keeps his head enough to assure everyone there is no danger, and settles back to contemplate the moving tableau: "Wolmar lui-même, le froid Wolmar se sentit ému. Ô sentiment!, sentiment! douce vie de l'âme! Quel est le cœur de fer que tu n'as jamais touché? Quel est l'infortuné mortel à qui tu n'arrachas jamais de larmes? Au lieu de courir à Julie, cet heureux époux se jeta sur un fauteuil pour contempler avidement ce ravissant spectacle" (p. 585). There follows a general delirium, celebration of reunion and of resolidarization in their tight little collectivity now complete.

More typically their company is calm, and even less verbal than in this scene. Indeed it seems most in its element when the atmosphere is not gay.[110] Intimate societies in Paris must talk all the time and about everyone, "comme si leurs cœurs n'avaient rien à se dire" (p. 255); at Clarens one needs no outside referents and not even very many words, since much communication is implicit or exquisitely gestural:

> Sentiment vif et céleste, quels discours sont dignes de toi? Quelle langue ose être ton interprète? Jamais ce qu'on dit à son ami peut-il valoir ce qu'on sent à ses côtés? Mon Dieu! qu'une main serrée, qu'un regard animé, qu'une étreinte contre la poitrine, que le soupir qui la suit, disent de choses, et que le premier mot qu'on prononce est froid après tout cela! [p. 543]

There are moments of intense silence where an uncommon number of things are "said": "Que de choses se sont dites sans ouvrir la bouche! Que d'ardents sentiments se sont communiqués sans la froide entremise de la parole!" (p. 546).[111] Julie in dying anticipates the ideal, a "communication immédiate" (p. 716) for which the metaphor is not speech but silent reading — now unmediated.[112] Silence is the mark of plenitude, of self-sufficiency. The metacommentary about it thus occurs only in the narrative retrospective of a linguistic medium, for a letter cannot *represent* silences.[113]

---

[110] "L'indifférence et la froideur trouvent aisément des paroles, mais la tristesse et le silence dont alors le vrai langage de l'amitié" (p. 168); "la communication des cœurs imprime à la tristesse je ne sais quoi de doux et de touchant que n'a pas le contentement" (p. 385).

[111] Julie had said of herself and Claire: "nous sentions sans nous rien dire combien le tendre langage de l'amitié a peu besoin du secours des paroles" (p. 235); and Saint-Preux, of the three of them: "Te souvient-il, ma Julie, ... comment à chaque réflexion touchante, à chaque allusion subtile, un regard plus vif qu'un éclair, un soupir plutôt deviné qu'aperçu, en portait le doux sentiment d'un cœur à l'autre?" (p. 225).

[112] "... une communication immédiate, semblable à celle par laquelle Dieu *lit* nos pensées dès cette vie, et par laquelle nous *lirons* réciproquement les siennes dans l'autre, puisque nous le verrons face à face."

[113] The *style entrecoupé*, which imitates silence theatrically by suspension points, is not used in *Julie* to represent lulls in conversations, but only to suggest pauses and sighs *in the process of letter-writing* itself (as in the fragments, pp. 172-73). It is no less factitious for that, but the difference in usage is important.

Sentiment is also the strait gate through which only can pass the elect reader. For the novel, asserts the preface already, "ne plaira médiocrement à personne," and those whose hearts are not in the right place are curtly told, although indirectly, to look elsewhere. The text plays upon the fact that it does not offer the conventional novel reader the excitement he expects; and whether what it does offer is adequate compensation for that is in effect the shibolleth which determines not *its* adequacy, but that of the reader. As if commenting on *Julie* itself, Edouard says, after hearing Saint-Preux's story, "Il n'y a ... ni incidents ni aventures dans ce que vous m'avez raconté, et les catastrophes d'un roman m'attacheraient beaucoup moins; tant les sentiments suppléent aux situations, et les procédés honnêtes aux actions éclatantes!" (p. 140).[114] In this way the text supplies the appropriate — and the *only* appropriate — reader reactions. A similar kind of remark by Saint-Preux, this time dealing with the texture of the letters themselves, acts to reach out and englobe the reader: "je soutiens qu'il n'y a point de lecture aussi délicieuse, même pour qui ne te connaîtrait pas, s'il avait une âme semblable aux nôtres" (p. 220). Of course there is something tautological about that assertion, and about this stance in general. The Editor/Author returns for a last word, to express the pleasure of not having to frequent ugly characters, and repeat that any "lecteur d'un bon naturel" will be satisfied (p. 733). The good reader belongs to the society of Clarens.

To some degree, empathy abrogates absence. After their night in Julie's room, the lovers will not meet again, except during Julie's delirium, for over six years. But, according to Julie, they can look on absence as a form, perhaps the best form, of presence:

> Oui, mon ami, nous serons unis malgré notre éloignement; nous serons heureux en dépit du sort. C'est l'union des cœurs qui fait leur véritable félicité; leur attraction ne connaît point la loi des distances, et les nôtres se toucheraient aux deux bouts du monde. Je trouve comme toi que les amants ont mille moyens d'adoucir le sentiment de l'ab-

---

[114] The second preface serves up the recriminations of a less enthusiastic respondant, and part of "R"'s reply is: "Mes jeunes gens sont aimables; ... le sentiment y est; il se communique au cœur par degrés, et lui seul à la fin supplée à tout. C'est une longue romance" (p. 744).

sence et de se rapprocher en un moment; quelquefois même on se voit plus souvent encore que quand on se voyait tous les jours; car sitôt qu'un des deux est seul, à l'instant tous deux sont ensemble. [p. 212]

Julie's letters constitute now a spiritual simulacrum of Julie and reanimate the memory in almost hallucinatory fashion:

> À chaque phrase ne voit-on pas le doux regard de tes yeux? À chaque mot n'entend-on pas ta voix charmante? Quelle autre que Julie a jamais aimé, pensé, parlé, agi, écrit comme elle! Ne sois donc pas surprise si tes lettres, qui te peignent si bien, font quelquefois sur ton idolâtre amant le même effet que ta présence. En les relisant je perds la raison, ma tête s'égare dans un délire continuel, un feu dévorant me consume, mon sang s'allume et pétille, une fureur me fait tressaillir. Je crois te voir, te toucher, te presser contre mon sein... [p. 220]

In comparison, the portrait Julie sends with the partly jocular claim that a portrait can "communiquer à l'un l'impression des baisers de l'autre à plus de cent lieues de là" (p. 242), seems mildly disappointing; paradoxically, it is too resembling for someone with such intimate knowledge of her to fail to perceive how inexact it is (pp. 269-70).[115] In fact the act of giving it seems to have a greater effect upon her than on Saint-Preux:

> Oui, mon ami, le sort a beau nous séparer, pressons nos cœurs l'un contre l'autre, conservons par la communication leur chaleur naturelle contre le froid de l'absence et du désespoir.... Cent fois le jour, quand je suis seule, un tressaillement me saisit comme si je te sentais près de moi. Je m'imagine que tu tiens mon portrait, et je suis si folle que je crois sentir l'impression des caresses que tu lui fais et des baisers que tu lui donnes; ma bouche croit les recevoir, mon tendre cœur croit les goûter. Ô douces illusions! [p. 268]

The terms used come close to making it more fetish than talisman, except that they apply rather to its sender than possessor. In quite

---

[115] Cf. Christie Vance's observations on their non-verbal communication and the talisman as their symbol, op. cit., p. 112.

interesting circumstances, these ideas develop into a full-blown theory of spiritual presence:

> On ne voit point les esprits, je le veux croire; mais deux âmes si étroitement unies ne sauraient-elles avoir entre elles une communication immédiate, indépendante du corps et des sens? L'impression directe que l'une reçoit de l'autre ne peut-elle pas la transmettre au cerveau, et recevoir de lui par contre-coup les sensations qu'elle lui a données?... Pauvre Julie, que d'extravagances! Que les passions nous rendent crédules! [p. 309]

Like the previous quotation, this one ends on a wistful but demystifying note. What Julie is really doing here is trying to rationalize what she *believes to have been* a genuine hallucination of Saint-Preux at her bedside. Since the event really took place, however, her whole notion is empirically founded on a misperception: the passage is thus symbolic both of an extreme form of poetic belief in the communication of souls, and of the flaws inherent in a value system that does not entirely have its feet on the ground.

To interpret such a passage doubly, in such a way that it casts doubt on its overt content while affirming it, may appear to do some violence to an ideological structure which after all does have its fairly clear premises. The point is just that these are axiomatic, and that objectively viewed, the text does not function unequivocally to demonstrate them: there is an undertow, although it does not for the characters experientially invalidate data which to them are in the line of self-evident truths. No character in the book would deny this conclusion of Julie's: "La sensibilité porte toujours dans l'âme un certain contentement de soi-même indépendant de la fortune et des événements" (p. 713): it identifies the fundamental autonomy of their dearest values. Yet one can hardly examine such an assertion closely without noticing that it describes a state which has little need of outside corroboration; it constitutes finally a closed circuit, and encourages self-complacency and self-congratulation — hardly a prescription for virtuous citizenry.

In point of *fact,* it is not true of Wolmar to say as Julie does that he is incapable of dissimulation (p. 350), for he has hidden for several years, for example, his knowledge of Julie's intimate past.[116] In a sense, that does not matter: he is *nonetheless* incapable of dissimulation because such is his essence, and that is that. Events do not have to prove the remark. Similarly, the terms in which Saint-Preux and Julie in particular are depicted are a matter of a priori definition. When Julie says, "vous n'êtes pas capable d'user d'artifice avec moi" (p. 28), one can say that she is merely manifesting her naïveté, saying something she would not affirm at some later point; one can also note that this permits her to act henceforth *as if* what she posits were true and not to bother with the niceties of verification. These are perfectly reasonable observations, yet at the same time what may transpire in fact has little bearing on such a statement by her, just as when she writes, many experiences later, "ton âme est encore innocente et saine" (p. 135), and tells herself, "je suis coupable, mais il est vertueux" (p. 186). Nor does this concession make her guilty either; but it is her function to maintain the integrity of his innocence, and vice versa.[117] How the self is qualified might in such contexts be considered a variable, but the *other* must remain a constant.

For Saint-Preux, how could Julie be guilty? "Le crime pourrait-il approcher de ton cœur?" (p. 315). The *pourrait-il?* shows that there is no concrete instance envisaged of the phenomenon referred to: it is, by definition, excluded. Thus, "tu ne peux rien vouloir que d'honnête" (p. 203) essentially means that whatever she wants *is* "honnête." A sentence such as: "Cet effort de courage qui vous ramène à toute votre vertu ne vous rend que plus semblable à vous-même" (p. 345) may appear as an accidental and awkward tautology, but it simply allows that, whereas Julie may stray by minute degrees from her essence, nothing she *does* can change that *essence*. Saint-Preux later remarks that his idea (*image*, in a literal visual sense) of virtue came to *look like* Julie (pp. 469-70). And Claire even asks Julie, after her fall, "le danger dont tu sors n'est-il pas une preuve

---

[116] He has had the letters of Saint-Preux all along, although it is never precisely explained how they got from Mme d'Étange's hands into his without either Julie or d'Étange knowing about them.

[117] Julie again: "ne pouvant plus m'estimer moi-même, j'aime à m'estimer encore en toi" (p. 98).

de ta vertu?" (p. 72).[118] There is thus no conceivable sense in which she could "fail" to be virtuous.

The quality of the soul is a given. When Wolmar says to the former lovers that "le vice pouvait entrer dans des cœurs comme les vôtres, mais non pas y prendre racine" (p. 478), what may seem to him an empirical statement will not so strike the reader (who has known them for "longer" than has he). Vice would simply not be what we call "vice" if it *could* take root in them: no exterior standard has any purchase on this rhetorical situation. Saint-Preux and Julie may be shortsighted or make mistakes, but they cannot have bad intentions: "ils sont toujours de bonne foi, même en se démentant sans cesse" (p. 492). That innocence once so posited cannot thereafter be subject to alteration is more than suggested by Claire's assurance to Julie: "on ne prend guère de baisers coupables sur la même bouche où l'on en prit d'innocents" (p. 629). Again, this is a question of definitions.

The same kind of rhetorical absolute obtains in matters not related to personal essences. If a boy grabs a toy drum from his little brother, Fanchon takes it from him; but the lesson must stop there: the drum must not be restored to the first brother. Why? "En perdant le tambour, le cadet supporta la dure loi de la nécessité; l'aîné sentit son injustice; tous deux connurent leur faiblesse, et furent consolés le moment d'après" (p. 565). *Consolés le moment d'après?* Easily said. The narrative does not so much designate thus the result of a validated experiment as it identifies for us a system which *must* work. Moral lessons derive from the same essentialist premises as do the characters; the rules function not in "life" but in the text, according to predestined design. It is purely a matter of principle, for instance, for Saint-Preux to state, for purposes of a certain argument, that the Chinese "parlent beaucoup sans rien dire" (p. 396): how could he know? The allusion serves as a rare reminder of his travels, but they hardly included extensive training in Chinese. It obviously makes no sense, however, to call such statements lies, which again would erroneously suppose some objective,

---

[118] Likewise later, in retrospect, "Ta faiblesse, que je blâmais, me semblait presque une vertu" (pp. 390-91); she says too that Julie's mother "s'en prend de vos fautes à la vertu même" (p. 288).

referential control. They are autonomously self-defining axioms of the text.

In other words, the essential character of a thing or person is not composed of facts and acts, which can only confirm what is already there. That is, in part, why words and events in this novel seem sometimes to go their own separate ways. Saint-Preux has made love to Julie, but he certainly without outright prevarication can make it sound as if he had not:

> Dis si, dans toutes les fureurs d'une passion sans mesure, je cessai jamais d'en respecter le charmant objet.... Quand un transport indiscret écarte un instant le voile qui [couvre tes charmes], l'aimable pudeur n'y substitue-t-elle pas aussitôt le sien? Ce vêtement sacré t'abandonnerait-il un moment quand tu n'en aurais point d'autre? Incorruptible comme ton âme honnête, tous les feux de la mienne l'ont-ils jamais altéré? [p. 115]

The veil of *pudeur*, a merely verbal construct which does not quite, all the same, cover one up the way clothing does, is a hedge against facts; but the facts have not altered their perceptions of their innocence. "J'abjure, je déteste un forfait *que j'ai commis,* puisque tu m'en accuses, mais auquel ma volonté n'a point de part" (p. 116): this is what Saint-Preux writes to Julie following whatever indecencies she reproaches him for during his inebriation. The statement puts as much distance as possible between him and offense, while making amends as chivalry requires. After his misadventure with a Paris prostitute — wine again aiding — Julie replies, "Une erreur involontaire se pardonne et s'oublie aisément" (p. 283). An involuntary crime (Saint-Preux uses this expression too on p. 290) is by definition one for which one is not responsible. No one here is ever disturbed by hidden implications of such episodes, by the thought for example that what one does under the influence of alcohol has anything at all to do with one's will, manifest or repressed. A Freudian slip here does not mean a thing.

Frequently one finds a train of thought which makes its way around a circular path to its starting point, recuperated for goodness' sake by a certain rhetorical strategy. As her parents are preparing their departure, Julie is plotting a tryst with Saint-Preux, and she remarks: "Il fallait feindre de la tristesse, et le faux rôle que je me vois contrainte à jouer m'en donne une si véritable, que le remords m'a presque dispensée de la feinte" (p. 86). So she is sad on the right occasion, and, but for her subtle discriminations, no one would be the wiser.[119] Those plans do not quite come off as intended, though, because of Julie's compassionate intervention on behalf of Fanchon; whereupon Julie once more scores a good result obliquely obtained:

> Quand nous aurions fait par adresse ce que nous avons fait par bienfaisance, nous n'aurions pas mieux réussi.... Quelle ruse avons-nous employée pour écarter une trop juste défiance? La seule, à mon avis, qui soit permise à d'honnêtes gens, c'est de l'être à un point qu'on ne puisse croire, en sorte qu'on prenne un effort de vertu pour un acte d'indifférence. [pp. 97-98]

They are more or less rewarded for being good by being lucky; the flawed motive again achieves the same positive result as the good would have. And in a more than incidental way it is itself on the side of virtue: remorse in the previous instance, charity here.

Or let us take the matter of physical perfection. It is an aspect of both Julie's closeness to nature and of her modesty that she is most beautiful when least beautified. As Saint-Preux objects once after they have been in a company together: "Que de contraventions à tes engagements! Premièrement, ta parure; car tu n'en avais point, et tu sais bien que jamais tu n'es si dangereuse. Secondement, ton maintien si doux, si modeste, si propre à laisser remarquer à loisir toutes tes grâces" (p. 104).[120] The usual rhetorical structure of such a comparison is reversed here because Julie cannot be improved upon. Much later at Clarens, Saint-Preux recalls the paradox of her beauty in these terms:

---

[119] She follows up with this after her parents' departure: "Ces amères réflexions m'ont rendu toute la tristesse que leurs adieux ne m'avaient pas d'abord donnée" (p. 89).

[120] Claire refers to Saint-Preux's smallpox scars as a "dangereux fard" (p. 415), but not out of any equivalence between ugliness and beauty: rather because the disease, contracted willfully from contact with Julie, is a visible reminder of their days of passion.

> La seule vanité qu'on lui ait jamais reprochée était de négliger son ajustement. L'orgueilleuse avait ses raisons, et ne me laissait point de prétexte pour méconnaître son empire. Mais elle avait beau faire, l'enchantement était trop fort pour me sembler naturel; je m'opiniâtrais à trouver de l'art dans sa négligence; elle se serait coiffée d'un sac que je l'aurais accusée de coquetterie. [p. 530]

With detachment and some irony he now demystifies the enthrallment which motivated the earlier passage. He nonetheless draws from it the logical conclusion that if it was vain not to dress fancily, then it is more modest to do so. At present, therefore, Julie can dress up *more* in order to be *less* attractive: "Je trouve qu'elle se met avec plus de soin qu'elle ne faisait autrefois ... et je dirais qu'elle affecte une parure plus recherchée pour ne sembler plus qu'une jolie femme, si je n'avais découvert la cause de ce nouveau soin." The explanation is that she does this only for Wolmar's benefit, and when he is away she dresses in yet another quite different, intermediate style. It is clear from Saint-Preux's minute analysis that none of these three manners, however, is unstudied: she still always knows exactly what she is doing, and for whom. She may gain thereby in feminine charm,[121] but she can no longer avoid the implication of artifice — just as he thought in the first place — even when she feigns the middle and most unassuming ground.

Virtue in this context does not mean that one is less likely to be induced into sin; on the contrary. "Notre maître n'est pas seulement un homme de mérite; il est vertueux," writes Claire, "et n'en est que plus à craindre" (p. 18). Virtue is the absolute antecedent, the only reason why the attachment exists to start with; in her very first response, Julie enunciates this principle: "crois-moi, si ton cœur était fait pour jouir en paix de ce triomphe, il ne l'eût jamais obtenu" (p. 13). She seems to confront Saint-Preux with a no-win impasse: "j'espère encore que, [si ton cœur] était assez lâche pour abuser de mon égarement et des aveux qu'il m'arrache, le mépris, l'indignation, me rendraient la raison que j'ai perdue, et que je ne serais pas assez lâche moi-même pour craindre un amant

---

[121] "Elle usait seulement du talent *naturel aux femmes* de changer quelquefois nos sentiments et nos idées par un ajustement différent."

dont j'aurais à rougir" (p. 14). In other words: you can do with me what you will; but if you are the sort of person who could take advantage of such a situation, the offer no longer obtains. This results syllogistically from the premise that only his virtue makes him capable of inspiring her desire. Essential virtue always continues flowing, though, even when conventional, formal "virtue" is gone: "N'est-ce pas toi qui nourris dans mon âme le goût de la vertu, même après que je l'ai perdue?" (p. 89).[122] They are not vulnerable to vulgar attractions;[123] the high qualities attributed to the other both rationalize one's own weakness for him/her and reinforce self-assurance of one's own exceptional nature. Love first constitutes its object as a unique being, then invokes its uniqueness as the cause and justification of the love. "S'il n'était qu'un homme ordinaire, Julie n'eût point péri" (p. 185), Julie writes to Bomston, who has no trouble with this sort of logic. She needs cite no *evidence* for Saint-Preux's exceptional nature, because a person needing evidence would not in any event understand the essential truth of the attribution.

Thus a complex network of shared values and mental processes provides self- and mutual reinforcement to the central characters and their fixations. A tortuous, enthymematic chain underlies such a simple assertion as Saint-Preux's "si j'étais resté coupable, vous ne me seriez pas aussi chère" (p. 662), and it involves assumptions about the way Julie thinks as well as he. The fact that you are so dear to me proves the sinful attraction is gone. In this system, it could not possibly prove anything else. What evidence could even theoretically be adduced to demonstrate the contrary? Nor does such a statement serve to establish for the reader the reliability of its own conclusion, which must needs be a *foregone* conclusion if the sentence is to be understood at all. The fact that these privileged souls all love each other is proof that they are worthy of each other, and vice versa. The reciprocity is needed sustenance for each: Julie writes, after Saint-Preux's return, "Je sens qu'il s'honore de

---

[122] To Julie, Saint-Preux remarks: "Hélas! un cœur moins pur [que le tien] t'aurait bien moins égarée! Oui, c'est l'honnêteté du tien qui nous perd; les sentiments droits qui le remplissent en ont chassé la sagesse" (p. 315).

[123] "Je ne crains pas que les sens et les plaisirs grossiers te corrompent; ils sont des pièges peu dangereux pour un cœur sensible, et il lui en faut de plus délicats" (p. 200; cf. also, p. 277).

mon estime; je m'honore à mon tour de la sienne" (p. 410).[124] The economic system of Clarens works on the same basis as this sentimental solidarity, with a slightly larger population base which enables it to constitute a completely self-sufficient universe.[125]

The magnanimousness of thought, the almost Corneillian generosity they afford each other has its price in intellectual clarity even for the most level-headed brain among them. Wolmar absents himself with the express purpose of testing Julie and Saint-Preux alone together, saying, "je veux devoir la fidélité de ma femme à son cœur et non pas au hasard." His confidence, he further explains, is based upon what he has read in their letters: "Je confie Julie épouse et mère à celui qui, maître de contenter ses désirs, sut respecter Julie amante et fille" (p. 481). On the surface, this sentence makes it sound as if Saint-Preux had preferred respect *over* desire, which is objectively untrue; if anything, the precedent is one Wolmar should logically cite for keeping the two of them under surveillance. But semantically, by making an abstract absolute out of the verb *respecter*, it gives full credit to the tautological terminological system Saint-Preux and Julie had established for themselves, and renders them not only innocent but *essentially* so and thus incapable of betrayal. Again, tangible data would seem to prove the contrary of the conclusions the characters draw; there is no room for any such notion as countervailing evidence.

One footnote is interestingly revealing in this regard; it comes just after Julie has explained to Saint-Preux the importance of not

---

[124] She extends this to all present further on: "tout l'univers est ici pour moi; je jouis à la fois de l'attachement que j'ai pour mes amis, de celui qu'ils me rendent, de celui qu'ils ont l'un pour l'autre" (p. 677). Saint-Preux similarly stresses the multiple ties and their completeness when he writes to Bomston, after Claire's return: "Chaque jour [prépare notre réunion], en ramenant ici quelqu'une de ces âmes privilégiées qui sont si chères l'une à l'autre, qui sont si dignes de s'aimer, et qui semblent n'attendre que vous pour se passer du reste de l'univers" (p. 584; cf. p. 588).

[125] If this were not explicit in the passages cited in the previous note, the symbol of "les vins de tous les pays" (p. 593) would sufficiently suggest this sense of autonomy, of possessing everything necessary not only for everyday living but for exotic sensations (the Élysée also providing that). Notes Jean Starobinski: "Clarens est précisément une île, un asile, un jardin clos, une petite communauté étroitement repliée sur le bonheur qu'elle a su inventer. C'est le refuge terrestre des belles âmes, à l'intérieur duquel elles se sont *exclues* du reste du monde" (op. cit., p. 126).

teaching vanity to children: "Si jamais la vanité fit quelque heureux sur la terre, à coup sûr cet heureux-là n'était qu'un sot" (p. 561). The mutual reinforcement of character and Editor works to leave the reader no alternative response; but more significant is the nature of the assertion itself, which, paraphrased, amounts to this: if ever a vain man esteemed himself happy, he was wrong. The possibility of introducing empirical evidence is foreclosed by its disqualification in advance: if you can cite a contrary instance, it is ipso facto invalid. The thought system is completely self-corroborating.

The coherence of a text is realized through rhetorical strategies; it is to identify how they function here, and not simply to depreciate the text by exposing its contradictions, that these examples are worth examining. A tautology is an argument, in the formal sense, whose conclusions are already contained in its premises; a system which revolves on its own axes, generating only various manifestations of itself, is a tautological system. Any literary work considered in its own terms would be found to some extent to conform to this definition, but not in all could one isolate specific instances of formal, logical tautology. *Julie* seems to be a particularly remarkable case for this.

Example 1. Creation and solution of a problem ex nihilo: "la religion, qui lui rend amère l'incrédulité de son mari, lui donne seule la force de la supporter" (p. 578). Only faith gives her the courage to bear a suffering it has itself created; in its absence, there would be neither the courage nor the problem.

Example 2. Saint-Preux, explaining the secrecy surrounding Wolmar's agnosticism: "L'athéisme, qui marche à visage découvert chez les papistes, est obligé de se cacher dans tout pays où, la raison permettant de croire en Dieu, la seule excuse des incrédules leur est ôtée" (p. 579). What this confusing sentence (perhaps the form mirrors the contortions of the thought) seems to indicate is that religious constraint in a Protestant country is not really constraint, because Protestants are in the right (reason dictates you believe as they do); therefore, in those countries the atheists must go underground. This is a typical mindset of religious absolutism: repression of error forces people to be right, and is therefore liberating.

Example 3. Saint-Preux, describing the happiness reigning at Clarens: "Mais les instruments du bonheur ne sont rien pour qui ne sait pas les mettre en œuvre, et l'on ne sent en quoi le vrai bonheur consiste qu'autant qu'on est propre à le goûter" (pp. 512-13). This is a lot like the old argument about heaven, where everyone is filled to his capacity for happiness — but there are different capacities. You therefore, quite literally, don't know what you're missing. After the sentence Saint-Preux could have added: "et vice-versa: l'on n'est propre à goûter le vrai bonheur, qu'autant qu'on sent en quoi il consiste."

Example 4. After asserting that women naturally like dairy products and sugar while men prefer strong flavors and spirits, Saint-Preux concludes: "En effet, j'ai remarqué qu'en France, où les femmes vivent sans cesse avec les hommes, elles ont tout à fait perdu le goût du laitage, les hommes beaucoup celui du vin; et qu'en Angleterre, où les deux sexes sont moins confondus, leur goût propre s'est mieux conservé" (p. 435). Now the initial "En effet..." seems to suggest that what follows will in some way corroborate the previous remarks; whereas what this sentence contains is a *valid* observation on France and England *only if* the premises are already granted. Its conclusion, that "leur goût propre s'est mieux conservé," is an acceptable proposition only to someone who agrees on the definition of *goût propre* as a natural sexual characteristic.

Example 5. Wolmar explains that the servants are free not to like the entertainment offered at Clarens:

> Que s'il se trouve parmi nos gens quelqu'un, soit homme, soit femme, qui ne s'accommode pas de nos règles et leur préfère la liberté d'aller sous divers prétextes courir où bon lui semble, on ne lui en refuse jamais la permission; mais nous regardons ce goût de licence comme un indice très suspect, et nous ne tardons pas à nous défaire de ceux qui l'ont. Ainsi ces mêmes amusements qui nous conservent de bons sujets nous servent encore d'épreuve pour les choisir. [p. 437]

This is freedom only if you want to stay; it is slightly reminiscent of Wolmar's contemporary, the Baron de Thunder-ten-tronckh, whose servents "riaient quand il faisait des contes." The liberty offered is in fact an elimination test; therefore everyone present is in agreement. There is a similar liberality with regard to consumption of wine at the harvest festival: "On boit à discrétion; la liberté n'a point d'autres bornes que l'honnêteté.... Que s'il arrive à quelqu'un de s'oublier, on ne trouble point la fête par des réprimandes; mais il est congédié sans rémission dès le lendemain" (p. 596). The system at Clarens turns on a whole series of tautological structures like these, fail-safe mechanisms designed to make any dissension self-destruct. The perimeter of the property describes a vicious circle.[126]

Another strategy of thought and word is that which evades duplicity only by means of what one might call double talk: the displacement of consequences or responsability onto a rhetorical figment distinct from the person threatened. The most egregious case of this is Saint-Preux's implausible explanation for his drunken behavior: "Non, Julie: un démon jaloux d'un sort trop heureux pour un mortel a pris ma figure pour le troubler" (p. 116). This almost comic remark in an otherwise very serious letter is a virtual quotation from *Pathelin;*[127] given its obviousness, it is scarcely subversive. Such is not the case with the instance where a respectful Saint-Preux, who would have great difficulty expressing explicit desire, sends a double of himself to convey the message at less risk:

> Je n'ai traîné dans mon exil que la moindre partie de moi-même: tout ce qu'il y a de vivant en moi demeure auprès de vous sans cesse. *Il* erre impunément sur vos yeux, sur vos lèvres, sur votre sein, sur tous vos charmes; *il* pénètre partout comme une vapeur subtile, et *je* suis plus heureux en dépit de vous que je ne fus jamais de votre gré. [pp. 42-43]

Julie serves permissively as an object of desire without any direct overture on Saint-Preux's part; "il pénètre partout comme une vapeur subtile" conjures a wispy deflowering where the lover is satisfied but nothing has happened to her. The vapor is conceptually similar to the veil which later verbally preserves the essence of her chastity.

---

[126] As Jean Starobinski well observes, "Les maîtres gardent le privilège de *se sentir égaux* si bon leur semble; mais ce privilège n'appartient qu'à eux, et non aux serviteurs. Le sentiment de l'égalité reste ainsi un luxe de maître" (op. cit., p. 122).

[127] In that farce, Guillaume the clothier concludes that the devil and not Pathelin has stolen his goods: "Le dyable en lieu de ly a prins mon drap pour moy tenter."

This sort of immaculate penetration, with or without the interpretation that it also constitutes a masturbatory fantasy, is typical, although it is usually Julie rather than Saint-Preux who in such passages is doubled. First of all, in a comic echo (this time of Tartuffe), Saint-Preux displaces desire for the body onto a plane of purely spiritual adoration ultimately aspiring for the Creator: "Eh! si j'adore les charmes de ta personne, n'est-ce pas surtout pour l'empreinte de cette âme sans tache qui l'anime, et dont tous tes traits portent la divine enseigne?" (p. 15). Further on, grappling more openly with the question of desire, he takes an ostensible stand against desecration of Julie but mounts an attack on her absent body through its rhetorical clone:

> Ah! soyez heureuse aux dépens de mon repos; jouissez de toutes vos vertus; périsse le vil mortel qui tentera jamais d'en souiller une! ... Si j'ose former des vœux extrêmes, ce n'est plus qu'en votre absence; mes désirs, n'osant aller jusqu'à vous, s'adressent à votre image, et c'est sur elle que je me venge du respect que je suis contraint de vous porter. [p. 27]

This kind of erotic fantasizing stays with him right up to the moment preceding their night together, as the "vestiges" of Julie replace the purely wishful double and bring imagination to its most voluptuous point: "Toutes les parties de ton habillement éparses présentent à mon ardente imagination celles de toi-même qu'elles recèlent.... Empreintes délicieuses, que je vous baise mille fois!" (p. 121).[128] Thereafter, as if this represented in itself a developmental climax followed by diastole, there is less need for his letters to bear to Julie the particularly erotic functions of memory. Then he speaks more generally of "cette empreinte adorable dans [m]on âme ... ce fidèle miroir de Julie, sa pure image" (pp. 205-6), first inspired by her letters and subsequently through the portrait. On the other hand, Saint-Preux's "copy" is in her womb, a process he labels "tripler mon être" (p. 141) in order to preserve, and extend, the metaphor of Julie as another part of himself.

---

[128] In a sentimental rather than lubricious parallel, Julie enters the room of her mother and kisses her linens (p. 89). See too, on the wardrobe scene, Peggy Kamuf, "Inside *Julie*'s Closet," in *Romanic Review*, 69, No. 4 (1978), 296-306.

The question of whether this pair of lovers can be successfully transplanted to England also is posed in terms of finding an adequate equivalent for their natural habitat. Bomston offers a copy not of the real Valais but of a certain Valais as represented by Saint-Preux, and minus its repressive aspects: "L'odieux préjugé n'a point d'accès dans cette heureuse contrée; l'habitant paisible y conserve encore les mœurs simples des premiers temps, et l'on y trouve une image du Valais décrit avec des traits si touchants par la plume de votre ami!" (p. 175). Moreover, Bomston himself can substitute there for the father. But on this score the alternative unmasks its insufficiency, as Julie declares: "je ne déserterai jamais la maison paternelle" (p. 185). [129]

Doubles have a binding function in the narrative, linking, on multiple levels, the characters on the one hand and thematic registers on the other. The metaphysical implications of the conscience, for instance, are evident when Julie characterizes it as "ce simulacre éternel du vrai beau" (p. 199). The "inséparables" are obviously cast as psychological and moral counterparts,[130] although Claire is more a derivative of Julie[131] than her equivalent, insisting as she herself does on her imitation of Julie, her devotion to her and her willingness to follow her to the grave (p. 183). Their alikeness and their difference (owing principally to Julie's outside attachment) are maintained in careful balance throughout the first half of the story. There is a small but significant asymmetry at Saint-Preux's return in that Claire is not present, as if Julie herself were only half represented,[132] and of course by the fact that Claire is now widowed. Her own return is feted very much as if it were a marriage of the two cousins, whose primary decoration is their garlanded, intertwined insignia (p. 586); it is complemented too by a merger of their households.

But finally comes a movement of the plot to substitute Claire for Julie in relation to Saint-Preux. Like Phèdre, retelling the tale

---

[129] See Tanner's remarks on "the essential fictitiousness of Lord Bomston's offer" in op. cit., p. 132.

[130] "Une parfaite conformité de goûts et d'humeurs" (p. 180).

[131] "Tous mes sentiments me vinrent de toi" (p. 628); "Tiens mon âme à convert dans la tienne; que sert aux inséparables d'en avoir deux?" (p. 635).

[132] "Je n'ai vu Julie encore qu'à demi quand je n'ai pas vu sa cousine" (p. 407); cf. p. 606: "mon cœur ne les distingue plus l'une de l'autre."

of the Minotaur but substituting herself and Hippolyte for Ariane and Thésée, Julie now rewrites their own story as one where Claire's love for Saint-Preux antedates her own and leads, from one hypothesis to the next and one conditional to another, eventually to an equivalence or even priority of Claire's claim to him.[133] Taking charge of the negotiations, she unintentionally reveals that she is designing a con-fusion in which she is herself thoroughly implicated: "ne soyez plus qu'un pour vous *et pour moi* ... ; et j'en serai plus sûre de mes propres sentiments, quand je ne pourrai plus les distinguer entre vous" (p. 621). A simple transaction, according to the way Julie puts it to Saint-Preux, one in which the original contract is honored but the debt is transferable:

> N'est-ce pas aussi Julie que je vous donne? N'aurez-vous pas la meilleure partie de moi-même, et n'en serez-vous pas plus cher à l'autre? Avec quel charme alors *je me livrerai* sans contrainte à tout mon attachement pour vous! Oui, portez-lui la foi que vous m'avez jurée; que votre cœur remplisse avec elle tous les engagements qu'il prit avec moi; qu'il lui rende, s'il est possible, tout ce que vous redevez au mien. Ô Saint-Preux! je lui transmets cette ancienne dette. [pp. 658-59]

Saint-Preux counters: "j'ai cessé de prendre le change," now that he feels he finally can distinguish Mme de Wolmar from her look-alike Julie. Claire for her part perceives the effect of the role reversal as one fundamentally benefitting Julie, and in reply quotes back to her her very words (from p. 617): "c'est pour vous donner droit de représailles que vous m'accusez d'avoir jadis sauvé mon cœur aux dépens du vôtre. Je ne suis pas la dupe de ce tour-là" (p. 635).[134]

---

[133] "Je soupçonne que tu as aimé, sans le savoir, bien plus tôt que tu ne crois, ou du moins que le même penchant qui me perdit t'eût séduite si je ne t'avais prévenue.... Conçois-tu ... qu'avec tant de conformité dans tous nos goûts celui-ci seul ne nous eût pas été commun? Non, mon ange; tu l'aurais aimé, j'en suis sûre, si je ne l'eusse aimé la première.... Ma Claire, voilà ton histoire" (p. 617).

[134] As Claire sees it, the problem of "fidelity" is raised for her as well (p. 634). An interesting symbolic disparity opposes the thoughts of Claire and Saint-Preux about each other: Claire remarks that "je trouve son image plus dangereuse que sa personne" (p. 632) whereas he reacts in the opposite

Another assimilation and substitution is that of Henriette for Julie, whom she not only resembles physically but is to be modelled after: "fais-en, s'il se peut, une autre Julie" (p. 421). She becomes their common daughter:

> En effet, toutes deux l'appellent Henriette, ou ma fille, indifféremment. Elle appelle *maman* l'une, et l'autre *petite maman*; la même tendresse règne de part et d'autre; elle obéit également à toutes deux. S'ils demandent aux dames à laquelle elle appartient, chacune répond: "A moi." S'ils interrogent Henriette, il se trouve qu'elle a deux mères. On serait embarrassé à moins. Les plus clairvoyants se décident pourtant à la fin pour Julie. Henriette, dont le père était blond, est blonde comme elle, et lui ressemble beaucoup. [p. 588, italics in text]

What is particularly curious about this passage is that "les plus clairvoyants" are objectively wrong, and their eyesight can only have to do with the idea that even while fooled they see beyond the facts to a more essential truth of identification. Thus too the physical substitution of Henriette in Julie's place at the table, with perfect imitation of gesture and voice (p. 727): Henriette stands for a spiritual prolongation of Julie in their midst, although this present form of illusion (and even more so the resurrection illusion of the peasants) must be transcended. In the textual syntagm, nonetheless, Julie gets the last word and she returns to the spiritual identity with Claire: "Songez qu'il vous reste une autre Julie" (p. 729).

In speaking of rhetorical strategies, then, I am not just concerned to point up devious maneuvers which make the text waffle on its unsound foundation; it is a matter of trying to get at the devices by which any text can and must pull together its fundamental disparities, what Paul de Man calls its referential and its "messianic" functions. For *Julie* both purports to tell us about some authentic human beings (in an essential if not literal-historical sense) whose experiential truth is captured and offered for our appreciation, and on the other hand spins a legend about ultimate goodness if not divine grace. Patterns exists in all texts, and a pattern is, minimally,

---

way: "je la vois plus belle que je ne l'imagine" (p. 664). She finds the direct attraction insufficiently compelling; he is put off by the inadequacy of the idealization.

a repetition. Repetitions play a role in all narrative structure, most obviously in the refrains of oral epic; they also play a central ritual role in any sacred text. Both as novel and as bible, *Julie* is a text which repeats, corrects, corroborates, and problematizes itself: for even a faithful repetition questions to some degree the adequacy of the original utterance, never "means" precisely what the first occurrence did. Repetition is an essential structuring aspect of *Julie* and, as we shall see, it has a thematized significance as well.

Repetition can take many forms. That of doubling or copying has just been discussed, and itself has many kinds of manifestations, some of which emphasize resemblance and some difference. In an even more general way, redundancy underlies the whole text: *Julie* is an extraordinarily, pervasively repetitive text in that its tenets constantly return in various permutations; thematically, this insistence posits the ultimate singleness of their truth.[135] One of its most evident forms is that of citation, as in the passage quoted above where Claire repeats terms from Julie's letter. This is not infrequent, particularly to the degree that the characters have learned significant things from each other: "Souvenez-vous de ce que vous m'avez dit vous-même..." (p. 131). When Saint-Preux writes his critique of Paris, he gets back in return "la critique de ta critique" (p. 215) — a joint endeavor, by the way, of the *inséparables*. The following are four other avatars of repetition, in no particular hierarchical order.

1) *Imitation*. There is an evil manifestation of imitation represented by Paris, where the impoverished duplication of imperious fashion reduces all individuality to identity: "Tout le monde y fait à la fois la même chose dans la même circonstance; tout va par temps comme les évolutions d'un régiment en bataille: vous diriez que ce sont autant de marionnettes clouées sur la même planche, ou tirées par le même fil" (p. 227). And there is a positive one,

---

[135] The second preface concedes repetitiveness but turns it into an asset and sign of veracity. "N" presents the negative case: "Ce recueil est plein de choses d'une maladresse que le dernier barbouilleur eût évité: les déclamations, les *répétitions*, les contradictions, les *éternelles rabâcheries*." "R"'s version: "une lettre que l'amour a réellement dictée, une lettre d'un amant vraiment passionné, sera lâche, diffuse, toute en longueur, en désordre, en *répétitions*. Son cœur, plein d'un sentiment qui déborde, dit *toujours la même chose*, et n'a jamais achevé de dire" (pp. 755, 741).

emulation: the main characters elevate each other by their examples, and raise all lesser ones to their better selves. Everyone, by imitating Julie's qualities, moves closer to virtue and truth.

2) *Recapitulation.* Julie's 25-page letter 18 in part III is the best-known example of the need felt within the story to return to the past: to relive it, but also to re-evaluate it and indeed to revise it. Recapitulation is always a taking of stock; one never narrates the past in the same way it was experienced, nor can it be told twice the same way; it must be shaped and, in a word, imbued with meaning. "Résumons un peu" (p. 386), writes Claire at the beginning of part IV, where after a long interval things need some redefining, some *mise au point*. Some of Saint-Preux's résumé to Bomston, also early in part IV (p. 400), is technically absurd, because he tells his addressee things he already knows; but that is to overlook again the thematic importance of recapitulation for its own sake, the matter of how the various events, in Saint-Preux's eyes, relate to each other. Julie's "courte récapitulation de sa vie entière" (p. 711) in her very last letter is again a recapitulation, and repetition of the act of recapitulation.

3) *Repeat events.* Numerous scenes in the novel are replicated at some later stage, including the dramatic letter at the end, itself an echo of the decisive one in part III. Usually too the text calls attention to the repetition. Twice Saint-Preux has entered Julie's room: in part I, to make love to her, and in part III, during her smallpox. He himself underscores not only the recurrence but recalls the erotic nature of the first visit: "je reconnais les mêmes lieux. Une fois en ma vie je les ai traversés... à la même heure... avec le même mystère... j'étais tremblant comme aujourd'hui... le cœur me palpitait de même..." (p. 312). Naturally, the differences in the two situations are just as important, as is the fact that he will never return there again (nor indeed to the same house again). Twice Saint-Preux visits the same hotel room in Sion ("je la reconnus pour la même que j'avais occupée autrefois") and there he repeatedly stands humiliated in the presence of Edouard: "pour la seconde fois de ma vie je me vois devant lui dans la confusion que vous pouvez concevoir" (pp. 602-4). The memorably romantic bower at Clarens has its antithetic réplique in the Élysée, but the kiss will be repeated in the selfsame bower in the wilting presence of Wolmar. There is a further kind of repetition of the same scene, this time

also at Clarens and imitating its double nature: whereas Claire earlier prepared the way for Julie, this time Julie kisses Saint-Preux first with the surprise (and embarrassment) of the complementary kiss falling upon Claire (p. 586). Twice Julie brings Fanchon and Claude Anet together. And of course there are two trips to Meillerie, the second a sentimental but coercive pilgrimage with Julie to "les monuments des anciennes amours" (as the legend on the engraving styles it) where Saint-Preux once suffered and dreamed alone.[136] Doubtless there are other examples.[137]

4) *Uniformity*. In marked contrast to Paris, where Saint-Preux summarizes the frenzy of life by saying, "je ne puis être sûr un seul jour de ce que j'aimerai le lendemain" (p. 233), the inhabitants at Clarens enjoy an "immobilité d'extase" (p. 544). There the stories one tells are not exciting (p. 540) and one sings in unison (pp. 596-97); the "règles inaltérables et sûres" (p. 536) never need changing, and men and women know and adhere to their natural place.[138] Since all is well, it needs no improving and can only be repeated from day to day as its own ideal. "Tous les soirs, Julie, contente de sa journée, n'en désire point une différente pour le lendemain, et tous les matins elle demande au ciel un jour semblable à celui de la veille; elle fait toujours les mêmes choses parce qu'elles sont bien, et qu'elle ne connaît rien de mieux à faire" (p. 539).

All such events also serve to a certain extent as guideposts in the plot; they suggest that a cycle has been completed, and thus, along with length and pace of events, contribute to the rhythm of the narrative. Many other sorts of things also figure in, some of

---

[136] The repetition is underscored here by a number of terms constructed on the prefix *re*: *rappeler, retracer, revenir* (twice), *revoir*; cf. the commentary on this passage by Yves Le Hir in *Styles* (Paris: Klincksieck, 1972), pp. 54-61.

[137] Cf. Godelieve Mercken-Spaas, "La Répétition à la deuxième puissance," in *Studies in Eighteenth-Century Culture*, No. 5, pp. 203-13. Her discussion of the contrast between literal and symbolic repetitions is quite useful, but I have not followed her schema because she treats only two repetitions of events, and because there does not seem to be a formal criterion (non-arbitrary) for identifying a "symbolic" repetition where no event is repeated.

[138] The feminine code in particular is not merely alluded to but frequently insisted upon in *Julie*, where again it forms a part of the opposition to high and urban society: the overlap and confusion of masculine and feminine functions is to be rejected in favor of conformity with the natural divisions: cf. especially pp. 432, 435, 484-85, 530, 564.

them anticipatory. When Edouard writes to Saint-Preux at Clarens: "Continuez vos descriptions: malgré le mauvais ton de vos lettres, elles me touchent et m'instruisent; elles m'inspirent des projets de retraite et de repos convenables à mes maximes et à mon âge" (p. 511; cf. p. 574), one can be rather sure that the lengthy letters thus authorized will continue (Saint-Preux's following is 31 pages) and besides it seems likely that Edouard can himself be expected to end his own adventures by joining their circle. Premonitions too anticipate probable developments, for they can hardly serve any other purpose unless they draw attention to particular illusions the characters harbor. "Ainsi tout déconcerte nos projets, tout trompe notre attente, tout trahit des feux que le ciel eût dû couronner! Vils jouets d'une aveugle fortune [etc.]" (p. 119): here Julie is being humorous, but simply by parodying one of their real styles; usually such language is indeed a sign of something significant, as when she writes, "Jamais je n'eus si grand besoin de te voir, ni si peu d'espoir de te voir longtemps" (p. 142), or "le temps de l'amour serait-il passé, et faut-il ne se plus revoir?" (p. 152). These are omens that any reader recognizes, even if they do not necessarily carry a high reliability index — they suggest what may lie ahead, but not unambiguously.

Sometimes, however, the gist is more clearly prophetic or the tone more sententious. One can take it as pompous or defiant rhetoric (like the "eternal" vow never to drink again) when Saint-Preux intones: "jamais les nœuds ni de l'amour ni de l'hymen ne m'uniront à d'autres qu'à Julie d'Étange" (p. 203); but the centrality of the subject matter suggest that the vow may have a long-range signification as a function of the narrative, one not entirely limited by the psychological determination of the character at the specific moment it is uttered. The odds increase when other characters contribute similar pronouncements. Claire, after telling Saint-Preux that everything is lost in advance because "le ciel [really referring to the father] vous l'avait ôtée même avant qu'elle se donnât à vous" (p. 290), also records as countervailing truth that Julie's mother now realizes "combien votre amour porte un caractère naturel de sympathie que le temps ni les efforts humains ne sauraient effacer" (p. 293), and Julie too says that "ce cœur ... te restera jusqu'à mon dernier soupir" (p. 313).

On the other hand, there are more muted messages that also play a narrative control function. No one comes forth to corroborate Saint-Preux when he makes this threat/prophecy: "Elle passera ses jours dans la douleur, tourmentée à la fois de vains regrets et de vains désirs, sans pouvoir jamais contenter ni l'amour ni la vertu" (p. 297): in a less straightforward way than other predictions, it will nonetheless prove accurate. The difficulty in evaluating it when first encountered is precisely that it hovers somewhere indecisively between prophecy (in which case it could be — narratologically — trusted) and spite (which makes it just an expression of his displeasure).

For there are obscure and ambiguous signs, and the plot plays with and against these anticipations too. Julie believes, and therefore leads one to believe, that through disease she has lost her beauty and that this will cool Wolmar's ardor; in conjunction with this, she seems to believe that what she takes for a vision or dream may be the sign that Saint-Preux is perhaps able to resume his former position as lover. Unless, that is, the apparition instead portends Saint-Preux's death, in which case it is tantamount to a symbol of their implicit death pact.[139] But all these mistaken alternatives merely serve to lend dramatic value to the illusion.

Another quasi-prophecy of Julie's in part V is worth considering: "Si le ciel, dit-elle souvent, me refuse la conversion de cet honnête homme, je n'ai plus qu'une grâce à lui demander, c'est de mourir la première" (p. 578). This has been cited as evidence that the novel's end is meant to anticipate Wolmar's conversion, so that that expectation may be assumed as part of the work's conclusion. This amounts, however, to giving full faith and credit to only half of Julie's sentence. If the first part is taken instead as simply wishful thinking, then it is rather the last part that serves a prophetic function: and since it is indeed realized, there are grounds for saying that the ambiguity favors not the foreshadowing of Wolmar's conversion but simply of Julie's death. There are indeed some elements of suspense in the plot, although the keys to most of the "mysteries" and "secrets" referred to by the characters are known, or nearly

---

[139] "Est-ce un pressentiment de la mort du meilleur des hommes? Est-ce un avertissement qu'il n'est déjà plus? Le ciel daigne-t-il me guider au moins une fois, et m'invite-t-il à suivre celui qu'il me fit aimer?" (p. 309).

so, by the reader.[140] The reason for Julie's silent anguish in parts IV-VI is long held in abeyance — both for us and for correspondent Edouard, who must ask more than once for an explanation — yet repeatedly alluded to (e.g., pp. 496, 512) even in footnotes (pp. 490, 512). Only its precise nature remains in doubt.[141]

On the other hand, however blurry the signposts may be on other questions including Wolmar's putative conversion, they are rather clear on one event that is well prepared so as finally *not* to take place, and that is the marriage between Claire and Saint-Preux. As early as part one there are suggestions that Claire may lie in reserve as the *pis-aller* for Saint-Preux, especially his exclamation: "Ah! qu'en ce moment j'eusse été amoureux de cette aimable cousine, si Julie n'eût pas existé" (p. 90). That, plus the fact of their triangular intimacy,[142] and the way Saint-Preux eventually consolidates the cousins — "mon cœur ne distingue plus l'une de l'autre" (p. 606) — creates the expectation, even before the explicit marriage project is enunciated, that Saint-Preux and Claire may gravitate toward each other and effect more or less spontaneously the very kind of double substitution that Julie finally proposes. Claire's distraction (p. 584), their apparent emotion when forced to embrace,[143] certain glances (p. 596), hints by Wolmar (pp. 609, 633), and most of all the kiss he plants conspicuously on Claire's hand (p. 631) all point to a not even faintly concealed swing toward mechanical plot resolution. Instead, it is all thrown off the track by an intervening vow of Saint-Preux's to Bomston: "je te suivrai partout: j'en fais le *serment solennel* à la face du Dieu vivant, je

---

[140] For instance, Julie's mysterious project for marriage is more easily divined by the reader than by Saint-Preux, and her "dangereux secret ... odieux mystère" (pp. 288-89) is a (presumed) secret to Wolmar only — though in fact he too knows, and that is the *real* secret for the reader, although it again is suggested more than once (e.g., p. 391).

[141] The second preface gives voice to the feeling that the plot is all too transparent: "rien d'inopiné, point de coup de théâtre. Tout est prévu longtemps d'avance, tout arrive comme il est prévu" (p. 739).

[142] Jean H. Hagstrum sees in this situation a tension between heterosexual and homosexual forms of love, romance and friendship: see *Sex and Sensibility: Ideal and Erotic Love from Milton to Mozart* (Chicago: University of Chicago Press, 1980), pp. 227-41.

[143] "[Claire] prit en rougissant le parti d'imiter sa cousine. Cette rougeur que je remarquai trop me fit un effet que je ne saurais dire, mais je ne me sentis pas dans ses bras sans émotion" (p. 586).

ne te quitte plus qu'à la mort" (p. 641). This prior commitment in no-nonsense language in effect takes away his freedom to give his own hand in marriage, and thus, removing the consolation and security that their union might have offered to Julie, perhaps seals her death. This marriage plot is important: it plays the absolutely crucial role of being the happy ending that did not happen, the narrative's facile, coasting path that it refused to follow.

There also has intervened by this point Saint-Preux's ominously repeated dream of Julie's face veiled in death (pp. 603-4). Its portent is quite unmistakeable and its effect is not lost on Claire, who responds as someone who, especially as a denizen not of real life but of narrative, knows such a sign cannot be lightly dismissed: "Ce rêve a quelque chose d'effrayant qui m'inquiète et m'attriste malgré que j'en aie.... Je n'approche pas de Julie sans trembler de la perdre; à chaque instant je crois voir sur son visage la pâleur de la mort; et ce matin, la pressant dans mes bras, je me suis sentie en pleurs sans savoir pourquoi. Ce voile! Ce voile!..." (p. 607). For the potency of this omen she holds Saint-Preux doubly implicated, first for having failed on his panicky return to Clarens to cross over the wall (behind which he hears Julie's voice) so as to gain immediate assurance of her good health, and/or for having been unable in the dream itself to lift the veil: [144] "Non, je ne puis vous pardonner d'avoir pu l'écarter sans l'avoir fait, et j'ai bien peur de n'avoir plus désormais un moment de contentement que je ne vous revoie auprès d'elle" (p. 608). She will in fact never see them together again, and in some obscure way Saint-Preux remains responsible for having foreseen and thus précipitated the death of Julie.

Neither Claire nor anyone else can give a logical account for this question of causality: "Je ne suis pas crédule, mais craintive. Je sais bien qu'un songe n'amène pas un événement, mais j'ai toujours peur que l'événement n'arrive à sa suite" (p. 632). Finally Claire herself must seal Julie's death with a veil, and the Editor points out the explicit realization of the dream, with the healthy Enlightenment comment: "L'événement n'est pas prédit parce qu'il

---

[144] It is unclear whether the second idea is merely a metaphor for the first, but it hardly matters, inasmuch as the crossing of the wall itself would have been a purely symbolic assurance, not a literal one: after all, it was Claire herself Julie was talking to at the time when Saint-Preux heard them.

arrivera; mais il arrive parce qu'il a été prédit" (p. 725). It begs the question, of course, because the dream does explain why Claire produced the veil, but not why Julie died. The Editor is not raising philosophical questions about fate here, but rather about which function takes precedence in narrative, where just possibly the event is predicted in order to happen.

There is certainly a conversion motif in the last half of the book, but that is not the same thing as a conversion. Wolmar's obvious right to membership in the select pool of Clarens in the first place makes him "deserve" to be a believer: that is a normal part of their baggage. Saint-Preux breaks the news of Wolmar's unbelief to Bomston adding, "je n'avais pas conçu le moindre soupçon" (p. 579), as if the long-delayed secret were a matter of cancer or venereal disease. Bomston's aid is enlisted because being English he is, by conventional assimilation, a philosopher, and can therefore meet Wolmar on his own terms and thus complement Julie's sentimental approach; refuting Julie's and Saint-Preux's arguments is child's play to Wolmar, who can even feed them arguments to use against him. But Wolmar, having "si peu de cette ironique fierté des esprits forts" (p. 581), is no Voltaire. Julie asserts, "d'un ton ferme et persuadé," that the right moment will come and, however obliquely, she links this thought to that of her death: "Puissé-je l'acheter aux dépens de ma vie! mon dernier jour serait le mieux employé" (p. 583).

That is reason enough for considering carefully what transpires that last day. But the religious aspects of all this are really rather confusing. For one thing, Saint-Preux cautions Julie because she for her part seems to be on the path leading to visions and fanaticism (p. 673); on the other hand, the dying Julie never mentions the Lord (only God), and even less Jesus. The indices all prepare for some dramatic change; in his last letter, Wolmar tells how his doubts grew during Julie's last days, about the need to believe in her continued existence, about his first tears. And Julie's own final letter leaves only, apparently, the finishing touches for Saint-Preux to supervise: "Soyez chrétien pour l'engager à l'être. Le succès est plus près que vous ne pensez: ... ma confiance ne me trompera pas" (p. 730). This would be a more decisive indication of the imminent conversion, perhaps, were it not for the fact that the same letter appears equally confident about the ill-fated marriage between Saint-Preux and Claire. And the next letter — and last of the novel — which again calls on Saint-Preux to "achever ce grand ouvrage" simultaneously puts a blunt end to talk of marriage. One could say that all this constitutes a program for a conversion in the finale, if in fact such a conversion took place. As is it, however, what is significant about the theme may be precisely that its consummation is evidently lacking: that a narrative procedure leads one to expect a possible result but leaves it ultimately problematic. Diegetically, Wolmar's conversion as event is no more part of the text than is Rodrigue's and Chimène's betrothal part of *Le Cid*.

From that standpoint, in consequence, *Julie* is a story of a sacrifice which does not guarantee redemption. For Julie herself, however, perhaps it does. For her, five parts out of six of her story constitute a saga of sacrifice. What is meant by that word in part one belongs merely to troubadour vocabulary or amorous hyperbole; Julie does say, for instance, "il faut que ce mot de vertu ne soit qu'un vain nom, ou qu'elle exige des sacrifices" (p. 93), but the one she alludes to is only a postponed tryst. In part two, though, Julie becomes the victim sacrificed and offering itself (pp. 176-77), and in part three Saint-Preux joins her as one who must sacrifice (pp. 289-93): "Tel est, mon ami, le sacrifice héroïque auquel nous sommes tous deux appelés" (p. 342). This sense of grandeur itself provides support, as Julie henceforth gives of herself to provide the happiness of Wolmar, her children, Claire, and the rest of her entourage.[145] But despite the greater contentment she always claims this has resulted in, she makes a revealing comparison at the end: "Après tant de sacrifices, je compte pour peu celui qui me reste à faire, ce n'est que mourir une fois de plus" (p. 729). Julie's sacrifices were tantamount to as many deaths.

"On meurt ainsi par degrés" (p. 380), confesses Julie. The real problem is to identify what survives these stages. Part three brings a relaxation in tempo which the characters themselves comment upon: "Cette éternité de bonheur ne fut qu'un instant de ma vie," writes Saint-Preux to Claire; "Le temps a repris sa lenteur" (p. 296). What is referred to is, as the quotation suggests, entirely a matter

---

[145] Laure has at least this much in common with Julie, "le sacrifice de tout mon bonheur à un devoir si cruel" (p. 640).

of subjective time, since parts one and two each encompass objectively more chronological span than the whole last half of the novel, which is lived nonetheless at a slower pace. The rhythmic transition has thematic implications which Claire underscores in her answer to Saint-Preux. The compressed, intensive past ("vous avez épuisé durant une année les plaisirs d'une vie entière") is vulnerable to decay, and the stasis now imposed affords a preservation of that experience's beauties from the ravages of time:

> Le temps eût joint au *dégoût* d'une longue possession le progrès de l'âge et le *déclin* de la beauté: il semble se *fixer* en votre faveur par votre séparation: vous serez *toujours* l'un pour l'autre à la fleur des ans; vous vous verrez sans cesse tels que vous vous vîtes en vous quittant; et vos cœurs, unis jusqu'au tombeau, prolongeront dans une illusion charmante votre jeunesse avec vos amours. [p. 300]

And Julie will add that love, if it is not pure illusion, seems at least restricted to youth: "depuis que le monde existe on n'a jamais vu deux amants en cheveux blancs soupirer l'un pour l'autre" (p. 352).

Past versus present is one of the dominant motifs of part four. The danger for the former lovers, according to both Claire and Wolmar, lies in memory and not in the present attraction as such: "Il l'aime dans le temps passé: voilà le vrai mot de l'énigme. Ôtez-lui la mémoire, il n'aura plus d'amour" (p. 492). The exact effect of visiting Meillerie seems for both of them difficult to define, although this confrontation with concrete "monuments" is in some way crucial. It contributes to Saint-Preux's happiness because he seems afterward to have renounced ulterior motives: Julie, on the other hand, is probably affected mostly by a feeling of vulnerability, which will not be entirely evident until part six, where she will prove to have been on the verge of succumbing just when she was most unambiguously asserting her security. But "les monuments à craindre," says Julie later, "existent partout où nous sommes; car nous les portons avec nous" (p. 655). Perhaps equally upsetting is the unanticipated Proustian intrusion of the past when Saint-Preux sets foot in the room at Sion, the only moment when anyone in this novel expresses such an uncanny sensation of collapsing time: "je crus redevenir à l'instant tout ce que j'étais alors; dix années s'effacèrent de ma vie, et tous mes malheurs furent oubliés"

(p. 602). There is no redeeming euphoria, however, for the present instantly reasserts itself. With a certain fidelity to memory, Saint-Preux concedes that the present no longer lives, yet at the same time says it cannot fade (p. 663).

The emphasis in the second half, as we have seen, is on permanence, not exactly arresting time but nullifying the threat of change by means of uniformity: "Un état aussi permanent laisse peu de vicissitudes à craindre" (p. 495). Happiness seems to consist principally in this sense of *durée*. "Se plaire dans la durée de son état, n'est-ce pas un signe assuré qu'on y vit heureux?" (p. 539). Yet that rhetorical question is not innocuous: what would constitute a *sure* sign that one "is" happy? The whole matter of *guérison* which structures the second movement of the story suggests replacing a temporary, abnormal state with a stable and felicitous one; and it targets Saint-Preux primarily, upon the assumption that Julie's need is already less acute. Yet it is she who in dying radically questions the success of the search for stability, and her words are obsessed with the vulnerability to decline: "Mon bonheur monté par degrés était au comble; il ne pouvait plus que déchoir; il était venu sans être attendu, il se fût enfui quand je l'aurais cru durable.... Non, quand on a tout acquis, il faut perdre, ne fût-ce que le plaisir de la possession qui s'use par elle" (p. 714). Claire had already said to Saint-Preux earlier that possession "s'use à force d'en jouir" (p. 299): *usure* has eroded even Clarens. The new cycle which was assembling the major characters together there is in fact arrested by the departure of Edouard and Saint-Preux; the process of dispersal has already begun, and Julie's death contributes to it. Saint-Preux is invited back (p. 728), but we never see his reply, and Julie's last words look forward instead to reunion with him in death. Nor can we assess the supposed "recovery" of Saint-Preux, who never sees Julie after the moment Edouard pronounces him healed; indeed he is suddenly eclipsed at the end, and we know nothing more of him.

Bonheur is another term that assumes, early on, a primarily sexual meaning; [146] even otherwise, it is a fragile notion, for Julie

---

[146] Julie and Saint-Preux share this conventional use of the terms *bonheur* and *heureux*. "Seriez-vous tombé dans cette erreur cruelle, que *l'amour heureux* n'a plus de ménagements à garder avec la pudeur, et qu'on ne doit plus de

after crying that "le bonheur a fui loin de nous" (p. 76) can also oscillate toward euphoria: "j'ai le regret de [n']avoir qu'une [âme] pour jouir de tout mon bonheur" (p. 99) — and back: "Ah! misérable fille, c'est bien à toi de parler de bonheur! En peut-il jamais être où règnent la honte et le remords?" (p. 111). Finally hope of happiness is abandoned all around. Saint-Preux: "il faut immoler le bonheur au devoir" (p. 291); Julie: "je suis morte au bonheur, à la paix, à l'innocence" (p. 295); Claire: "vos feux et votre bonheur ne pouvaient plus que décliner" (p. 300). Once more, the happiness at Clarens depends upon leaving vicissitudes behind, replacing pleasure with tranquillity. "La douce chose de couler ses jours dans le sein d'une tranquille amitié, à l'abri de l'orage des passions impétueuses!" (p. 422, cf. p. 470). The city, paradoxically, by comparison, is stilted and uninteresting: "ils ne connaissent jamais qu'une manière de vivre, et s'en ennuient toujours" (p. 589), whereas the calm of Clarens is absorbing and gratifying. Above all, it is collective: "Venez, hommes rares, augmenter et partager le bonheur de cette maison" (p. 643), writes Wolmar. Clarens is thus the last imaginable abode for *ennui*.

It is a long way from the end of the book, however, in part four, that Julie lets drop the sobering realization, "il n'y a point de vrai bonheur sur la terre.... Je ne suis pas heureuse" (p. 496). She relates this state to her husband's religious scepticism, but it is not long before she gives her dissatisfaction much more general and fundamental implications: "l'*ennui* d'être toujours à son aise est enfin le pire de tous" (p. 530). This remark in truth is not from a passage where she is discussing unhappiness, but she frequently reveals her uncertainties precisely when she is ostensibly addressing the opposite topic. "Faites enfin le bonheur l'un de l'autre, et rien ne manquera plus au mien" (p. 680) is said just when her sense of happiness is rapidly crumbling under her. It is desire now, and not fulfillment, which appears dreamily attractive; she

---

respect à celle dont on n'a plus de rigueur à craindre?" (p. 112); then she invites Saint-Preux to her room with: "non, nous ne quitterons point cette courte vie sans avoir un instant *goûté le bonheur*" (p. 120). And when Saint-Preux bewails that "il ne restera sur la terre aucun monument de mon *bonheur*" (pp. 160-61), he is referring to offspring.

denies that happiness can be satisfactorily self-contained,[147] and the very same letter bears the startling revelation which undermines in one swoop a large part of the rhetoric of Clarens: "Je ne vois partout que sujets de contentement, et je ne suis pas contente: une langueur secrète s'insinue au fond de mon cœur; je le sens vide et gonflé. . . . Mon ami, je suis trop heureuse; *le bonheur m'ennuie*" (p. 682). "Le chant du cygne," remarks the footnote. The "comble du bonheur permis sur la terre" (p. 711) which she will once more attest to on her deathbed cannot stave off the avalanche of anxieties (p. 714), ones which really, to her, require her death. Doubtless we are to take this as a metaphysical thirst, an aspiration to an ultimate fulfillment;[148] but what it says about life on earth in the best of circumstances, surrounded by prosperity on the one hand and virtue on the other, is no more reassuring for that. And it was precisely that possibility of earthly happiness that was so long insisted upon.

Such subversive revelations oblige us to reread radically much of what has previously flowed by as a harmonious vision. What can one think of passages like these, once the outcome of Julie's *bonheur* is known?

> Les noirs soucis, l'ennui, la tristesse, n'approchent pas plus d'ici que le vice et les remords dont ils sont le fruit. [p. 512]
>
> S'il est au monde une vie heureuse, c'est sans doute celle qu'ils y passent. [p. 512]
>
> Le ciel semble l'avoir donnée [Julie] à la terre pour y montrer à la fois l'excellence dont une âme humaine est susceptible, et le bonheur dont elle peut jouir dans l'obscurité de la vie privée. [p. 516]
>
> Elle jouit du bien qu'elle fait, et le voit profiter. Le bonheur qu'elle goûte se multiplie et s'étend autour d'elle. [p. 517]
>
> Si le bonheur et la paix ne sont pas dans l'âme de Julie, où sera leur asile ici-bas? [p. 572]

---

[147] "Malheur à qui n'a plus rien à désirer! il perd pour ainsi dire tout ce qu'il possède. On jouit moins de ce qu'on obtient que de ce qu'on espère et l'on n'est heureux qu'avant d'être heureux" (p. 681).

[148] This is suggested elsewhere, for instance in Saint-Preux's remark: "On dirait que rien de terrestre ne pouvant suffire au besoin d'aimer dont elle est dévorée, cet excès de sensibilité soit forcé de remonter à sa source" (p. 576).

To be sure, with regard to chronology and psychology, these remarks come from characters who at the time they were pronounced did not know better; that is no problem. The difficulty comes on the level of the ideological message inherent in the work as a whole. For if we are supposed to accept the establishment of happiness through virtue where only a ruined ideal once stood, then there has been a dreadful erosion of the underpinnings of the basic idea almost since the time it was first sketched out. At some unknown point, in terms of the secret evolution of her own thought processes, Julie has written to Saint-Preux of their present happiness: "Voyez ... quelle est notre situation présente. En est-il au monde une plus agréable? ... À qui devons-nous un bonheur si rare?" (p. 652). It is now at least possible to read this passage as if all were false, knowingly false: her letter's expressions then become only a desperate gesture of recuperation. Edouard's question quoted at the end of the series above, intended rhetorically, becomes disturbing in this light, effectively the key to the antitext contained in the edifying *Julie:* for if the conditional clause must finally be answered negatively, the text has no resolution to offer to the dilemma: *where* indeed will be "leur asile ici-bas?" Of all the things cascading together at Julie's death, two of her utterances stand out almost as if she had died in order to say them: one is, of course, her electrifying closing line reaffirming her love for Saint-Preux; the other consecrates the rescue, via the other world, of her fragile quasi-happiness: "Je fus heureuse, je le suis, je vais l'être: *mon bonheur est fixé, je l'arrache* à la fortune; il n'a plus de bornes que l'éternité" (pp. 714-715).

Julie's significance has always extended beyond herself and her acknowledged idolater. Although not much detail is ever given about the small community of Vevay and Julie's relations with it, the well-founded rumors which circulate about her sexual attachment do not prevent an allusion to her "réputation sans tache" (p. 154) nor the adoration which her generous and loving heart evokes in the town (p. 180). Many men may resemble Saint-Preux, says Edouard, "mais il n'y a qu'une Julie au monde" (p. 174). At Clarens she becomes a public institution: "vous êtes pour tout le pays un dépôt cher et sacré" (p. 594). The fact that she is inscrutable and ultimately unknown [149] contributes to the constitution of a queen-like figure [150] whose taste and charity spread round about her contageously. Julie never travels — only others, and she is the one who waits and welcomes. She becomes the archmother, not of her children alone but of Claire's and of the whole neighborhood, ministering to all, goddess of justice (p. 584), distributor of alms and pardons *(gratia plena),* [151] protector of all suffering creatures. [152] She is in short the mother superior of Clarens, en route to becoming its patron saint (or its Protestant equivalent). The tearful Julie kneeling in prayer for her husband's salvation fixes her image as an uxorial saint. Impurity withers at the very sight of her. [153]

The principal job of the text is to transform Julie into a legend. It starts its work almost unnoticed, camouflaging its mythmaking language in the hyperbolic trappings of amorous discourse: "Ah! je l'ai dit cent fois, tu es un ange du ciel, ma Julie! Sans doute, avec tant d'autorité sur mon âme, la tienne est plus divine qu'humaine. Comment n'être pas éternellement à toi, puisque ton règne est céleste? et que servirait de cesser de t'aimer s'il faut toujours qu'on t'adore" (p. 97). Nothing at this stage suggests that in time everyone will talk about Julie the same way. Another of this function's disguises is levity, still borrowing on the same register as before:

---

[149] It is Wolmar who says of her, "on n'en peut parler que par conjecture; un voile de sagesse et d'honnêteté fait tant de replis autour de son cœur, qu'il n'est plus possible à l'œil humain d'y pénétrer, pas même au sien propre" (p. 492).

[150] Saint-Preux: "j'aurais baisé le bord de sa robe" (p. 404); Claire: "Ma Julie, tu est faite pour régner. Ton empire est le plus absolu que je connaisse" (p. 390); Wolmar: "il y a longtemps que nous sommes tous vos sujets" (p. 545).

[151] "Quand M. de Wolmar a dit: 'Je vous chasse', on peut implorer l'intercession de madame, l'obtenir quelquefois, et rentrer en grâce à sa prière; mais un congé qu'elle donne est irrévocable, et il n'y a plus de grâce à espérer" (p. 429).

[152] "Ce sont, dit-elle, des animaux qui souffrent; délivrons-les" (p. 498).

[153] Of Laure, Claire says: "La pauvre malheureuse oserait-elle mêler son haleine à la tienne, oserait-elle respirer près de toi? Elle y serait plus mal à son aise qu'un possédé touché par des reliques; ton seul regard la ferait rentrer en terre; ton ombre seule la tuerait" (p. 627).

> Dites, quelle est donc cette mortelle unique dont le moindre empire est dans sa beauté, et qui, semblable aux puissances éternelles, se fait également adorer et par les biens et par les maux qu'elle fait? [p. 195]
>
> Combien je m'applaudis d'y revoir briller dans tout son éclat l'image de la vertu, d'y contempler la tienne, ô Julie, assise sur un trône de gloire et dissipant d'un souffle tous ces prestiges! [p. 233]

Despite the teasing irony, Julie seems, for reasons that may vary locally, to attract this sort of terminology. She is the first, indeed, to apply to herself allegorical figures which in many ways are vintage *Roman de la Rose:*

> Cent fois mes yeux furent témoins de ses combats et de sa victoire; les siens étincellaient du feu de ses désirs, il s'élançait vers moi dans l'impétuosité d'un transport aveugle, il s'arrêtait tout à coup; une barrière insurmontable semblait m'avoir entourée, et jamais son amour impétueux, mais honnête, ne l'eût franchie. [Julie, p. 70]
>
> Ah! quel sentiment coupable eût pénétré jusqu'à elle à travers cette inviolable escorte? [Saint-Preux, p. 470]
>
> Comment le rempart qui défend ta personne n'a-t-il pu te garantir d'une crainte ignominieuse? ... Regarde tout autour de toi, tu n'y verras rien qui ne doive élever et soutenir ton âme. Ton mari ... tes enfants ... ton vénérable père ... ton amie ... sa fille ... ton ami ... toi-même enfin ... [Claire, p. 485]
>
> Elle s'environnait de la majesté suprême; je voyais Dieu sans cesse entre elle et moi. Quel coupable désir eût pu franchir une telle sauvegarde? Mon cœur s'épurait au feu de son zèle, et je partageais sa vertu. [Saint-Preux, p. 580]

Metaphor alone seems able to express anything essential about Julie. About her sin: "Une tache paraît-elle au soleil?" (p. 73), asks Claire. A Saint-Preux no longer in the throes of infatuation still exclaims: "Julie! femme incomparable! vous exercez dans la simplicité de la vie privée le despotique empire de la sagesse et des bienfaits" (p. 594). His voyage around the world serves as an abstract indicator of experiences garnered, but very little concrete brings it to mind except a banal allusion here and there to a tropical island or China;[154] largely, on the contrary, it serves to authorize the mythical rhetoric since it rationalizes the assertion that Julie's realm really is unique in the world (p. 397), that the entire globe has but two regions, where Julie is and where she is not: the rest is void (p. 401). The kind of adoration that erotic love once inspired is now evoked under other rubrics in terms whose pomp, even with its grain of salt, plays upon the legend that Julie and all those around her know is taking form before their eyes: "Chère amie, ouvrez-moi votre maison sans crainte; elle est pour moi le temple de la vertu; partout j'y vois son simulacre auguste, et ne puis servir qu'elle auprès de vous. Je ne suis pas un ange, il est vrai; mais j'habiterai leur demeure, j'imiterai leurs exemples: on les fuit quand on ne leur veut pas ressembler" (p. 666). The comparison with the palace of a queen is never made; instead what suits Julie is the clean but orderly spareness of the temple of a divinity.

As if there were a particular grace which flowed through Julie or emanated directly from her, her influence spreads to all about her, assimilating them to her own merit. And like that of the king whose touch can heal, sometimes this magnetism is endowed with a cleansing, purifying power:

> Voilà ce qui doit arriver à toutes les âmes d'une certaine trempe; elles transforment, pour ainsi dire, les autres en elles-mêmes; elles ont une sphère d'activités dans laquelle rien ne leur résiste: on ne peut les connaître sans les vouloir imiter, et de leur sublime élévation elles attirent à elles tout ce qui les environne.... Vous donnerez le ton à tous ceux qui vivront avec vous; ils vous fuiront ou vous deviendront semblables, et tout ce que vous aurez vu n'aura peut-être rien de pareil dans le reste du monde. [Claire, p. 180]

> Je ne sais quel enchantement secret règne dans ta personne; mais tout ce qui la touche semble y participer; il ne faut qu'apercevoir un coin de ta robe pour adorer celle qui la porte. [Saint-Preux, p. 272]

---

[154] As Lionel Gossman put it, "The journey round the world has been but an episode in the village drama" ("The Worlds of *La Nouvelle Héloïse*," in *Studies on Voltaire and the Eighteenth Century*, 41, pp. 235-76, p. 255).

> Sitôt que j'approche d'elle, sa vue apaise mon trouble, ses regards épurent mon cœur. Tel est l'ascendant du sien, qu'il semble toujours inspirer aux autres le sentiment de son innocence et le repos qui en est l'effet. [Saint-Preux, p. 495]
>
> Ne voyez-vous pas que ce concours dont vous vous félicitez est votre ouvrage, et que tout ce qui vous approche est contraint de vous ressembler? [Saint-Preux, p. 571]
>
> Soit que l'exemple de ton retour à toi-même me donnât plus de force pour t'imiter, soit que ma Julie épure tout ce qui l'approche, je me trouvai tout à fait tranquille. [Claire, p. 630]

Claire, in the first of the above passages, includes Saint-Preux with Julie in a combined influence,[155] tempering thus the starkness of the myth in its more or less nascent stages; thereafter, no one confuses Saint-Preux with the divine light.

Her aura only augments as death approaches; when she speaks, something like a transfiguration takes place for all to witness:

> Ce discours, prononcé d'abord d'un ton grave et posé, puis avec plus d'accent et d'une voix plus élevée, fit sur tous les assistants, sans m'en excepter, une impression d'autant plus vive, que les yeux de celle qui le prononça brillaient d'un feu surnaturel; un nouvel éclat animait son teint, elle paraissait rayonnante; et s'il y a quelque chose au monde qui mérite le nom de céleste, c'était son visage tandis qu'elle parlait. [p. 704]

This progressive isolation of Julie as a pillar of light, both symbolically on a thematic plane and in local prestige on a diegetic one, culminates in the death of a saint: "vous avez vécu pour la charité; vous mourez martyre de l'amour maternel" (p. 705). The phrase sounds hagiographic, as the two levels, popular adoration and mythic apotheosis, coalesce around her deathbed. Her own discourse be-

---

[155] Bomston, in a similar vein at this early stage, combines them both as mythical lovers and spiritual beacons: "Ces deux belles âmes sortirent l'une pour l'autre des mains de la nature; c'est dans une douce union, c'est dans le sein du bonheur, que, libres de déployer leurs forces et d'exercer leurs vertus, elles eussent éclairé la terre de leurs exemples" (p. 169).

comes at times very nearly messianic: "Non, mes amis, non, mes enfants, je ne vous quitte pas, pour ainsi dire, je reste avec vous; en vous laissant tous unis, mon esprit, mon cœur, vous demeurent. Vous me verrez sans cesse entre vous; vous vous sentirez sans cesse environnés de moi... Et puis nous nous rejoindrons, j'en suis sûre" (p. 714). These words are beautifully hedged, enough to sound not quite like a biblical quotation — just enough, indeed, to resemble more those of a dying saint. "Que son esprit nous anime" (p. 732), writes Claire, prayer-like, in her last letter; and she evokes a kind of adoration of Julie's tomb, "cette terre sacrée." [156] These more or less Catholic notions are easily desacralized without blasphemy in the Protestant setting, and situate Julie's sainthood in a vague area between sacred and profane myth, with implications which are at once, paradoxically perhaps, non-theological and extra-terrestrial.

A series of not-quite-literal and obviously symbolic miracles also ushers Julie to a martyr's end. First, the sudden return of the wayward Claude Anet suggests again the magnetic qualities of Julie's virtue. More obviously biblical in its overtones is the "miracle" of the wine: "Après quelques autres informations, il fut clair que la provision d'un seul jour en avait duré cinq, et que le vin manquait sans que personne s'en fût aperçu, malgré plusieurs nuits de veille" (p. 719). There is not the slightest suggestion here or elsewhere that anything genuinely supernatural occurred; the wedding at Cana is a carefully controlled analogy, suggested by parallel terminology but explicitly denied (the footnote helps in this attenuation of the allusion by rerouting the discussion onto the sobriety of the servants). Similarly, Julie's whispered "On m'a fait boire jusqu'à la lie la coupe amère et douce de la sensibilité" (p. 721) recalls the metaphorical cup of the Garden of Gethsemane.

Julie's resurrection, the most evident of these, raises enormous interpretive problems. It still functions symbolically in the mythologization of Julie, and diegetically, as an extremely concrete manifestation of the adulation surrounding her; nonetheless, in the latter respect, its excess is logically undermining — "cette extravagante scène," "une illusion si grossière," Wolmar, although profoundly

---

[156] "Holy" ground associated with burials is normally consecrated ground for burial; here the holiness comes from the *contents* of the tomb: note the distinction between *terre sainte* and *terre sacrée*.

shaken and moved, calls it (pp. 723, 725; the footnote p. 725 calls attention to the superstitious aspect). Exhaltation and demythologization stand in uncertain counterpoint; the delirium which consummates Julie's legend must be confronted with her decomposing body, as Claire poses the veil declaring her official, unequivocal death.

Thoughts of death begin in the novel's early pages and, once more, are primarily concerned throughout part one and beyond with love. It is moot where the idea of a suffering impelling one toward death shades off into emotional blackmail; Saint-Preux (it is usually his death that is implied) moves between the poetic: "ce baiser eût été mon dernier soupir, et je serais mort" (p. 7) and the threat to leave, which is a veiled one of death: "M'ordonnez-vous de mourir?" (p. 9); "comptez sur vous, ou chassez-moi, c'est-à-dire ôtez-moi la vie" (p. 22).[157] Julie reacts to prevent his death/departure and immediately thinks of death herself: "je serai respectée, ou guérie. Voilà l'unique espoir qui me reste avant celui de mourir" (p. 14). They are treading well-beaten rhetorical paths here, and the "baiser mortel" (p. 37) remembered by Saint-Preux dimly evokes legends of fatal passions and heroic death-pacts.[158] Another round of death evocations makes it into an erotic suggestion: "je sens qu'il faut enfin que j'expire à tes pieds... ou dans tes bras" (p. 39). And the letter from Meillerie which exclaims, "Il n'y a rien, non, rien que je ne fasse pour te posséder ou mourir" lends relief to the terms with the threatening, graphic conclusion: "la roche est escarpée, l'eau est profonde, et je suis au désespoir" (pp. 66-67). In Julie's expressions of her dilemma the death hyperbole is a common furnishing, for instance when she defines her final choice this way: "il fallait donner la mort aux auteurs de mes jours, à mon amant ou à moi-même" (p. 70); but in the light of the novel's conclusion some of these remarks take on longer-range implications, as for example: "il faut que j'aime avec transport, ou que je meure

---

[157] Cf. p. 27: "Cependant un mal réel me tourmente, je cherche vainement à le fuir; je ne voudrais point mourir, et toutefois je me meurs; je voudrais vivre pour vous, et c'est vous qui m'ôtez la vie."

[158] "Ne vaudrait-il pas mieux cent fois se voir un seul instant et puis mourir?" (p. 82).

de douleur" (p. 83). [159] But Saint-Preux's return from Meillerie which precipitated this situation, according to Claire, also saved her life.

Julie's thoughts take a tragic turn where death becomes a concrete option. In explaining this drift to Saint-Preux, she writes, "il ne s'agit pas d'éteindre un amour qui doit durer autant que ma vie, mais de le rendre innocent ou de mourir coupable" (p. 111): she is already plotting to force her father, if possible, to let them marry; but knowing that might fail, she includes an alternative strategy which might be anything from provoking murder to suicide. Her invitation to her room insists clearly on a freely assumed risk which might well entail sudden death together:

> Non, mon doux ami, non, nous ne quitterons point cette courte vie sans avoir un instant goûté le bonheur: mais songe pourtant que cet instant est environné des horreurs de la mort; que l'abord est sujet à mille hasards, le séjour dangereux, la retraite d'un péril extrême; que nous sommes perdus si nous sommes découverts, et qu'il faut que tout nous favorise pour pouvoir éviter de l'être. [p. 120]

In short, the odds favor discovery and prompt, brutal assassination by her father: this night is less a libidinous abandon by Julie than a desperate solution, one way or another, to her dilemma. Nothing heroic: she does not want a defensive stand, and forbids him to bring a sword "car, si nous sommes surpris, mon dessein est de me précipiter dans tes bras, de t'enlacer fortement dans les miens, et de recevoir ainsi le coup mortel pour n'avoir plus à me séparer de toi, plus heureuse à ma mort que je ne le fus de ma vie" (p. 121). [160] When Saint-Preux is about to duel Bomston, a better swordsman than he, Julie vows (in her letter to Edouard) not to survive him. Separation itself brings back a suggestion of suicide which lends some weight retroactively to its earlier evocation: "Ô rochers de Meillerie, que mon œil égaré mesura tant de fois, que ne servîtes-vous mon désespoir!" (p. 167). When all hope is really lost, in

---

[159] Such a terminological line will not bear too much emphasis, however; Claire underscores, for example, Saint-Preux's last words when faced with the separation: "nous ne vivrons pas longtemps séparés" (p. 160) — yet they both manage to live separated for six years, most of it without any communication.

[160] In Tanner's reading, the essence of this scene for Julie is precisely "to indulge her imagination of the aroused and irresistable father" (op. cit., p. 121).

part three, this becomes the subject of a long-meditated design and a theoretical discussion thereon with Edouard. Julie's faint upon receipt of Saint-Preux's letter of renunciation symbolizes death, and when her mother dies soon thereafter she exclaims, "ma tendre mère, hélas! je suis bien plus morte que toi!" (p. 295). She hopes that her oncoming illness will be the end,[161] and Saint-Preux arrives apparently at a death-bed.[162] And his visit is, from his standpoint, equivalent to the accomplishment of a death pact, for he is attempting to join her in death by voluntarily contracting the same disease. If he does not die as a result, it is, literally speaking, because she does not. When she then surrenders in principle but reveals that she will none the less marry, Saint-Preux solemnly threatens a murder-suicide (pp. 315-16). And of course the return trip to Meillerie provokes a series of fantasies of death, first Julie's, imagined during the storm, then reminiscence of the temptation of the cliff (with a possible urge to repeat the risk), and finally the narrowly averted wish to force a double drowning.

These many menaces of and brushes with death in melodramatic or even tragic consequence of fated love justify, at least in a general way, Denis de Rougemont's assimilation of this story to the Tristan legend in *L'Amour et l'Occident*. The intimate association between the motifs of love and death here needs no more demonstration, nor even the more precise element of common death uniting the lovers. Meanwhile, however, another whole cycle of death suggestions develops within the text of *Julie* which has nothing ostensibly to do with this vein. Happiness itself, at least such as she experiences it, inspires thoughts (wishes?) of death: "En vérité, me dit-elle d'une voix émue, des jours ainsi passés tiennent du bonheur de l'autre vie; et ce n'est pas sans raison qu'en y pensant j'ai donné à ce lieu le nom d'Élysée" (p. 469). A great deal has been written about the Clarens Élysée with very little notice taken

---

[161] "Je suis forcée de me mettre au lit, et me console dans l'espoir de n'en point relever.... Ah! si je ne dois plus vivre pour toi, n'ai-je pas déjà cessé de vivre?" (p. 307). Cf. p. 202: "Dis-moi, que serions-nous si nous n'aimions plus? Eh! ne vaudrait-il pas mieux cesser d'être que d'exister sans rien sentir...?"

[162] "L'image du trépas, un appareil de douleur, la vertu malheureuse et la beauté mourante!" (p. 312).

of this explicitly funeral association of its name.[163] Julie has carefully, lengthily elaborated a select haven which speaks to her of eternal repose, of a removal from the anxiety of contingency. It is as if she cannot muse on her many blessings without instinctively evoking death in their wake:

> Mon imagination n'a plus rien à faire, je n'ai rien à désirer; sentir et jouir sont pour moi la même chose, je vis à la fois dans tout ce que j'aime, je me rassasie de bonheur et de vie. Ô mort! viens quand tu voudras, je ne te crains plus, j'ai vécu, je t'ai prévenue; je n'ai plus de nouveaux sentiments à connaître, tu n'as plus rien à me dérober. [p. 677]

"J'ai vécu": this enclosed past tense is the utterance of a woman about thirty; and "je t'ai prévenue" will turn out to have more exactly premeditated connotations than it at first appears.

For Julie's last letter before her accident already resonates like a voice from beyond the tomb, with all the detachment of one who has already decided to die and awaits but the occasion. Indeed she will die a most antiseptic death, accompanied by doctors but by as little apparent suffering as symptoms. Warned of the impending end, she replies, " Croyez-vous me l'apprendre? ... la mort me presse, il faut nous quitter" (p. 696). Explaining her intention to inform Claire, she suggests a scenario already in place: "Je destine la nuit prochaine à ce triste devoir." "Quant à la préparation à la mort, Monsieur," she says to the minister, "elle est faite" (p. 703). More than that, Julie has meticulously planned this scene and learned it by heart:

> Oui, me dit-elle tout bas, je parle trop pour une malade, mais non pas pour une mourante, bientôt je ne dirai plus rien. À l'égard des raisonnements, je n'en fais plus, mais j'en ai fait. Je savais en santé qu'il fallait mourir. *J'ai souvent réfléchi sur ma dernière maladie;* je profite aujourd'hui de ma prévoyance. Je ne suis plus en état de penser ni de résoudre; *je ne fais que dire ce que j'avais pensé,* et pratiquer ce que j'avais résolu. [p. 707]

---

[163] An exception is Tony Tanner, who goes on to take Elysium as an emblem for all of Clarens: "Clarens is, in a certain sense, a house of the dead" (*Adultery in the novel,* pp. 144-53).

Throughout, she is entirely in control of the situation. Observing her "secrète joie" (p. 698), her "air de contentement" (p. 700), her "air assez gai" (p. 717), Wolmar reproaches her: "vous vous réjouissez de mourir" (p. 707). Threatened with survival — the doctor has said he will answer for her life if she makes it till morning — after clear signs of improvement, Julie steals away furtively at the last moment ("sur le matin") as Claire tries futilely to snatch her from death's maw.

Julie has saved for the last line of her last letter, this time to be read only when she is authentically beyond danger, her most dramatic article of (self-) knowledge. Magnificently calculated, it falls with a mysterious hush and then is heard no more, like Julie herself: "Je meurs dans cette douce attente: trop heureuse d'acheter au prix de ma vie le droit de t'aimer toujours sans crime, et de te le dire encore une fois!" Its effect comes mostly from the single verb *aimer*, highly charged in any case by centuries of literary tradition, and unanticipated here because it has so long been held in reserve. Its absence was a sign of the control which dominated the last three parts of the story. Julie's statement at the beginning of the letter that she is not indeed *guérie* "says" the same thing, but the poetic victory of love is not sealed until the sacred formula itself appears.[164]

Of that victory, of course, much has deservedly been written. The very least one can concede is that it throws into some confusion the ideological line of at least the second half of the text. Not alone because love has persisted — that seemed always permissible beneath the surface, provided the love assert no claim to recover the prerogatives of an earlier period — but because the control has been lost. For what gives the *t'aimer toujours* its extreme ramifications is really the concession made earlier in the same letter: "Un jour de plus peut-être, et j'étais coupable!" Julie cannot trust herself to live, because the absolutely unbearable possibility of adultery

---

[164] "C'est la mère à la fin qui est sacrifiée à l'amante," remarks Lecercle (op. cit., p. 112); cf. Starobinski's interesting recall here of the Tristan connection: "Julie, il est vrai, ne meurt pas d'une mort d'amour, mais pour avoir accompli son *devoir* de mère: Rousseau a transposé sur le plan de la vertu un acte qui, selon le mythe de l'amour-passion, aurait dû être motivé par la volonté de destruction inhérente à la passion elle-même. Une ambivalence subsiste néanmoins" (op. cit., p. 140).

can no longer be forestalled: eight years of virtue, and with them the whole meaning she has imprinted on her life and world, are within a day of complete ruin. Death thus comes as a rescue: "le ciel ne m'ôte plus rien de regrettable, et met mon honneur à couvert. Mon ami, je pars au moment favorable...."

There are, of course, positive interpretations that can be given, even aside from the gratification of the love plot. Julie aspires to a metaphysical fulfillment which allows her to die an attitudinally exemplary if not doctrinally scrupulous death. It underscores the fact that virtue is never given nor definitively acquired but is always vulnerable, and must be constantly achieved. The culmination of her institutional role in the plot is intact, and she has only become more human in allowing to appear this one sign of weakness after it could no longer really compromise her. But we must remember too, in conjunction with this, that happiness has failed Julie, and this failure must reflect back upon the whole of the rhetoric the reader assimilates even after learning that that of the novel's first half was itself substantially erroneous.[165] In consequence a fundamental uncertainty will govern the whole; for, as Paul de Man points out, referring back to Julie's recapitulative letter following her marriage,

> The retrospective clarity gained at midpoint does not extend to the second part: no equivalent recapitulation is possible at the end of *Julie,* for it can be shown that the religious language of the last chapters is nowhere held up as being free of delusion, in the way the beginning of Letter 18, Part III, can be said to be. The readability of the first part is obscured by a more radical indeterminacy that projects its shadow backwards and forwards over the entire text. [op. cit., pp. 216-17]

Moreover, in terms of the book's form, the ending we have does not bring the kind of closure that might have been anticipated but rather, by plunging Saint-Preux in particular into a sudden oblivion, breaks up the tightly-knit circle which Julie just before her death

---

[165] "What appeared at first as a sequence of lyrical moments ... becomes, in the recapitulation, a narrative chain of successive errors, as misleading for the reader as they were for the character" (de Man, op. cit., p. 212).

had planned to draw definitively together: "Cette réunion n'était pas bonne" (p. 728).

Julie did not write that last letter without *knowing* that it compromised an integral understanding of things. "Je me suis longtemps fait illusion. Cette illusion me fut salutaire; elle se détruit au moment que je n'en ai plus besoin." The fact that the illusion was *salutaire* does not, perhaps, affect her own salvation; but what does the fact that it was nonetheless an illusion do to her survivors? Could one still preach unamended the value system of Clarens, aware that eight years in its practice had not produced virtuous lucidity? And, as de Man notes, nothing at this point can set things straight, right the illusions, explicate the truth of signs.

Still, it is not just a matter of retroactive reading in the light either of this ending or of the mid-way revision of III.18. There never was an unambiguous point of view, insofar as every level and theme of the text bore disguised contraindications to the main line if not simply a contradictory or marginally coherent discourse. The meanings of *Julie* are indeterminate because the text as a whole allows them to be. From the evasive and ironic preface and from the second preface which, while parrying criticisms, gives full vent to outraged and logical objections, through to that last letter of Julie's which Wolmar could as well have suppressed, we are confronted with a text which always wavers when asked to vouch decisively for its own truth. But its truths, let us recall, are not doctrinal but sentimental. Despite its philosophical overtones, empathy is a literary quality, and above an ostensible appeal to the convertible reader who has "conservé quelque amour pour l'honnêteté" (preface) there is ultimately an appeal to the reader pure and simple, to take a part in this story.

CONCLUSION

With books of criticism as with literary texts, the close examination of procedures calls premises into question. The critic cannot escape in his own writing the constraints of rhetoric which he identifies as operating in the target works. It follows that if the literary work cannot be tidily summed up, the same would likely be true of criticism. Apart from the profound "blindnesses" which Paul de Man has described as the inherent condition for the most insightful criticism, there are the more or less conscious operational simplifications which simply make it easier for the critic to do his work. No argument of any kind can be sustained if all possible qualifications are admitted at every point. In this sense all criticism, like all fiction, involves sleight of hand; the deftest writers in both genres only make it harder to detect. I am not making that claim for myself, but it might be useful to extend somewhat the parameters of the discussion so willfully contained until now.

For example, my original, pragmatic assumption that the text is a defineable entity — a necessary supposition for "intrinsic" criticism of any stripe — is obviously a kind of convenience which these three novels themselves serve to problematize. Depending on how you look at it, *Marianne* is or is not a closed text (the several contemporaries who composed sequels to it obviously did not think so). The "preface" of *La Religieuse*, which I as a matter of critical judgment have chosen to treat in a qualified sense as part of the text, is not always so considered even if the most recent criticism does tend in that direction. Even *Julie* is not immune from such problematics, for the second or dialogic preface is sometimes incorporated, not to mention the marginal — and appended — adventures of Bomston. *Mutatis mutandi*, the same reservations could be voiced at some level about a great number of literary texts, however great the consensus on their standardization. The eighteenth century has a rather high percentage of formally incomplete novels, but that is not the subject at issue.

Also, *mutatis mutandi,* the same double reading, constructive and deconstructive, can perhaps be performed with equal validity on any text, literary or otherwise. Has this exercise, which I of course hope has illuminated particular works, isolated any phenomenon peculiar to the period from which they are drawn; or has it in the process implicitly established anything about the functions of the female subject? Both questions remain open. Empirically, it appears to me that great clarity of thesis, the hallmark of the general category of *romans à thèse* to which *La Religieuse* and *Julie* at least belong, lends itself exceptionally well to the discovery of a parallel and resistent discourse, precisely to the degree that all certainties are arrived at through a rhetorical containment of unfriendly data. Thus, a text which like *Marianne* appears thematically to recognize ambiguity and complexity is perhaps less likely than those others to harbor nasty secrets unknown to itself.

An intrinsic reading — and this encompasses numerous kinds of critical practice, not a single doctrine — studies the text much as one would an organism, with the assumption that somehow all its bewildering subtlety is largely contained in the DNA of each and every cell. Now a text need not be assumed to have generated itself, like an embryo, from some original particle. It came into being as an artifact that was indeed, at some specific historical juncture, someone's creation. Truly the text does not spawn itself; but no matter how it got there, it does generate all its own meaning. To some, it might be important to establish whether or not Rousseau, for example, "knows" that his novel manages to undercut its most overtly declared aims, as if our esteem for his artistry (or intelligence) were at issue in the response. The only plausible answer to that query, however limited in scope, is that Rousseau presumably wrote every word of the book. Beyond that, Rousseau's brain is of little help to any reader. As far as we can tell it is the text alone which "knows," whether the text in play be the individual work (as in this book), the whole of the writer's corpus, novels of a particular type or period, and so forth.

Our function, to be sure, is not merely to decode that knowing and expose it to daylight, content finally to "know" for our own sakes what went into it. What we do is more like comparing and testing what we think we know against what the text thinks it knows and what we think it knows. That is a risky process only if we were expecting definitive results; what we always risk is not so much the future reversal and repudiation of our insights as the likelihood that they themselves will one day be understood in a different light. But that will not be because the truth of the text, finally established, has rejected our misreadings.

Is there then no way to *mis*read? We are all committed to the rationality of critical discourse, and obviously are concerned to discriminate between sound and specious arguments. Although there may be ways in which language may be made to say anything, we recognize contortion at some point because we listen for meaning every day and depend in a practical way upon our ability to sense when that faculty is being abused. In criticism we do not deal much in propositional truths and falsehoods; we try to grasp the complexity of things and this entails endless subtleties. Nonetheless, we make assertions in the form of rational statements, and these can be subjected to empirical or logical verification of some kind; no reading can stand which does not receive a modicum of reinforcement from other readings.

Besides, to complicate a surface reading is not to nullify that superficial sense, any more than awareness of the larger submerged portion of an iceberg denies the part that is visible above the surface. It is still there, although the individual reader may cease to notice it much after delving into the more ambiguous reaches of meaning. In language, however, no neat distinction between the parts thought to be above and below the surface will stand up. Even with *Julie,* the point is not that a work which purports to mean one thing really turns out to mean something quite different. It is that the work contains all these meanings, either in tension with each other or operating at separate levels. When Diderot says of Greuze's maid weeping for her dead bird, "Cette enfant pleure autre chose, vous dis-je," he is not eradicating the dead bird. He is reading allegorically (and much more), but even that reading depends upon the functional meaning-production of the evident subject. Meanings interfere with each other only in the sense that, like certain optical illusions, they cannot always be perceived in all ways at once. Enriching perspective is what reading is all about.

WORKS CITED

Brooks, Peter. *The Novel of Worldliness,* Princeton: Princeton University Press, 1969.
Catrysse, Jérôme. *Diderot et la mystification,* Paris: Nizet, 1970.
Coulet, Henri. *Marivaux romancier,* Paris: Armand Colin, 1975.
Davidson, Hugh. "Dialectical order and movement in *La Nouvelle Héloïse,*" in Alfred J. Bingham and Virgil W. Topazio (eds.), *Enlightenment Studies in Honour of Lester G. Crocker,* Oxford: The Voltaire Foundation, 1979.
Démoris, René. *Le Roman à la première personne,* Paris: Armand Colin, 1975.
De Man, Paul. *Allegories of Reading,* New Haven and London: Yale University Press, 1979.
Diderot, Denis. *La Religieuse,* Paris: Garnier-Flammarion, 1968.
Edmiston, William F. "Sacrifice and Innocence in *La Religieuse,*" in *Diderot Studies,* 19 (Geneva: Droz, 1978), 67-84.
Fort, Bernadette. *Le Langage de l'ambiguïté dans l'œuvre de Crébillon fils,* Paris: Klincksieck, 1978.
Genette, Gérard. "Discours du récit," in *Figures III,* Paris: Seuil, 1972.
Gilot, Michel. Introduction to Marivaux, *La Vie de Marianne,* Paris: Garnier-Flammarion, 1978.
Gossman, Lionel. "The Worlds of *La Nouvelle Héloïse,*" in *Studies on Voltaire and the Eighteenth Century,* Vol. 41 (Geneva: Institut et Musée Voltaire, 1966), 235-76.
Hagstrum, Jean H. *Sex and Sensibility: Ideal and Erotic Love from Milton to Mozart,* Chicago: University of Chicago Press, 1980.
Jugan, Annick. "*La Vie de Marianne* de Marivaux: l'équivalent littéraire d'un art de la fugue," *Degré Second,* No. 1 (1977), 59-95, and No. 2 (1978), 67-99.
Kamuf, Peggy. "Inside *Julie*'s Closet," *Romanic Review,* 69, No. 4 (1978), 296-306.
Lecercle, Jean-Louis. *Rousseau et l'art du roman,* Paris: Armand Colin, 1969.
Le Hir, Yves. *Styles,* Paris: Klincksieck, 1972.
Lotringer, Sylvère. "Le Roman impossible," in *Poétique,* 3 (1970), 297-321.
———. "Manon l'écho," in *Romanic Review,* 63, No. 2 (1972), 92-110.
Marivaux, Pierre Carlet de. *La Vie de Marianne, ou les aventures de Madame la comtesse de* *** (Frédéric Deloffre, ed.), Paris: Classiques Garnier, 1963.
May, Georges. *Diderot et "La Religieuse,"* New Haven and Paris: Yale University Press and Presses Universitaires de France, 1954.
Mercken-Spaas, Godelieve. "La Répétition à la deuxième puissance," *Studies in Eighteenth-Century Culture,* No. 5 (1976), 203-13.

Mylne, Vivienne. *The Eighteenth-Century French Novel*, Manchester: Manchester University Press, 1965.
Poulet, Georges. *La Distance intérieure*, Paris: Plon, 1952.
Rex, Walter E. "Secrets from Suzanne: The Tangled Motives of *La Religieuse*," in *The Eighteenth Century: Theory and Interpretation*, 24 (1983), 185-98.
Rosbottom, Ronald. "A Matter of Competence: The Relationship between Reading and Novel-Making in Eighteenth-Century France," in *Studies in Eighteenth-Century Culture*, 6 (1977), 245-63.
Rousseau, Jean-Jacques. *Julie, ou la nouvelle Héloïse: lettres de deux amants habitants d'une petite ville au pied des Alpes, recueillies et publiées par Jean-Jacques Rousseau* (René Pomeau, ed.), Paris: Classiques Garnier, 1960.
Rousset, Jean. *Forme et signification*, Paris: José Corti, 1962.
Rustin, Jacques. "*La Religieuse* de Diderot: mémoires ou journal intime?" in V. del Litto et al., *Le Journal intime et ses formes littéraires*, Geneva: Droz, 1978.
Sherman, Carol. "Changing Spaces," in Jack Undank and Herbert Josephs (eds.), *Diderot: Digression and Dispersion*, Lexington: French Forum Publishers, 1984.
———. "The Deferral of Textual Authority in *La Religieuse*," in *Postcript*, 2 (1985), 57-65.
Spink, J. S. "The Social Background of Saint-Preux and d'Étange," in *French Studies*, 30, No. 2 (1976), 153-69.
Spitzer, Leo. "À propos de *La Vie de Marianne*," in *Romanic Review*, 44 (1953), 102-26.
———. "The Style of Diderot," in *Linguistics and Literary History*, Princeton: Princeton University Press, 1967.
Starobinski, Jean. *Jean-Jacques Rousseau: la transparence et l'obstacle*, Paris: Plon, 1957, reed. Gallimard, 1971.
Stewart, Philip. *Le Masque et la parole*, Paris: José Corti, 1973.
———. "A Note on Chronology in *La Religieuse*," in *Romance Notes*, 12, No. 1, 149-56.
Suleiman, Susan. "La Structure d'apprentissage," in *Poétique*, 37 (1979), 24-42.
Tanner, Tony. *Adultery in the Novel*, Baltimore and London: Johns Hopkins, 1969.
Todd, Janet. *Women's Friendship in Literature*, New York: Columbia University Press, 1980.
Vance, Christie. "The Extravagant Shepherd: A Study of the Pastoral Vision in Rousseau's *La Nouvelle Héloïse*," *Studies on Voltaire and the Eighteenth Century*, Vol. 105, Banbury: The Voltaire Foundation, 1973.
Van Laere, François. *Une Lecture du temps dans "La Nouvelle Héloïse,"* Neuchâtel: La Baconnière, 1968.

NORTH CAROLINA STUDIES IN THE ROMANCE LANGUAGES AND LITERATURES

I.S.B.N. Prefix 0-8078-

Recent Titles

A STUDY OF NOMINAL INFLECTION IN LATIN INSCRIPTIONS, by Paul A. Gaeng. 1977. (No. 182). *-9182-7.*
THE LIFE AND WORKS OF LUIS CARLOS LÓPEZ, by Martha S. Bazik. 1977. (No. 183). *-9183-5.*
"THE CORT D'AMOR". A THIRTEENTH-CENTURY ALLEGORICAL ART OF LOVE, by Lowanne E. Jones. 1977. (No. 185). *-9185-1.*
PHYTONYMIC DERIVATIONAL SYSTEMS IN THE ROMANCE LANGUAGES: STUDIES IN THEIR ORIGIN AND DEVELOPMENT, by Walter E. Geiger. 1978. (No. 187). *-9187-8.*
LANGUAGE IN GIOVANNI VERGA'S EARLY NOVELS, by Nicholas Patruno. 1977. (No. 188). *-9188-6.*
BLAS DE OTERO EN SU POESÍA, by Moraima de Semprún Donahue. 1977. (No. 189). *-9189-4.*
LA ANATOMÍA DE "EL DIABLO COJUELO": DESLINDES DEL GÉNERO ANATOMÍSTICO, por C. George Peale. 1977. (No. 191). *-9191-6.*
RICHARD SANS PEUR, EDITED FROM "LE ROMANT DE RICHART" AND FROM GILLES CORROZET'S "RICHART SANS PAOUR", by Denis Joseph Conlon. 1977. (No. 192). *-9192-4.*
MARCEL PROUST'S GRASSET PROOFS. *Commentary and Variants*, by Douglas Alden. 1978. (No. 193). *-9193-2.*
MONTAIGNE AND FEMINISM, by Cecile Insdorf. 1977. (No. 194). *-9194-0.*
SANTIAGO F. PUGLIA, AN EARLY PHILADELPHIA PROPAGANDIST FOR SPANISH AMERICAN INDEPENDENCE, by Merle S. Simmons. 1977. (No. 195). *-9195-9.*
BAROQUE FICTION-MAKING. A STUDY OF GOMBERVILLE'S "POLEXANDRE", by Edward Baron Turk. 1978. (No. 196). *-9196-7.*
THE TRAGIC FALL: DON ÁLVARO DE LUNA AND OTHER FAVORITES IN SPANISH GOLDEN AGE DRAMA, by Raymond R. MacCurdy. 1978. (No. 197). *-9197-5.*
A BAHIAN HERITAGE. An Ethnolinguistic Study of African Influences on Bahian Portuguese, by William W. Megenney. 1978. (No. 198). *-9198-3.*
"LA QUERELLE DE LA ROSE": Letters and Documents, by Joseph L. Baird and John R. Kane. 1978. (No. 199). *-9199-1.*
TWO AGAINST TIME. *A Study of the Very Present Worlds of Paul Claudel and Charles Péguy*, by Joy Nachod Humes. 1978. (No. 200). *-9200-9.*
TECHNIQUES OF IRONY IN ANATOLE FRANCE. Essay on *Les Sept Femmes de la Barbe-Bleue*, by Diane Wolfe Levy. 1978. (No. 201). *-9201-7.*
THE PERIPHRASTIC FUTURES FORMED BY THE ROMANCE REFLEXES OF "VADO (AD)" PLUS INFINITIVE, by James Joseph Champion. 1978. (No. 202). *-9202-5.*
THE EVOLUTION OF THE LATIN /b/-/ụ/ MERGER: A Quantitative and Comparative Analysis of the *B-V* Alternation in Latin Inscriptions, by Joseph Louis Barbarino. 1978. (No. 203). *-9203-3.*
METAPHORIC NARRATION: THE STRUCTURE AND FUNCTION OF METAPHORS IN "A LA RECHERCHE DU TEMPS PERDU", by Inge Karalus Crosman. 1978. (No. 204). *-9204-1.*
LE VAIN SIECLE GUERPIR. A Literary Approach to Sainthood through Old French Hagiography of the Twelfth Century, by Phyllis Johnson and Brigitte Cazelles. 1979. (No. 205). *-9205-X.*
THE POETRY OF CHANGE: A STUDY OF THE SURREALIST WORKS OF BENJAMIN PÉRET, by Julia Field Costich. 1979. (No. 206). *-9206-8.*

When ordering please cite the *ISBN Prefix* plus the last four digits for each title.

Send orders to: University of North Carolina Press
Chapel Hill
North Carolina 27514
U. S. A.

NORTH CAROLINA STUDIES IN THE ROMANCE LANGUAGES AND LITERATURES

I.S.B.N. Prefix 0-88438

Recent Titles

NARRATIVE PERSPECTIVE IN THE POST-CIVIL WAR NOVELS OF FRANCISCO AYALA "MUERTES DE PERRO" AND "EL FONDO DEL VASO", by Maryellen Bieder. 1979. (No. 207). *-9207-6.*

RABELAIS: HOMO LOGOS, by Alice Fiola Berry. 1979. (No. 208). *-9208-4.*

"DUEÑAS" AND "DONCELLAS": A STUDY OF THE "DOÑA RODRÍGUEZ" EPISODE IN "DON QUIJOTE", by Conchita Herdman Marianella. 1979. (No. 209). *-9209-2.*

PIERRE BOAISTUAU'S "HISTOIRES TRAGIQUES": A STUDY OF NARRATIVE FORM AND TRAGIC VISION, by Richard A. Carr. 1979. (No. 210). *-9210-6.*

REALITY AND EXPRESSION IN THE POETRY OF CARLOS PELLICER, by George Melnykovich. 1979. (No. 211). *-9211-4.*

MEDIEVAL MAN, HIS UNDERSTANDING OF HIMSELF, HIS SOCIETY, AND THE WORLD, by Urban T. Holmes, Jr. 1980. (No. 212). *-9212-2.*

MÉMOIRES SUR LA LIBRAIRIE ET SUR LA LIBERTÉ DE LA PRESSE, introduction and notes by Graham E. Rodmell. 1979. (No. 213). *-9213-0.*

THE FICTIONS OF THE SELF. THE EARLY WORKS OF MAURICE BARRES, by Gordon Shenton. 1979. (No. 214). *-9214-9.*

CECCO ANGIOLIERI. A STUDY, by Gifford P. Orwen. 1979. (No. 215). *-9215-7.*

THE INSTRUCTIONS OF SAINT LOUIS: A CRITICAL TEXT, by David O'Connell. 1979. (No. 216). *-9216-5.*

ARTFUL ELOQUENCE, JEAN LEMAIRE DE BELGES AND THE RHETORICAL TRADITION, by Michael F. O. Jenkins. 1980. (No. 217). *-9217-3.*

A CONCORDANCE TO MARIVAUX'S COMEDIES IN PROSE, edited by Donald C. Spinelli. 1979. (No. 218). 4 volumes, *-9218-1* (set); *-9219-X* (v. 1); *-9220-3* (v. 2); *-9221-1* (v. 3); *-9222-X* (v. 4.)

ABYSMAL GAMES IN THE NOVELS OF SAMUEL BECKETT, by Angela B. Moorjani. 1982. (No. 219). *-9223-8.*

GERMAIN NOUVEAU DIT HUMILIS: ÉTUDE BIOGRAPHIQUE, par Alexandre L. Amprimoz. 1983. (No. 220). *-9224-6.*

THE "VIE DE SAINT ALEXIS" IN THE TWELFTH AND THIRTEENTH CENTURIES: AN EDITION AND COMMENTARY, by Alison Goddard Elliot. 1983. (No. 221). *-9225-4.*

THE BROKEN ANGEL: MYTH AND METHOD IN VALÉRY, by Ursula Franklin. 1984. (No. 222). *-9226-2.*

READING VOLTAIRE'S "CONTES": A SEMIOTICS OF PHILOSOPHICAL NARRATION, by Carol Sherman. 1985. (No. 223). *-9227-0.*

THE STATUS OF THE READING SUBJECT IN THE "LIBRO DE BUEN AMOR", by Marina Scordilis Brownlee. 1985. (No. 224). *-9228-9.*

MARTORELL'S "TIRANT LO BLANCH": A PROGRAM FOR MILITARY AND SOCIAL REFORM IN FIFTEENTH-CENTURY CHRISTENDOM, by Edward T. Aylward. 1985. (No. 225). *-9229-7.*

NOVEL LIVES: THE FICTIONAL AUTOBIOGRAPHIES OF GUILLERMO CABRERA INFANTE AND MARIO VARGAS LLOSA, by Rosemary Geisdorfer Feal. 1986. (No. 226). *-9230-0.*

SOCIAL REALISM IN THE ARGENTINE NARRATIVE, by David William Foster. 1986. (No. 227). *-9231-9.*

When ordering please cite the *ISBN Prefix* plus the last four digits for each title.

Send orders to: University of North Carolina Press
Chapel Hill
North Carolina 27514
U. S. A.

The Department of Romance Studies Digital Arts and Collaboration Lab at the University of North Carolina at Chapel Hill is proud to support the digitization of the North Carolina Studies in the Romance Languages and Literatures series.

www.ingramcontent.com/pod-product-compliance
Lightning Source LLC
Chambersburg PA
CBHW022019220426
43663CB00007B/1133